"I flew through the pages of this book! Stephanie's story about nannying for the upper class is equal parts juicy, funny, and insightful. Her career goals being derailed by the all-too-real need to make money will resonate with anyone who's had to make their own way in the world."

—Stefanie Wilder-Taylor, author of *Sippy Cups Are Not for Chardonnay* and *Drunk-Ish*

"Raw, vulnerable, and reminiscent of many young women chasing the NYC dream, Stephanie gives us a peek into her experiences navigating the foreign world of east coast elitists while searching for an authentic sense of self. It's the totally unapologetic coming of age story you never knew you needed."

—Deuxmoi

"Stephanie Kiser's emotionally honest memoir about nannying for New York's elite is a thoughtful meditation on the way social class separates our realities, even amid the universality of motherhood and maturation."

—Blythe Grossberg, author of *I Left My Homework in the Hamptons*

WANTED: TODDLER'S PERSONAL ASSISTANT

WANTED: TODDLER'S PERSONAL ASSISTANT

HOW NANNYING FOR THE 1%
TAUGHT ME ABOUT THE MYTHS OF
EQUALITY, MOTHERHOOD, AND
UPWARD MOBILITY IN AMERICA

STEPHANIE KISER

sourcebooks

Published by Sourcebooks
P.O. Box 4410, Naperville, Illinois 60567-4410
(630) 961-3900
sourcebooks.com

Cataloging-in-Publication Data is on file with the Library of Congress.

Printed and bound in the United States of America.
KP 10 9 8 7 6 5 4 3 2 1

For Gram,
Who has never let me know a day without
unconditional love

For Lila,
How lucky I've been to grow through life with you

For my mom,
Who had the hardest job in the world and I've
never remembered to thank

And for the Kisers
FB, AP, Slimmy, Lid, and Bob P

1

WE'RE ALL RICH HERE

I'M WAITING OUTSIDE THE SCHOOL pickup line sandwiched between Drew Barrymore and a cousin of George W. Bush. Steve Martin and his wife are a few spots ahead, close enough that I can hear their conversation. But this is no longer of any particular interest to me. I have seen them enough times now that the initial shock has passed. Steve is always pleasant, though slightly aloof, and his wife bears an uncanny resemblance to Tina Fey. I'd overheard some of the moms whispering about this once, as if it were somehow offensive, but I disagree. Tina Fey is a trailblazer, a national treasure. Steve Martin is seventy-two years old and wearing Harry Potter-esque spectacles. As far as I can tell, Steve has hit the jackpot, and here I am casually standing feet away from him. Apparently, I too have hit the jackpot.

Black Escalades and Suburbans line the 64th Street block between Park and Madison. Hermès bags swing from the shoulders of women whose outfits cost upward of ten thousand dollars. Rings dazzle on dainty manicured fingers weighed down by huge stones. It's just another Tuesday afternoon in New York City, but for the parade of mothers who wait to pick up their children from The Episcopal School, every day is a runway show.

Not all the mothers passing through are attractive, but that matters very little. What the less fortunate ones lack in natural beauty, they make up for in sophistication. I watch wide-eyed as women stroll down the street in Jimmy Choos with four-inch heels. Some wear leather pants despite it being three in the afternoon on a weekday, and they all seem allergic to the sun, hiding their eyes behind thick-framed sunglasses. I attempt with little subtlety to peek into the Chanel shopping bag that one carries. Whatever is inside, I want it. All of these people have more money tied up in one diamond earring than I have in my checking and savings accounts combined.

"Oh, my God, Ellie, you look amazing! How long has it been?" I turn and catch two stay-at-home moms embracing. Their Cartier bracelets ding against one another as they pull back from a stiff hug.

"How was your summer?" Ellie asks. "Were you guys out East?"

I have seen Ellie at the school a handful of times, watching as her chauffeur curbed an oversized Range Rover. Ellie would appear just moments later, strutting one gorgeous Christian Louboutin in front of the other, her salon-blown hair fanning out in the wind as she headed to the waiting area. Ellie wasn't beautiful, perhaps not even pretty, but she was marvelous.

"Oh, yes! We were out East for August."

By "out East" they were of course referring to the Hamptons.

Ellie mentions a celebrity who bought the house next door and name-drops a billionaire she had drinks with in Montauk. Her friend reveals she snagged a reservation at the pop-up restaurant that *everyone* had been dying to try out and they sat right next to Beyoncé and Jay-Z, but she didn't recognize them. She leans in, confessing, "Really, I'm hardly sure who they are!" They laugh, and the friend asks about Ellie's husband, who, I learn, managed to work from home all of July and so they had been fortunate enough to enjoy their summer together, but Ellie knows lots of women who'd only seen their husbands on weekends.

I feel like I've listened to a hundred variations of this conversation from the women who wait here daily, enough to predict how it wraps up. For all their differences, Ellie and the other mothers have one universal agreement: it is really *very* hard surviving a summer in the Hamptons.

"The traffic in Southampton this year—it was brutal."

"I know," Ellie sighs. "It's just so much harder out there."

Still, despite all their suffering, one thing could be counted on: these mothers would return to both their misery and their massive beachside mansions the following June.

Their grievances are ridiculous, but I can't help listening. I like imagining what life would look like if these were my concerns. *God, things would be easy,* I think.

I hear laughter from the start of the line, where a group of nannies is clustered. I'm curious what's so funny and feel like a kid myself, desperate to be part of their friend group. The last few weeks, it's felt like regardless of who I target, who I smile at or attempt small talk with, no one is interested. I consider approaching the nanny circle, but I sense they are no more open to inviting me into their crew than Ellie would be inviting me into hers. I do not fit into either category, the typical Upper East Side mother or the typical Upper East Side nanny and, as a result, I have absolutely zero friends here.

"Oh, but have you tried the Tracy Anderson gym?" Ellie squeals to her friend.

"No, I haven't. Wait, how is it?"

"Honestly, it changed my life. My backside has never looked better, and the membership is only twelve thousand a year."

At three thirty on the dot, the six-foot-five school security guard opens the heavy wooden doors and steps aside. We are free to go in and collect our children now, but the guard eyes us carefully. He reminds me of the nightclub bouncers I see on weekends in the Meatpacking District, except that he is not denying me entrance, and most of the people here are sober. This man takes his job very seriously, as he should. He is, after all, the protector of America's wealthiest toddlers.

I thought it was all a bit absurd the first few times I picked up Ruby from school. The precautions felt over the top, but these are not your average little ones. These are the children of politicians, celebrities, and athletes. I have difficulty comprehending the privilege inherent in this sort of childhood. As I walk up a flight of stairs to the five-year-olds' classroom, I try to think back to my first day of nursery school and remember something important: that I never had one.

Ruby skips toward me and immediately asks if we can go to the playground, listing her favorite ones as I follow her down the steps. Outside, I take Ruby's hand, and we begin our eight-block stroll up Fifth Avenue. We pass perfectly maintained buildings on a pristine sidewalk. In a city notorious for its filth, here is a single street so well kept, one would not fear going barefoot.

It is early October, six months since my college graduation and my fourth month in New York City. Walking Ruby home, I think how lucky I was to find this job.

I'd been living in an apartment in East Harlem, where safety is questionable, but I shared it with my best friend, Lila. We'd gone from high school weekends binge-watching *Downton Abbey* on my grandmother's beat-up couch to frequenting New York's trendiest nightclubs. In my mind, I was thriving.

Two months into my new life, the federal government began sending me notices for my student loans. Each week came an email reminding me of the burden. I had a *lot* of student debt—more than the total of two brand new BMWs. I'd never handled more than a couple hundred dollars when I took out the six-figure loan at eighteen, so it hadn't seemed like a big deal.

I searched tirelessly for a way to support myself while also keeping these loans out of default. I interviewed for various positions in the entertainment industry, having majored in writing for film and television in college, a degree that was proving incredibly useless in the real world. I wanted to write TV shows, dreamed of becoming the next Lena Dunham or Greta Gerwig.

I'd spent my senior year interning for a major producer from Lionsgate, reading incoming scripts and providing coverage on them. I found the whole thing exhilarating and knew I was going to make a career out of it. Then I arrived in New York and had my first job interview. It turned out that an entry-level job in the entertainment industry paid less than at most fast food chains.

Hollywood was essentially made of money. Where was it all going? I guess when Leonardo DiCaprio gets a salary of thirty million, it doesn't leave much for the people behind the camera. In the end, they went with a more experienced production assistant, anyway.

I decided to meet the job market halfway and apply for a temp job at a PR firm. It paid more—not much more, but perhaps enough to get by—and it had a creative component even if it wasn't necessarily the one I'd been seeking.

Then my student loan began rearing its ugly head, and I realized even the PR job wasn't going to cut it. I was making $1,450 a month—just enough to cover food, rent, subway fare, and, most importantly, eyebrow threading. Then the loan notice came, and I realized that, even if I stopped eating, walked to work, and crafted my own brows, I couldn't even cover half of it. Quick math told me I'd need to take home $2,500. I was terrified.

Then I found out that working for the wealthy allowed me to avoid the low entry-level salaries of professional careers, and I jumped at the opportunity.

Being a nanny was the last job I wanted, but necessity outweighed pride, and so here I am. Once, a first-generation college student and, now, just a toddler's personal assistant.

Somewhere around 73rd Street Ruby asks if we can stop for ice cream.

"What kind?" I ask.

"Mint chocolate chip."

It is what she always chooses, though it is, in my opinion, the worst of the flavors. Her mother seldom objects to treats and always leaves cash for random indulgences. In my childhood, ice cream was a rare luxury. It was an outing we couldn't often afford, but there were exceptions.

My father, separated from my mother at the time, had my sisters and me on Fridays, which also happened to be payday at the mill, where he worked as a mechanic.

"You have five dollars apiece," my father would tell us as we walked into Walmart. It felt like the shopping spree of a lifetime. I typically left with something useless, like press-on nails or a pack of fifteen ChapSticks. We'd end the evening by stopping at the ice cream shop down the road. My father would pull out an envelope of twenties from the check he had cashed at the bank, and we'd all pick cookie dough. Now *that* was a flavor worth ordering.

But unlike me, Ruby has ice cream nearly every day in the warm months. Today we spend her after-school hours running through the grass of Central Park and watching boats row around the Loeb. I watch as tourists snap photos and, because New York is still so fresh to me, I can't believe I am more than just a visitor. On the short walk home, Ruby spots the strategically parked ice cream truck and screeches with excitement. I'm grabbing a handful of napkins when my phone buzzes. Ruby is bouncing far ahead of me, and I pull the phone from my back pocket as I call out, "Ruby, hold on!"

I glance at the screen and see a text from Hope. I open the

message, irritated, but knowing my mother will continue to text me until I answer. She is nothing if not persistent.

> Dad took apart bathroom so we could remodel but we don't have enough for a new toilet. Can we borrow two hundred? It's annoying to go outside.

I sigh and slide the phone away as the doorman opens the door for Ruby and me. We enter the dimly lit foyer and, while we wait for the elevator, I watch as a candle flickers against a gold-framed painting. The painting isn't actually all that good, but it is framed nicely and has somehow found itself a spot in this exclusive dwelling. *We have a lot in common, this painting and me.*

In many ways I have outdone myself, that much I know. I've clawed my way out of a chaotic childhood. My mother's text, short as it is, opens a floodgate of memories that I've worked hard to lock away. It reminds me of the child I once was and of the life I have come from, growing up in a run-down apartment with young parents who had too little maturity and too much responsibility. I had no nanny or babysitter, only a grandmother who managed to care for me and her ailing father simultaneously. My clothes and shoes were purchased from Kmart only after they spent months collecting dust on a layaway shelf. Our family, me included, was very much into screaming and used profanities loosely. I was three the first time I flicked my mother off. There's even a photograph to prove it.

With Ruby, I eat gourmet sandwiches from Dean & Deluca and take Ubers across town to celebrated museums. My own childhood was calls from debt collectors, pets that never lasted more than a few months, and strict portion control that often sent my sisters and me to bed hungry.

The fact that I somehow ended up in this place—with this job—is hard for me to comprehend.

The elevator whisks us to the sixth floor, and Ruby enters the apartment, calling out for her mother. Sasha hurries down the hall, her delicate flats making hardly any noise at all.

"Coming," she assures Ruby.

Sasha pulls her daughter into an adoring hug before asking her about her day. It's strange, constantly witnessing a family's most intimate moments, and the scene often makes me long for moments in my own life that do not exist. I shake away the thought and try to convince myself I wouldn't have enjoyed such a tender exchange anyway.

In the world of Upper East Side mothers, Sasha is an anomaly. She is attractive, bright, and, at only thirty-five, exceptionally wealthy. Her parents went to Yale, as did she, as did her husband. I'm sure even her Havanese would have been accepted, had the little mop applied. Sasha does not work but is on the board of more fundraising committees than I knew existed. It's all part of a strange phenomenon on the Upper East Side, where women of great means spend decades preparing to attend prestigious schools like Princeton and Stanford, only to obtain degrees they never apply to a career. For these women education is not an economic necessity, it's a social status. The working mom is a rarity—and, in many instances, the least respected on the totem pole of motherhood.

Sasha's resume, combined with her family's name recognition, gives her a social currency most will never attain, but while I observe other moms gossip relentlessly, Sasha politely says hello to me and then promptly focuses her attention on her children.

The question of what it means to be a "good" mother has been top of mind since I took this job. It seems that the idea of women being able to have it all is still just that: an idea. I see all kinds of mothers in my day-to-day: working moms who have important jobs with impressive salaries and helicopter moms who obsess over every detail of their newborns' feeding schedules. But I have yet to discover the secret to raising a well-adjusted child, and I certainly haven't met an ideal mother.

Sasha is close, though. She adores motherhood and dedicates herself to it selflessly. Her only questionable parenting decision seems to be hiring me, a lost, self-loathing twenty-two-year-old, to help raise her children.

I'm unpacking Ruby's school bag when I decide that I'll lend my parents money for another toilet. My dad will pay me back, and this is the sort of favor one can't really refuse. Their home is no longer mine, so I won't have to use this new toilet, which is comforting because their bathroom never contained hand soap, and all the towels were filled with holes.

If I need to pee, there is a bathroom on Fifth Avenue waiting for me. It has floor-to-ceiling mirrors, jet-black marble, luxurious hand lotion, and an impeccable maid from Ecuador who folds the Charmin into tiny triangles and who keeps the toilet bowl perfectly sterile.

2

THE TODDLER KEEPER

WHENEVER SOMEONE ASKS HOW I became a nanny, I tell them the truth: that it was a complete and tragic accident. It was early fall when I miraculously landed myself an interview, weaseled my way past a white-gloved doorman, and unknowingly changed the entire course of my twenties.

"Hunter goes down for a nap around ten, and he usually sleeps until twelve or so. I'll write it down before you start on Monday, of course. He could sleep more or less, but what's most important is what time you get him down. Consistency is key."

I am following Sasha around her five-million-dollar apartment as she says this. I was hired to be their nanny about five minutes ago, and we're now ninety seconds into a house tour, but I'm finding it difficult to focus. My experience with children doesn't go much further than being an occasional date-night sitter, and I've just been given a job title that I'm both relieved and mortified by.

At the PR firm I'd watched the executives arrive in their suits, carrying green juices, and I'd wonder if I too could build a career there. But unlike the executives, I was taking home $408 a week and I needed something that paid more, not in ten years after I'd paid my dues, but right then. At twenty-two, and regardless of my income, the federal government expected a thousand-dollar monthly check from me later that month. I was every millennial you've ever met. And I was in a real bind. It was my best friend who came up with the genius plan.

"Babysit?" I asked, confused.

Lila and I were sitting at our kitchen table—all the doors locked and deadbolted. We had been inseparable for nearly a decade but had only lived together for two months and were still afraid of our new surroundings. On the first night in our New York apartment, we heard a series of pops from our balcony on 101st Street. We joked nervously that they were gunshots but eventually convinced ourselves it was fireworks. A few minutes later we heard the sirens.

"You babysat in college. Why not just do that for a while?" Lila was referring to Saturday night gigs when I was out of dining hall points and desperate for cash to get me through. I have no interest in babysitting, but the alternative is leaving New York, just like my parents said I'd have to. And the only thing worse than changing diapers would be telling them they were right.

•••••

"Do you have any idea how expensive New York City is?" my father asked when I told him my plan to move there.

We were standing over the hood of my car, dead on the side of the highway. He was messing around with the engine, trying to get it running again. I sat inside, leaning out the window, fist around the butter knife he'd taught me to hot-wire it with after I'd lost the keys too many times.

Periodically, he waved at me to give it a rev, and in between, we argued. "Do you?" I shot back. "You've been to seven states in your whole life."

"All right, dumb ass. You go to the dirty, crime-filled city, where everyone gets mugged and writes sad poetry about it in Starbucks and try, with the other billion people there, to find a place to work." He shrugged. "You won't make it. There are no jobs out there right now."

"You don't know anything," I said.

"No, kid. You don't know anything."

Both of us were right.

●●●●●

Lila's suggestion piqued my interest enough for me to pursue it. I figured babysitting would supplement my PR income. I had no idea how lucrative the nanny industry could be.

Sasha has offered me more than double what I am currently making, and my head is spinning as I try to follow along with the crucial details of her family's hyperscheduled, organized life. In the coming weeks I'll need to be aware of Hunter's dairy intolerance and Ruby's weekly lunch playdates. It is important that I remember what pediatrician they see and the names of the family's housekeepers and doormen. But in the foyer is a fifty-thousand-dollar painting, and instead of giving Sasha my full attention, I am busy wondering if I have ever seen it in the MOMA.

"This is Ruby's room," Sasha says as I trail behind her.

I reach out to touch the velvety flowered wallpaper that wraps the room like a tightly bound present. In the corner is a small white bed covered in stuffed animals and dolls, cashmere blankets, and fluffy pillows. Bookcases packed with children's classics cling to corners but are partially hidden by toys and a custom-made dollhouse— everything a kid could ever want all in one place. Ruby's bedroom, along with its en suite bathroom, is larger than most studio apartments. It is spacious, polished, and pristine, but it's also cozy. The perfection is mesmerizing.

"Oh, and these are all labeled," Sasha says while balancing a drowsy Hunter on one hip.

She points to shiny bins and explains what should go where. The labels say things like *Art Supplies, Doll Accessories*, and *Musical Instruments*. There are kid-sized electric cars and scooters, bowling sets, and a stuffed dog bigger than the child herself. Sasha apologizes for her tendency to over organize.

"No, that's great. I hope some of your organizational skills wear off on me," I say, laughing. But it's not funny, because they never will, and five years from this moment, I will still be "misplacing" my debit card every other week.

Sasha continues with details and explanations as I glance over at Ruby, who is pouring fake cups of hot tea around a child-sized table. The teapot is dainty and beautiful and looks like real porcelain.

Even in the private moment of pretend play, Ruby's manners are exemplary.

"Would you like a cup of tea, Barbie?" she asks.

"Yes, please," she responds in a deeper voice.

Ruby's long brown hair rests against a dark wool sweater. When a piece falls in front of her face, she flicks it away. She looks like the subject of a magnificent painting, a gorgeous child in an exquisite space. I'm hoping my expression doesn't expose the awe I'm feeling, but I can't help being stunned by Sasha's home. Not just by the obvious wealth but, oddly, by its warmth. I wonder what it must feel like to grow up here.

"Stephanie?" When Sasha calls my name, I snap back to reality.

"Yes, sorry," I smile. "I missed that last part."

"I just asked if you had any other questions."

The truth is I have *so* many questions. *What's it like to reside on the most prestigious street in the world? To never budget or be restricted to the clearance rack? How does it feel to have such a beautiful family and peaceful home and to be able to walk into a store and never want for anything? The ability to go anywhere, do anything, be anyone?* I can't imagine it, but I feel no jealousy. Only a burning desire to be just like them.

Of course, I say none of these things, for that would be extremely inappropriate, and it's then that Ruby interrupts.

"Stephanie, do you want to hear what my piano teacher taught me?"

"Definitely," I say, and she leads the way.

In the less formal of two living rooms lives a grand piano. Ruby sits with perfect posture and a wide smile, a sleek Yamaha positioned among antique furniture, and I think to myself that one shot of this scene would be too elegant for even a Pottery Barn catalog.

I'm intrigued by this child, by her talents, interests, and manners. It's become clear in our brief time together today that Ruby is the sort of child expecting parents dream of. I find that I'm not just charmed by Ruby's life: I'm charmed by her.

"You're getting really good, Ruby," Sasha tells her. "If you keep practicing, you'll be able to play the whole song in no time. I'm sure of it."

Ruby shuffles through a songbook. I don't know what the notes on the page mean, and I'm not convinced that she does either. Sasha's daughter blushes, takes a breath, then her hands begin to work. The song is butchered, years from perfection, and her fingers and mind struggle to stay in sync. But Ruby has resources and limitless encouragement. There is no doubt that she will eventually play the song in its entirety. I think back to myself at that age with regret. Who would I have turned out to be if I had what Ruby has? Intellectually, emotionally, socially, she is so far ahead of where I had been.

"We'll see you Monday, then," Sasha says as I leave later that day. "The kids really seem to like you; it should be an easy transition."

"Awesome. Yeah, I'm really excited."

But that's the thing about kids. Rich, poor, smart, fresh, happy, angry, it doesn't matter. *Children are universally difficult.*

3

FLIP-FLOP

"THAT'S NOT RIGHT," RUBY EXPLODES.

"Okay, okay, no problem," I say.

Ruby, typically angelic, is irate with me.

We are smack in the middle of our favorite pastime of transforming the kitchen into an art studio. We have every art supply in the house out (which is a lot considering Sasha keeps practically an entire Michael's craft store in the front hall closet). The table is littered with markers and paints, the floor covered in poster-size coloring sheets. There is confetti everywhere, including in my hair. Ruby has just finished bejeweling a cardboard princess crown when she asks me to make her a pair of flip-flops out of paper. I have no idea that this is something she and Sasha have done many times before and therefore have no way of anticipating the very specific vision Ruby has in mind.

"No, no, no. That's not right either," she moans after I show her an updated pair. She stands abruptly, belting, "MOMMMMMMMMY!" before sprinting away in hysterics.

I look down at the makeshift footwear. A flimsy piece of tape holds one shoe together. It lets go suddenly, causing the whole thing to fall apart. It is not entirely lost on me why Ruby considers this a job *not* well done.

A moment later Sasha leads a sniffling Ruby back into the kitchen.

"I'm sorry," I say sheepishly. "I'm not sure how she wants me to make them."

"Of course you're not," Sasha says, shooting me a sympathetic smile. "Ruby, Stephanie has never made flip-flops with you before. Do you know what that means?"

Ruby flicks a tear away and shakes her head no.

"It means that when someone isn't sure about something you want from them you have to use your words, be patient, and show them how it's done. Otherwise, you will hurt their feelings and they might not want to do a project with you next time. Okay?"

Sasha spends the next few minutes demonstrating how to create the flip-flops correctly. Once the shoes are done, she hands them to Ruby, who puts them on happily.

"I'm sorry, Stephanie," Ruby says. "Next time I will have more patty-tents."

"Patience," Sasha corrects, but Ruby is already out of the room and off to locate her favorite Rapunzel dress.

Sasha looks at the clock. "You can head out, Stephanie. It's almost six anyway."

"Okay, great. I'll just clean up, then I'll go."

Sasha always says not to worry about the mess, but I insist. At playdates, I often observe other moms giving their nannies outrageous directions. One nanny has to disinfect every toy that's been touched, down to each individual building block. I heard another describe her end-of-day routine and how she can't leave until she checks every hand soap dispenser in the house to make sure it's completely full. If it's not, she'll need to add just a touch more Diptyque to the dispenser before clocking out. The more I see and hear, the more grateful I am to be working for Sasha.

I text Lila on the elevator ride down to say I'll be just a minute. As a doorman holds open the door, I say I'll see him tomorrow. I catch a glimpse of Lila waiting and immediately feel a touch of embarrassment. Or maybe it's jealousy. It's become hard for me to identify the difference.

"Ready?" I ask, and we start walking.

Lila is wearing her usual uniform for her job as a paralegal at a downtown law firm. A conservative blouse, today cream-colored, her warm skin complementing it well. Her black pencil skirt falls just below her knees, and she wears bandages to protect the blisters caused by her ballet flats. She's well accessorized, as always, big gold hoops and a necklace adding to her polish. I look down at my nanny wear. My Emerson College sweatshirt is smudged with glitter glue and covered in stickers. Among my peers, I now exist in a perpetual state of mortification.

"How was your day?"

She always asks this, despite how boring and repetitive my

responses are. "We made chocolate chip cookies," I tell her or "Ruby had ballet class but has a runny nose so she skipped it. She was feeling better by the afternoon, though." Lila never makes me feel bad about my answers and responds with variations of "Wow, it sounds like a really nice day!" This almost makes me feel worse. "Stop being so nice," I want to scream. "Look at me. I'm failing!" But Lila has always been gentle in the face of my failures. Even in college, when I wrote my first "novel," which was essentially *The Hunger Games* but set in outer space, Lila read every single page with enthusiasm.

Lila and I met when she still had braces and I had an intense and ongoing battle with forehead acne. I was the new student with no friends, and she was a cool kid—the kind who almost seemed grandfathered in to the popular table—as if that seat had always been there waiting for her. But she was so kind, you'd have never guessed it.

In the early days of our friendship we had little in common. Our worlds existed only in opposition, but for whatever reason, our differences seemed only to draw us together.

I had been ecstatic the first weekend we had plans to hang out. I was playing in a basketball game Saturday night at an overheated and musty Boys & Girls Club in East Providence. Lila was supposed to meet me at the game then come back to my house after, but as the game carried on, there was no sign of her. I dreaded approaching my family after the final buzzer and was, as predicted, faced with immediate ridicule.

"Hey, where's your imaginary friend?" Stew asked.

I was about to call him a big-eared idiot when suddenly Lila appeared.

"I'm so sorry," she apologized, explaining that her mother had been in a fender bender on the drive over. "She has a car accident every few months. She's a really crazy driver," Lila laughed sheepishly. It turned out this was the understatement of the year since Joie totaled more cars in a decade than most did in a lifetime.

Stew stared at her like she had ten heads, "So you were just in a car accident and you still got yourself here to hang out with this kid?" He pointed a finger toward me.

Lila smiled and said of course, as if no other option had ever crossed her mind.

Now, as we breathe in the heavy New York air, I can't help but feel grateful for her friendship. Lila is the only person who has known me in my past, present, and hopeful future and loves each version same as the last, even when I don't. Because *I* can't help thinking how only one year ago Lila and I were nearly equals. Strolling the streets of Back Bay, both college students, our futures seemed equally bright. Now Lila is working at a law firm and becoming who she's meant to be. And I'm spending my days braiding a naked Barbie doll's hair and wondering what an interest rate is.

"What about you?" I ask. "How was yours?"

We're about ten blocks from Sprinkles Cupcakes. We often meet after work to walk there together. Neither of us has much spending money, me trying to navigate how finances and bills work, and Lila making only forty-five thousand a year in Manhattan. But Sprinkles serves a Campfire, which is a cupcake with ice cream on top of a s'more, and we split both the item and the price, so we consider this one very big bargain.

"I was prepping a case file for Karina today, but I don't know; I wasn't buying this couple."

Lila's law firm handles visa cases for large corporations. Her boss, Karina, is an exceptionally good lawyer but is thirty-two and single. We often question what's wrong with her and cannot imagine how she can be *that* old and not married. Still, she's great at her job, and she thinks Lila is brilliant at hers, even though Lila often finds her role boring.

"Do you think you'll go to law school?" I ask as I finish the last bite of ice cream and we begin our walk back uptown to East Harlem. We cut through Central Park. It's close to dusk now, and the paths are quiet. Lila considers the question.

"I think so? My dad would like me to." She shrugs. "I guess I probably will."

"But do you want to be a lawyer?"

She tilts her head, her expression slightly irritated as she says *yes, she does*, but this is Lila's tell. Whenever Lila is unsure of her answer or isn't proud of a decision, she becomes angry when discussing it.

"What about you?" she asks after a moment. "How long do you think you'll nanny for?"

The truth is I have no idea. I hope not long. I'm still writing every day, but it's getting harder. I'm tired from long days chasing after children, and the passages come out stale, words falling flat. I want so desperately to have a respected job; TV writing is glamorous, something that excites people, that they respond to with admiration. I thought I'd set myself up for that, but I saw quickly that landing a writing gig fresh out of college wasn't realistic. I'd hoped the PR work would at least hone those creative muscles, but now I'm someone's domestic staff. No matter how I try to spin it, I am simply the help. And no one respects that.

Yet, somehow, something's telling me that I can still do it. Either I'm a dreamer, or I'm a complete fool. Potentially a bit of both.

"Oh, my God," Lila screams, interrupting my thoughts.

"What?" I say, and she points to a commotion. Rats are popping out of a sandbox in droves, scurrying in front of us as if they're in a hurry to get somewhere. They're huge, they're creepy, and worst of all they're appearing in mass numbers. We look at each other, sheer horror in our eyes, then make a mad dash.

We run all the way to the 79th Street park exit before finally slowing down.

"Wow," Lila says, winded. "That was revolting."

Then I start laughing.

"What's funny?" she asks because one might not always consider a run-in with the rat pack a laughing matter.

"It reminds me..." I say, then laugh a little more. "Remember my sister caused a mouse infestation in the basement one time? That sandbox kind of looked like my house."

4

——

THE RACETRACK

THE YEAR WAS 1996, AND every grown-up I knew wore their hair in a mullet and drank excessive amounts of Coca-Cola. I was five years old, and my father had just introduced me to his new girlfriend. She wasn't the first one I had met, but she would be the most memorable. Sherri was different. Because Sherri was a bitch.

My parents had conceived me on my grandmother's couch when they were in their late teens. It was Christmas Eve, and the house was empty on account of my grandmother being at midnight mass. My mother was firm that she wanted to keep the baby, so they married shortly thereafter, and, unsurprisingly, were divorced two years later. They were barely old enough to drink and on a constant merry-go-round of partners. And me? Well, I was just along for the ride.

It was the late nineties, but Sherri still styled her hair in a classic eighties perm. The smell of Marlboros lingered on her clothes, even fresh from the washer. She cursed like a sailor and had a special affinity for making me miserable. Unlike most children, I never longed for my parents to get back together. I could not have cared less either way and had paid little mind to my father's choice in women up until this point.

Stew and Sherri were both amateur race car drivers, and they had met at the track one September weekend. The two of them wasted what little cash they earned building cars that would take them weeks to put together and seconds to destroy. It seemed a rather expensive hobby to take up, especially for a man who worked in a manufacturing plant and an unemployed single mother. But racing was my father's life. He loved it so much he'd buy a new carburetor instead of paying his electric bill. He'd pawn a ring before forfeiting a new transmission. It was all he knew. Stew came from a long line of mechanics and grew up at racetracks and in auto body shops. My parents fought constantly, but mostly about the fact that he spent all his money on a car he wasn't even permitted to drive on an actual road, not to mention that he hardly ever won his races. It was a rare day when he'd finish in the top three.

The only thing I despised more than Sherri was the racetrack where they'd met. Seekonk Speedway was filled with greasy men and women, most of whom were missing a couple of their teeth. My dad raced most weekends, and since Saturday was his court-appointed night with me, I frequented the fast-car track. During his races, he would leave me in the stands with whoever was free to watch over me, usually his racing buddies. One of them had a son, AJ, and together we'd search for treasures under the bleachers. Often we found only cigarette butts and wads of chewed gum, but occasionally I would snag a quarter or a half-eaten candy bar. Above us were men in Dale Earnhardt shirts drinking warm beers, making bets, and hollering after a few too many.

If I was lucky, though, Grandma Kiser and Aunt Patty would be at the track.

My dad's mom and sister each stood four feet eleven inches tall. Both had thick, fiery red hair, at least until the chemo turned Grandma Kiser bald. Neither had managed to graduate from high school, and Aunty Patty had an extra front tooth that she had always meant to get removed.

The two of them spoiled me greatly, or as well as they could, given their limited means. When they were there, I could buy the biggest popcorn at the snack bar and a giant Sprite, too.

"Hey, Junior!" Grandma Kiser called one night at the track.

Everyone at the track called my dad that because his father had raced there until his liver got so bad he couldn't get farther than the couch. Racing was a family tradition. My father's father was the oldest of ten siblings whose parents were so dirt poor, they couldn't afford to go to the hospital, even for difficult births. My great-grandmother had all eleven of her children at home. Larry came out the healthiest. The deliveries left five of his siblings disabled and one stillborn. Perhaps that's why Stew lived his life as if he had six to spare.

My memories of Grandpa Larry are scarce, but I do recall that he always wore the same beat-up red Budweiser baseball cap and that Grandma Kiser adored him. By the time I came along, they weren't together, and Grandpa Larry lived in a tiny Providence apartment with his new girlfriend, Dee Dee. Dee Dee owned six pet parrots and zero cleaning supplies. Their apartment was full of bird poop and cigarette ashes, empty beer cans and potato chip bags.

Despite their longtime separation, Grandma Kiser seemed to love Grandpa Larry as much as if they'd only just married, though I cannot speak to why.

People described him as charming, but the words that really lingered after he was gone were ones like womanizer, thief, and drunk. Still, despite his being unfaithful their entire relationship, Grandma Kiser's loyalty to Grandpa Larry knew no bounds. Even when a thirty-year-old Grandpa Larry was caught sleeping with her fifteen-year-old sister, Grandma Kiser still stood by her man.

"What is she wearing this pink coat for?" Grandma Kiser snapped at my dad as he passed me off to Aunt Patty in the stands. "Where's the blue one I bought her?"

She was always furious when I came dressed in frilly outfits or girly colors. Even after an ultrasound confirmed that I would be a girl, Grandma Kiser had insisted I was a boy. A grandson would have carried on the family name. It didn't matter that the name came with zero respect, assets, or admiration. What mattered was that a boy could do for the bloodline what a girl could not.

Stew shrugged, "Hope sent her in that one." He paused, then nodded to the cigarette in her hand. "Still haven't given up the poison pencils?"

"What's it going to do? Give me more cancer? Please." Grandma Kiser scoffed.

When the race began, I leaned my head against Grandma Kiser

and watched as the automobiles began looping around in circles. The stock cars were painfully loud, so I drowned out the noise by cupping my hands over my ears. I wore an adult-sized hat that my father had made me to match those worn by his crew or, more accurately, his friends. It was bright red, the words KID KISER MOTOR SPORTS sketched across the front. I was running my hand along the brim when, suddenly, a car clipped the wall and burst into flames. As the driver's crew worked to free him from the fire, I covered my eyes with the hat.

"Bastard!" someone screamed. I turned to catch a man throwing his drink across the bleachers before collapsing, his head falling into his hands.

"Don't worry about him," Grandma Kiser said as I looked on. "Pat just don't know how to pick winners is all."

This is how it was at the racetrack. The night would start cheerfully enough, but most patrons didn't have a lot of money to begin with, so when you mixed lost bets with four hours' worth of alcohol, you ended up with crashes both on the track and in the stands. The speedway was all pleather jackets, high fives, and laughs, until the favored driver fell into third place and half the bettors realized they'd just gambled away a month's rent.

As the bleachers began to clear, Grandma Kiser hoisted me up onto her tiny shoulders. It was absurd; this woman was so small, we were practically the same size. But Grandma Kiser was strong. Real strong. One had to be to have endured such a life.

"What should we do while we wait for your daddy and Sherri to meet us on out here?" she asked.

Just then I threw my body back dramatically, the force nearly tipping Grandma Kiser over. "I don't want to see Sherri," I wailed.

"Why not?" Grandma Kiser asked.

My eyes filled with tears. I was too young to identify these emotions. I knew only how Sherri made me feel, which was that I had been replaced in my father's life. So I shouted out the only thing that made sense to me: "Because I really hate her!"

Grandma Kiser let out one of her larger-than-life laughs. "Oh, you are bad to the bone."

She loved that line. I didn't know what it meant, but I knew that when my aunt and grandma were there at the racetrack, I never felt frightened. It felt no different from being at a playground. Instead of swinging from the monkey bars I was hanging on the bleachers. After the race ended, my dad stormed out, smelling like a Shell station and screaming about his goddamn motherfucking exhaust.

By the time we finally arrived back from dinner that night I was exhausted. It was late, well past ten, and I immediately grabbed my stuffed Simba and curled up on the couch. Stew threw a fleece blanket over me before turning to Hope.

"Hey, ah, by the way," my dad said, "I need to talk to you about something."

"About what?" my mom asked.

"About Sherri."

"Ugh," my mom groaned. Hope was the only person who possessed a hatred for Sherri deeper than my own. Hope dated as much as Stew did, but unlike him, she had never really moved on from their relationship. For her, dating was a distraction, not an end game.

Her love for my dad came in an obsessive form, but she had a weapon in her game of love: me. "What's she done now?" Hope laughed.

He took a second to answer. My mom had been putting some dishes away when he said it. She dropped a plate that shattered on the apartment floor, and I replayed what he said as she picked up the pieces.

Sherri's pregnant.

Now it will be Sherri. Her son. A baby. Plus me.

Sherri was sticking around after all.

5

CHURCH CHAT

KINDERGARTEN IN NORTH PROVIDENCE, RHODE Island was only a half day of school, and while my mom worked as a secretary in a nearby doctor's office, her mother—my Gram—would pick me up. I'd run straight to her, waving frantically, and we'd walk hand in hand through the parking lot before piling into her old Buick.

Gram would take me back to the house where my mother had grown up and whip me up a sandwich. The daughter of parents hit hard during the Great Depression, Gram grocery shopped and cooked with two things in mind: what items gave you the most food for the cheapest price and what she'd cut a coupon for. As a result, most meals consisted of delicious foods with outrageous nutrition labels. Bologna and hot dogs, frozen Banquet dinners, and Little Debbie snack cakes.

In the afternoon, I'd practice whatever my grandparents were teaching me at the time. During one week Gram was showing me how to tie my shoes, a supposedly easy task that I couldn't seem to grasp. We sat on the floor of the bathroom while Gram repeated the motion of bunny ears. When it was my turn, I'd make six knots, announce it looked wrong, then collapse in defeat. If my grandfather, Papa, was home, he'd take me into the yard and show me how to ride a bike without the training wheels. I'd never get farther than a few inches, and I spent more time running inside to get Band–Aids than I did actually riding.

Later, we'd head up to Gram's dad's house. Pop Pop was ninety-six and dying, so we couldn't do much together aside from watch TV and eat.

Pop Pop would shout over to Gram, "Hey, Mo. Get me and this little lady a couple of those mini apple pies. And turn on this here television."

Pop Pop had a little auto shop in Lincoln where he had worked as a mechanic all his life. He could fix any truck you brought him so long as the engine was still kicking, and even then, he could sometimes replace the whole thing. He had worked half his life to afford the tiny house in the woods where I spent most weekdays until I was six years old.

There wasn't a swing set or toys to play with. But he had lots of grown grandchildren, Gram's brother having had six kids, and so people were always stopping by. The house perpetually smelled like Folger's, a pot of coffee always ready for unexpected guests. I spent a time searching for lady slippers in the woods then convincing Gram to take out her disposable camera to photograph them. I certainly did not see tutors or learn to play musical instruments, activities far from my parents' radar.

We'd leave Pop Pop's by four thirty to make the five o'clock mass. Gram would lead us to the front, shuffling into her regular pew on the left. I tried to do what everyone else did, but the seats were hard, and, eventually, small thuds echoed as I tapped my feet along the bottom of the pew.

"Stephy, stop that," Gram shushed me.

Sigh.

I sat back in my seat and opened the hymnal. The words may as well have been hieroglyphs, so I watched Gram's mouth move in an attempt to make out the song the congregation was singing. When it ended, the priest stood up and said a bunch of words that Gram nodded along with.

These services seemed to last for days. Unlike the speedway, five o'clock mass was very safe, but it was painfully boring. Unfortunately, it was also where Gram spent a whole lot of time, and in turn, so did I.

"Did you hear what Deacon Louis said today?" Gram asked me on the short drive back to her house.

"That God will always take care of us?"

"That's right. As long as you pray, he will always listen."

Gram's life revolved around her religion. When she wasn't physically at mass, she was teaching catechism classes, delivering communion to nursing homes, or kneeling by her bed with a rosary in hand. It was as if she had a direct line to Jesus himself. Before having my mother, Gram had a miscarriage that nearly took her life. She often told the story of how she nearly died and how the doctors brought her back to life. As the attending physician fought to stabilize her, Gram saw a light, and it was Mary's voice that led her back to her body.

Hope said this story is embellished, and since Stew is an atheist, he thought it was bullshit, but Gram remained sure of the experience.

After church, Gram prepared dinner, delicious smells of melted butter wafting into the living room, where I was heavily invested in an episode of *Rugrats*. I'd nearly finished the episode when she called for me to come eat.

I was parked at Gram's table, happily digging into her shepherd's pie, when Hope pushed through the back door. She was scowling and launched into complaining to Gram about something that I tuned out, focused on my food and the hope that she'd let me stay at Gram's cozy house instead of piling us both into the car to go back to our cold apartment.

"What exactly did she say?" Gram pressed, something about her tone catching my ear.

Gram plopped another helping of shepherd's pie onto my plate, while my mom cringed. No one knew that my mother was fighting her own demons with food, or if they did, they didn't understand it.

"The teacher said she can't read," Hope said flatly. "That's what she said."

"Can't read what?" Gram asked.

"Anything!" My mom snapped. "She can't read anything! Not a single word."

My mom had just come from a conference with Mrs. O'Grady, my kindergarten teacher, who explained to my mother that I struggled to sound out even the simplest of syllables.

"She's younger than the other kids," my mom said. "She was only four when the school year started. The rest of the class was already five."

Mrs. O'Grady acknowledged this, but it wasn't just reading—I was failing to absorb most subject matter. I even had difficulty comprehending stories that were read aloud to me. She thought I should be put in the disabilities program. "Maybe with the extra support," the teacher said, "she'll have a shot at catching up."

Mrs. O'Grady wasn't wrong. My peers learned to count to ten in half the time that I did. They could write their names before I had memorized the letters in mine. It seemed like each time I finally understood one lesson, the class had already moved on to another.

"There's just one more thing," Mrs. O'Grady had said. My mom waited for her to continue. "The other kids, they've noticed that, well…" her voice trailed off. "Well, that she's overweight. They pick on her."

"Does it bother you," my mom later asked me, "that the kids call you fat?"

I told her no, and when she asked why, I was direct: "Because I *am* fat. I love food, and that's why I'm so big."

"People learn at their own speed," Gram told my mom. "And she's just big-boned. My father never liked a skinny minnie anyway, you know that."

My mom hated the way Gram made excuses for me, but Gram was my best friend. I liked hanging out with her more than any kid my own age.

"She's not just big-boned, Mom," Hope sneered, pulling my plate out from under me as I protested. "She's overweight and the pediatrician has told us both that multiple times."

Hope pulled my jacket off the coatrack, but I edged away. She followed me around the house, trying to get me to put it on.

"Come on, Stephy, listen to your mother," Gram said soothingly. But I wouldn't hear it. I never would. Each night by the time my mom swung by after work to pick me up, I'd already eaten dinner and taken a bath. There was nothing left to do but drive home and go to sleep, but I'd refuse. My mother, exhausted from a long day at work and often a restless night with me who often did not sleep, would nearly explode with frustration.

"I want to stay here!"

I never wanted to leave Gram's. My mother couldn't understand my resistance, but the answer was simple. It wasn't about the snacks or the TV time. It was that being with Gram was the only time when I always knew what to expect.

6

LITTLE LEARNING

THERE IS CONSISTENCY IN EVERYTHING Ruby and Hunter do. The children have a schedule, and everyone around them sticks to it. From the moment Sasha wakes them to the second they drift off to sleep, Ruby and Hunter follow a plan. They always know what to expect. When Sasha needs to run an errand, she makes clear not only when she is leaving but when she'll be back. They have weekly classes. Monthly playdates. Daily baths. Their lives are flawlessly structured. I imagine such predictability is a relief.

By the time I arrive at work at nine a.m., Sasha already has Ruby dressed in an Oscar de la Renta dress. Her hair is combed and neatly braided with a small bow pinning it back. Ruby is more elegant on weekday mornings than Queen Elizabeth was at a Sunday mass. I cannot recall any moment in my twenty-two-year history that I ever looked as graceful as Ruby does, and that is because there hasn't been one.

This is the sort of outfit she always wears on school days. The dress, embroidered with palm trees, is valued at four hundred twenty-five dollars. I know this because I removed the tag myself just days before. I place it in her closet, jamming it in among a row of similar dresses. I begin to wonder, even given the means, if I'd spend nearly a thousand dollars on an outfit that undoubtedly will not fit the child in less than a year. It seems both exquisite and wasteful.

"What's the plan for today?" I ask Sasha once I'm settled.

Most days Sasha takes Hunter to his prearranged activities, so I spend most of my time with Ruby, who took to me almost immediately. Sasha had explained that Hunter had never really had a sitter before and is very attached to her. This is fine by me, since Ruby is so consistently well behaved and easier to reason with.

"Ruby has Little Learning from ten to eleven thirty. Then she'll need a quick lunch before you drop her at school. She'll probably just want a hot dog."

"From where?" I ask.

"Just one of the food carts by Central Park."

"Yeah," Ruby cheers, "street hot dog!"

For a Fifth Avenue princess, Ruby is surprisingly humble. Despite their wealth and resources, Ruby's family is relatively low key. I often come in after a weekend to find empty Domino's boxes in the recycling bin or a melted Ben & Jerry's carton in the sink. Sasha and her husband both grew up on Fifth Avenue. They have only ever known this life of glamour, yet they poke fun at fancy dinner parties where the main courses are the size of gumballs and the guests spend the evening bragging about their private yachts.

Sasha and Ian should be the worst kind of Upper East Siders, but I find them unpretentious.

"I've left some cash on the table. Feel free to get yourself something to eat, too," Sasha instructs as she wrestles Hunter into *his* Armani coat.

"Wait, where is Little Learning?"

"It's just a few blocks away," she answers before heading out the door, "on the corner of East 81st and Fifth. You can't miss it."

When Sasha and Hunter leave, I turn to Ruby, who is a few licks into a lollipop that's turned her mouth the same color as Taylor Swift's signature lipstick. It's early in the day for candy, but Sasha's lax parenting philosophy allows it.

I help Ruby into a pair of black ballet flats and tie my Nikes before we head out to stroll, hand in hand. She calls out taxis that have their lights off. If one passes with its lights on, it is my responsibility to announce it. What the game lacks in complexity it makes up for in thrill. Ruby shrieks with surprise at an unoccupied cab that drives by. She and I continue the silly game until we reach our destination.

Number 4 East 81st Street is a three-story brownstone that sits directly across from one of the most prestigious art museums in the world. I cannot imagine what sort of children's class would require such a fancy facility, and for a second, I assume Sasha has mistaken the address.

"No, this is it," Ruby insists. "See?"

She points to the doorbell. Sure enough, on a sign no bigger than my pinkie finger are the words: *Little Learning*. I press the button, and we're buzzed in.

"Hello," a woman calls from behind her desk, to the right of a grand marble fireplace. The room looks more like a young heiress' bachelorette pad than it does a place for toddler education. The hardwood floor is covered in a fur rug, and beige furniture crowds the sitting area. Lines of bookcases display famous children's books. I think back to the elementary school in my hometown. The broken desks and the dim fluorescent lighting. The borrowed textbooks with penis doodles around the pages. Perhaps I would have learned better had I been studying in a chic penthouse instead of a medieval lair.

"Who do we have here?" The woman continues.

"Ruby Ross, in the ten o'clock class."

"All right, Ruby, you can go ahead downstairs and find your teacher." Then she lowers her voice as if she's about to reveal a secret. "I heard you're baking things that start with the letter *C* today."

Ruby, who is shy, stands timidly behind me. Eventually, with some gentle coaxing, she descends the stairs. I listen to Ruby's steps disappearing until it is silent. There are a few empty seats, and I choose one next to someone who is most likely a nanny, speaking quickly into a Bluetooth headset. She eyes me suspiciously as I sit down. I smile, but she doesn't return the gesture, and I assume she thinks I'm just another nosy Upper East Side mom trying to eavesdrop on her phone call. Maybe she's right about the nosy part, at least.

"*Ah, si, si.* Katherine is at Little Learning now, but her class only goes another fifteen minutes."

With a closer look, I realize that I recognize the nanny from Ruby's school. Her name is Elissa, and she watches a sweet-faced girl with freckles and a front tooth gap.

"Oh, yes, it'll be an early night. I should be out of work at seven, home by eight."

She spends the next few seconds nodding in agreement with whomever speaks from the other side.

As Elissa's conversation carries on, I Google the cost of Little Learning classes. *Five hundred dollars.* I feel my eyes grow wide. Five hundred dollars *a class*?

How long is this class? How many kids? Surely, the student-teacher ratio must be one-to-one for that sort of money. Even then, it seems absurd.

"Katherine is almost done," Elissa says, beside me. "We have to go to ballet now. I'll call you on my way home. *Si. Si. Nos vemos.*" Elissa clicks off the phone.

As she begins to gather her things, I decide it's my chance to finally make a nanny friend. Nannying isn't the sort of job that provides coworkers. While my friends enjoy chatting with work friends over weekly lunches of catered Chipotle and hearty salads from Sweetgreen, I eat my lunch with a two-year-old on my lap. When my weekday commute ushers me past the hustle and bustle of the offices in midtown, I picture a group of twenty-something professionals at a happy hour. Lila often describes outings with her paralegal coworkers; they can't afford fancy spots just yet, but they happily drop five dollars a beer at an East Village watering hole when they can. While I've grown to enjoy my workdays, this is not where I want to be. I wanted a career, not just a job, and this hardly qualifies as either. Everyone I encounter during my workday seems either too young or too old to be a friend. I'm becoming desperate, so I take a breath, gather my confidence, and introduce myself.

"Hi, I'm Steph. I'm Ruby's nanny," I say holding out my hand. Elissa looks at me with reservation but eventually accepts the greeting.

"Elissa. Katherine's nanny."

"I've seen you at school a few times," I continue.

"The girls are not in the same class," she says flatly.

I feel the sting of embarrassment—of social ineptitude—but I am confused. In college, I could roam the hall of my dorm and have five new friends in minutes. Here, only a year later, all the money in the world wouldn't get this sixty-year-old woman to converse with me. This is some sort of rock bottom. The woman in front of me is not interested in the cute Zara sweater I'm wearing or the downtown clubs where I know the bouncers. I'm not like her. I'm also not like the mothers around here. *So where do I fit in?*

"Where are you from?" she asks after a moment.

Glad to see a flicker of interest, I quickly respond, "Rhode Island."

"Long Island?"

"No, Rhode Island. Like near Boston."

She stares at me blankly.

Just then, a class is released, and I watch a group of three-year-olds stumble up the stairs. I count two teachers and five students. Katherine is one of them. The teachers hand the children off to their stay-at-home moms or nannies who have trickled in as Elissa and I attempt conversation. When it's Katherine's turn, one of the teachers bends down to meet her at eye level.

"Katherine, do you want to tell your nanny what you read to the class today?" Sheepishly, Katherine nudges her chin into her shoulder. "Come on," the teacher encourages. "Show Elissa what you read."

Slowly, the three-year-old pulls out a book that had been tucked underneath her arm. I recognize the cover. *Chicka Chicka, Boom Boom.* I too had once learned to read the beloved story—when I was eight years old and in the second grade.

"I read all the pages but one," she says proudly.

"Last week she had trouble with the *T, U, V* pages, but our teaching assistant recognized today she was simply confusing *U* and *Y* sounds. We corrected it in no time." Her teacher smiles.

I watch as the teacher and nanny clap in celebration. Everyone is so proud. Even I, a complete stranger to this child, am impressed. I wonder, *What if I had gone to Little Learning?* I'd spent my entire childhood being labeled "delayed." But was I? Was little Katherine a uniquely fast learner or is this what you get for five hundred dollars an hour?

I begin to think maybe I hadn't been slow after all. Maybe I had just been born into the wrong class.

7

BABY GALA

WE ARE STANDING BY THE entrance of the Natural History Museum's annual children's gala. Robert De Niro brushes past me, a Kobe beef slider in his hand, sneaking bites as he chases his daughter through a dinosaur exhibit. I have seen him in the school pickup line, though never this close. Here in this setting, with a head of unkempt hair and wrinkled clothes, Rob is nearly unrecognizable. In the bubble of wealthy Manhattan, he appears to be just another dollar-heavy dad. A prehistoric dad—*but still*—just a dad.

When I asked Sasha about the dress code for the gala her answer was simple—: "Some people might get dressed up, but a lot will just come in nice jeans. Wear whatever you feel comfortable in." But now as I stand under the dim lighting, in the Hall of Ocean Life, I feel embarrassed. I look down at my cream-colored Target blouse to find it is lost in a sea of chic black Givenchy midis. It turns out that I have misunderstood the event. Sure, the gala is for children, but it also provides an opportunity for Upper East and West Siders to showcase their family's wealth in a space that allows all family members, young and old, to play a role. The mothers here are taking notes. *Which children had the best manners? Which families arrived in black cars? Which husband had the nicest Rolex?* This isn't a children's party. It is a talent show for family status.

I pass mothers who are so decked out I wonder if they've enlisted help from a stylist. They wear sharp diamonds and thin heels and wrap their shoulders in layers of skin-soft silk. The fathers, straight from their offices on Wall Street or in Midtown, come in their finest Italian suits. They shoot out brief emails on their BlackBerrys and speak quickly into iPhones. When they pass by one another, they exchange firm handshakes, and say things like "How about the hit the stock market took this week?" Even the children, high on sugary treats and drowning in tears of their own tantrums, have come red carpet ready. It is one thing to be at the gala. It's another to *stand out* at the gala.

I am very concerned that I am standing out, and not in the way I would have hoped. I have never been to a fancy party, let alone one that suggests a donation on top of the ticket price. I look around at the decorations and photographers, pop-up bars and staff, and suddenly feel overwhelmed. It's exhilarating to be here, but I also find myself uneasy, my feelings contradictory yet intertwined.

"What should we do first?" Sasha asks the children.

In her petite fingers is a thick brochure highlighting the activities for this year's event. The possibilities are many: animal encounters, world-famous magicians, a dessert bar sponsored by Shake

Shack. I feel envy coming on, and so I quickly remind myself that I once had my seventh birthday party at Papa Gino's. As the guest of honor, I was allowed to make my own pizza. I know a thing or two about childhood excitement myself.

This museum party, held from six to nine p.m. only once a year, is every child's dream. It's more magical than Disney World's parade down Main Street. But it's exclusive. A ticket to the gala will cost you three times what a ticket to Epcot would, and that's only if you can get one. Family packages run up to $25,000 for the evening, and tickets are not mailed in advance but held by security in a list at the door.

"I want to do the fossil digging!" Ruby declares.

"Okay, let's see," Sasha runs her finger down the map. "That's on the third floor. Stephanie, do you want to take her to that, and I'll take Hunter to face painting?"

"Oh, you want us to separate?" I ask, the idea of being on my own inducing panic. At least if we stay together, I can hide behind Sasha and go unnoticed. On my own with Ruby, I risk exposure. I don't belong in this world, and I'm constantly waiting for the moment when I slip up. As a child or a teenager, I would have found all this so ridiculous it would have been laughable, but that was before. Before I became so envious.

I turn over my Forever 21 purse in an attempt to hide the word *fabulous* that is etched across one side. I think of Lila's Marc Jacobs purses sitting in our front hall closet and curse myself for not borrowing one.

"Just so they can fit in all the activities," Sasha says, but she senses my stress and adds, "but we can meet back up for dinner. Let's all be back at the buffet in an hour?"

"Okay, yeah, sure."

Ruby settles her hand into mine, and I decide that I'll need to play it cool. I have discovered the best way to fit into this world is to act as if the spectacular is all too familiar. When Ruby and I pass by waiters in black jackets and bow ties, who hold out fancy hors d'oeuvres to children no older than three, I keep my eyes straight ahead. I do not accept any of the endless swag that desperate sponsors keep shoving Ruby's way. I even decline the sparkling water that any mom who isn't sipping champagne has stopped to enjoy. The less I take, the less it will appear I need. Wealthy people can afford to look greedy. It's not unusual for them to be given free products, clothing, or experiences. These are the sort of people who companies want to be repping, and later buying, their merchandise.

But it's different for me. The more I take, the more I must not have. The more they take, the more they will have.

Two small voices call Ruby's name, and she shrieks with excitement. In the far corner are two of her schoolmates: Katherine and a dark-haired boy whose name I can't recall. I spot Elissa, and although our last exchange wasn't all that warm, I am happy to see a familiar face and decide to say hello.

"So," Elissa raises an eyebrow, "what do you think?"

"About the party?" I ask.

She nods. It is the first time all night that I feel at ease. I know that Elissa does not care if my shoes are real leather or what skin-care products I rely on. Like me, she is just a woman spending Thursday evening at work. I've found a safe ear.

"Okay, honestly…it's amazing. There are so many things to do and so much free stuff…and did you see the buffet? They have three kinds of chicken nuggets!"

Elissa laughs. "This is the first one you come to, *si*?"

I tell her that it is and that up until an hour ago, I hadn't even known that this sort of extravagant children's soiree existed.

"You could feed a whole family in Peru for a year with the food here," Elissa jokes, adding, "You know, the mac and cheese balls are very yummy." From a plate to the side of her, she offers one up. I thank her and pop it in my mouth.

"Let me give you one piece of advice, Stephania," Elissa says as we watch the children dust off a Brachiosaurus bone, "Make sure you enjoy everything these people bring you to."

"Why?"

"Because we couldn't afford to be here without them."

I wonder for a moment if that's true. Perhaps if Elissa and I work hard enough, make enough, we too could one day be real guests at this event. But most of the guests here are under age twelve. They didn't earn a spot on this guest list. They were born on it.

"Oh, I'll take one," Elissa whispers to a waiter carrying a tray of sushi.

Elissa is tiny. No taller than the average fifth grader, in fact. I tower over her so much that I often need to bend my knees just to meet her eyes. I can't be sure if her words have been said with hostility, but if they were, I would understand. Why would an immigrant from an impoverished village in South America find this scene any-thing but offensive? But from the smirk on her face, I realize that Elissa is not upset. She takes the parties and vacations, food and beach houses for everything they are. She knows how to make the most out of this job.

I realize I should be making my personal most of this, too. Someone here must know or even *be* a producer, writer, or director. But it seems disrespectful to Sasha to even consider networking with her peers while wiping leftover chocolate shake off her daughter's face. My goals and reality don't seem to align in this room together, so I decide against seeking connections.

"So you're saying that I should grab the sunglasses that the booths are giving away?"

"No, Stephania, don't take the sunglasses." Elissa laughs and turns to show me the contents of her purse. Inside it are dozens of items she has collected over the course of the evening: logoed stress balls, graphic T-shirts, and, in a napkin, cookies for later. "Don't take one thing. Take it all."

●●●●●

In the weeks following the gala, I am blessed with a new hope. Elissa and I are getting the girls together for weekly playdates, and she is no longer reserved in my company. Elissa speaks openly about her grandchildren, her family back in Peru, and how she transitioned from housekeeper to nanny in her late fifties. She is nearing seventy years old and still works sixty hours a week to make ends meet. We exchange stories from our workweek, pieces of my day that childless friends my own age can't understand, and I find comfort in the company of someone who knows what it means to be someone's nanny.

But my growing social circle isn't the only thing changing in my workday.

Despite his strong objections, Sasha has begun leaving Hunter and me together regularly. One afternoon, Ruby and I arrive back at the apartment and find Sasha waiting. Ruby has a birthday party to attend, and Sasha has decided to take her.

"We should be back no later than five thirty, but Hunter can have dinner before. Ruby will just eat at the party." Sasha pauses to give Hunter a quick kiss. "Feel free to do whatever with him, Stephanie. We'll see you later!"

Hunter no longer cries when left in my care, but he also does not celebrate. He eyes the door for some time after his mother leaves, and I do not dare speak or move. Months ago, I learned that, just like an animal in the wild, it is best to approach a reluctant toddler with caution and to always allow them the first move when engaging. Anything too sudden on my part has the potential to send Hunter spiraling.

I follow a safe distance behind Hunter as he enters Ruby's room. His room is cozy but dull compared to Ruby's second master bedroom, and he prefers her room to his own. Hunter and I have a little song and dance routine. He will enter the bedroom and pick out one of the hundreds of toys to entertain himself, though he remains wary of my presence. He will play for a minute before peeking over his shoulder to see if I am still there.

Usually, Hunter will pick through the bin of puzzles or comb over a bucket of action figures, but today he decides to change course. He finds his way to Ruby's bed, hoists himself up, and sits. A minute passes, and I'm unsure of what to do next, so I take a seat on the floor and wait. It's just us at home and the large apartment is otherwise quiet. I am sitting in the company of a tiny human who, without a diaper, would be dressed in his own feces, and yet *I* am the one feeling self-conscious and awkward. I'm finding it increasingly embarrassing to be me.

A stuffed animal lies on the ground near my leg. I watch as Hunter eyes it, likely contemplating whether he should ask me to send it his way. In the end, he must really want the fluffy bear, because he suddenly points assertively. I pick up the toy and gently toss it over, but Hunter has not yet mastered hand-eye coordination. The bear flies through his hands and bounces off his head with a soft thud.

While Hunter looks down at the fallen stuffed animal, I wait, certain my miscalculation will send him into a meltdown our afternoon will not recover from. With my jaw clenched tightly, I steel for the first sounds of screeching, only to be met with sweet baby chuckles.

Hunter is...laughing?

I let out a deep exhale. Feeling courageous, I pick up another stuffed animal and throw it toward him. Again, he erupts into laughter. It is odd, finding such relief in the approval of a boy who can barely pronounce his own name, but I find the shared moment uplifting. For the next fifteen minutes we continue the stuffed animal toss. It isn't much of a game, and it is one that we will play dozens more times before making any solid progress, *but today Hunter is laughing*. It's all the hope I need.

That night, I leave Sasha's feeling reassured. Ruby and I have already established a bond, and now a connection with her brother also appears promising. If I could get Hunter to not only accept my company but enjoy it, then phase one of my initiation would be complete.

•••••

On Friday evenings, I leave Sasha's Fifth Avenue apartment having made more money in one week than my mother's part-time secretarial work pays her in an entire month. I ride the subway home while mentally planning what portion will go to bills and how much I will put away to save. I have ideas on ways to invest and put the cash to good use. But I also don't have experience with money, so while my plans flourish, my bank account withers, and I burn through what I make just as fast as I earn it. I have just turned twenty-three, and for someone whose family often relied on dollar scratch tickets to afford gas, it feels like I've amassed a small fortune. But somehow I only ever pay my bills and don't save anything. The more money I'm exposed to, the more I want, and the more I make, the more I spend. I'm on a financial Ferris wheel and the only thing I know for sure is that I am no longer the ten-year-old once easily pleased with a single pair of new Skechers. New York City is a playground, each bar a slide I have to try, every restaurant a swing waiting for me to take a seat. I buy dresses from GUESS and Topshop, their Fifth Avenue flagships so bright and sleek they inspire me to drop a hundred eighty dollars on an outfit I wear only once.

●●●●●

"Thank you, Stephanie. Here is everything from this week," Sasha says. I rarely work on weekends but agreed to babysit so Sasha and her husband could attend a fundraiser. Sasha pulls a white envelope filled with hundreds of dollars in twenties from a vintage Birkin bag. I do not feel comfortable asking to leave my envelope of money there until Monday, mainly because I don't want to explain where I am headed at nearly midnight, so I take the cash out with me. "See you next week." I wave to their doorman as I leave.

I walk one block down before stripping off my *Golden Girls* T-shirt to reveal a black bodysuit, and I throw the T in a curbside trash can. It's too big to fit in my purse, and this club does not attract the sort of people who appreciate cheap pop-culture memorabilia. To wear it would be sexual suicide, and because I lack any sort of natural allure in the first place, I decide not to risk going any lower on the desirable woman food chain.

Lila and her boyfriend are waiting impatiently when my cab pulls up. "You are very late," Carlos fusses.

"Sorry, there was traffic in Times Square," I say, then turn to Lila. "I need you to stuff these in your bra." I hand over half the stack of twenties.

"Steph, what, no! Put them in your purse."

"I can't. You know purses disappear when I'm drunk, and I don't know how drunk I'm going to get."

There's a long pause. Lila is not happy, but she is *always* reliable.

"Look, it's a week's worth of money. Please. This is where it will be safest."

Lila sighs, then we both tuck our twenties in tight and go inside. Tonight, the manager gives Carlos a table right next to Jason Derulo. Jason checks out the girls around me all night long; he even goes home with one of us. I'm sure he considered me. If I had to guess, I'd say I was probably at the very top of his list, but in the end, he chooses Miss Ecuador 2015. I delete "Ridin' Solo" off my iTunes first thing the next morning.

Later, at nearly dawn, we eat thin slices of pizza in a shop in the East Village. My friends and I laugh until we finally hail taxis, dozing off on the ride home, and reaching our beds just as most of the city is waking up. My life has become spectacular, the exhaustion overshadowed by the exhilaration, and I don't notice how undisciplined I am becoming. The next morning I'm greeted by an unwelcome dose of reality.

"You're two weeks late on your loan. You need to pay it now, Steph," my mom yells through the phone.

It's Monday, so I am on my way to work after a boozy Sunday brunch in Soho that served stronger mimosas than I'd anticipated. I am hungover and tired, but I find my mother's repetitive line of conversation the most exhausting thing of all.

"Yup, got it," I say.

"No, Steph, today. We can't help you with these, okay? We have our own bills."

"Which you guys never pay," I hiss. "Do you know how hypocritical it is that you call me to pay my bills when one of you literally files for bankruptcy every five years?!"

My mother hangs up, which is a relief more than anything else.

It might be late, but at least I'll eventually make the payment I owe. I remind myself to pay the loan first thing Friday because I spent my last $260 on a ticket to a Pitbull concert. I sat in the fourth row while he belted out the modern classic "Timber" and drank shots on stage straight from a bottle. I regret nothing.

As I cross over to Lexington from Park, I think of how strained the relationship with family has become. My parents find my New York attitude arrogant. Each story I tell they perceive to be a brag. Every designer shirt I wear they interpret as a personal attack. They see my desire for finer things as a rejection of them and their lifestyle. It isn't, but what I'm finding is that there is a much bigger world out there than the one I grew up in. I enjoy foods they have never heard of and will never try. Our similarities have vanished, but the bigger issue is that they say I have also developed an air of superiority, mocking their home and town as if I too hadn't once been part of it. At first, that's only how they perceive it, but then I start leaning into it. I fear that any acknowledgment of who I used to be will prohibit me from fitting into my new surroundings. I barely return home now, and when I do it's far from pleasant. The truth is that I have yet to make anything of myself. I have only a crumb of what my employers have, and I'm squandering the opportunity anyway. I'm a nanny acting as if I'm a high-powered CEO. I'm a millennial in need of a reality check.

My sisters are still young, both in their early teens. They often call to report stories of particular absurdity, like when my mother had a dream that the youngest, Lydia, had suffocated in her sleep. By the time everyone woke the next morning they found their necks sore and their pillows missing. Hysterical with fear, my mother had thrown out every headrest in the house. Incidents like this are routine and lead me to believe I'm way too normal to be associated with them anymore.

"Stephanie!" Ruby screeches when she hears the front door open. I say good morning and listen to the pitter-patter of little feet making their way to me. I love that sound. When Ruby appears, my fatigue temporarily vanishes, and I wrap her in a hug that proves more powerful against my headache than Advil. "Mom doesn't feel good," Ruby reports.

"Oh, no," I say, "what's wrong with her?"

It is the third time Sasha has been ill in two weeks. "Her belly hurts. Come see."

Reluctantly, I follow Ruby into Sasha's room. Although I have worked for their family for a few months now, entering Sasha's bedroom still feels invasive. I stay out of her room as much as I can, but with her recent illnesses, it's become difficult to avoid.

"Hi, Stephanie." Sasha is in pajamas and the floor-length curtains are still pulled shut.

Hunter sits on the edge of the bed beneath a crystal chandelier, and he holds his arms out when he sees me. Hunter now seeks out my companionship, and I've come to adore him. My friends are tired of the dozens of pictures I send them, snapshots of moments in Hunter's day, a boy who isn't related to them, or to me either, for that matter. I kiss the top of his head as I lift him and balance him on one hip.

"Can I ask you a favor? Would you mind running to the grocery store and getting me some popsicles?" Sasha says.

"Of course," I say, though I am taken aback by the request. It's rare that Sasha asks me for anything outside of my general childcare duties. "What kind?"

"Cherry, if they have it. Will you just hand me my wallet?"

I carry it over from the bureau when Hunter pipes in, "I come, Stephanie?" I tell him that he can, and he runs off to find his coat. Sasha is fumbling through a thick wad of cash when she starts to explain why she's been feeling unwell lately. I am only half listening, busy trying to decide whether or not I should bother taking the stroller, when her last words pique my interest. "Wait, sorry. I missed the end. Did you say morning sickness?"

"Yes," she whispers, "but don't tell the kids. They don't know that I'm pregnant yet."

Stunned, I pause longer than what is likely acceptable. I can't remember if I manage to say congratulations. I know I mean to, but I am too panicked to locate any manners. I have only just won over Hunter, and I have never cared for a newborn. I can't be sure what the new addition will mean for me, their nanny, and more importantly for them.

I'd imagined that my mother hounding me about money would be the worst news of my day, but I remember who she was, a twenty-eight-year-old mother of three barely scraping by, lonely, and exhausted. I know the sort of damage new additions can bring to a family, and I am terrified for Sasha. The one thing I cannot understand when she tells me this is *why she looks so incredibly happy.*

8

GOLDFISH, GONE

BY THE TIME I WAS seven, most of the people I spent my younger years with were dead. Gram's dad, Pop Pop, was the first to go. His battle with bone cancer had been grueling. It crippled him first, his knuckles swelling to the size of clementines. Later, his speech began to slur, and then his appetite disappeared. When the hospice nurse came to explain the circle of life to me, I nodded along since I understood. I had seen *The Lion King*. At the wake, I reached into the casket to stroke his hand, but the coldness startled me, and I quickly pulled back.

Only a few months after Pop Pop died, it was Grandpa Larry's turn. Grandpa Larry had spent most of his life with a beer in his hand, and everyone assumed it would be his liver that would take him out. But when doctors found a brain tumor in his frontal lobe, the promise of death was irrefutable and fast. Grandpa Larry forgot who I was shortly after his diagnosis. He was found late one evening with a still-burning cigarette in the ashtray and a Bud Light on the nightstand. At least he died surrounded by his loved ones.

I was seven when Grandma Kiser passed. My parents, recently reconciled, woke me up one morning, and as I sat in my bed, they delivered the news. I didn't say anything when they told me, and my mother assumed I was still wrestling with the sensitive concept of death. On the contrary, I had come to understand death perfectly well, which is why I found there was nothing to say.

Grandma Kiser hadn't any money put aside for a burial, having blown nearly every penny she ever made at the casino. She played slots and bought scratch cards religiously. It was impossible that a woman with a middle school education would ever gain wealth from her cashier job, so perhaps gambling seemed like better odds. In the end it was cheapest to cremate her. At her request, her ashes were spread around the racetrack where she'd spent much of a hard life. Long after she was gone, people would still refer to her as white trash, as if she ever had a chance.

Two decades after her death, I would be nannying a five-year-old girl. When her first fish died, her parents spent the hours that followed in a frenzy, calling every pet store in a forty-block radius to get an identical replacement fish. When they couldn't find one with the same coloring, they decided to just throw the tank out, a bold attempt to protect their child from the harsh reality of loss of life. At first, Ruby didn't bring up the missing tank, but months later she confessed a secret to me.

"Steph," she whispered, "do you promise you'll never tell anyone?"

I nodded.

"I lost my fish. I don't want Mom to know because she'll think I'm a bad pet owner, but I don't know where I put him. One day he was here and then he was just gone."

At that moment I wondered which of us had been done more of a disservice at that age: me, who spent the next few years expecting everyone she loved to suddenly vanish, or the trust fund child, who went about her days believing she had misplaced a small aquarium.

Some of the losses in my childhood left voids. I missed Pop Pop and Grandma Kiser terribly, but others I'd seen off cheerfully, waving goodbye bigger than a prom queen to a crowd. Through it all, one thing remained constant: my parents' bickering.

"I have Nicky Saturday night this week," my dad said.

Things between my father and Sherri had not worked out. They broke up a few months after their daughter, Nicky, was born and my mother swooped in the moment the opportunity presented itself. Hope was determined to get Stew back, and she did. He'd barely moved back in with us before Hope was pregnant. Nicky was nearly two years old, too young to cause any real trouble, but my mother despised her.

My mother frowned, resting her hand on the swollen melon that had once been a flat stomach. "Saturday's not going to work," Hope said. "We have to build the crib."

"What do you mean, build the crib?" he frowned. "We have four weeks to build the crib."

"Stewy, I already had to ask my mother to help out. How much more can I do?"

Earlier in the day, my mother and I had met Gram for lunch. We sat down at Twin's, the family restaurant where my parents had met, in a booth that my mother had once delivered food to. I was only allowed one slice of pizza, and I poured on handfuls of grated cheese and dipped it in ketchup in hopes of making the slice denser.

"Sherri's getting three hundred dollars a month in child support, and Nicky doesn't even live with her," my mother complained.

This was true. Sherri was pregnant again and her first two kids had both moved in with their grandparents. By now Sherri and my father were both in their midtwenties, with both expecting their third child.

"If it's what the court says," Gram tried to reason, but my mother wouldn't hear it. For weeks she had been obsessing over money.

"How are we supposed to afford a new baby if all of his check is going to a kid that doesn't even live with him? We can't do it."

Gram sighed as she put down her utensils. She'd inherited a decent sum of money when Pop Pop died, selling the large plot of land he once lived on to a company that would destroy his woods and develop the space into offices. She knew my young parents were barely managing their monthly rent. They both worked, but still the bills added up. If I had to guess, my grandmother knew exactly what was coming when she asked my mother what she needed. Five minutes later they had a deal. Over the years Gram would help out as needed—money for a new boiler to keep us warm or a used car to keep us moving. The issue was that while Gram would do anything for Hope, she'd also never stop reminding her of as much. It was my earliest lesson on how money creates just as many problems as it solves.

Hours after the lunch had ended, my mom and I returned home, and the argument between my parents picked up right where it had left off.

"All I'm asking is for you to build the crib this weekend," Hope persisted.

When Stew offered to do it on Friday, she continued to protest. He lost his patience somewhere between Hope's fourth and fifth excuse for why Friday wouldn't work.

"I'm not going to fight with you every goddamn week about this bullshit," Stew yelled. "I see this kid on Saturdays. End of story."

"But weekends are our time together."

Stew fumbled around the apartment looking for his keys. It's what he did when their fighting became too tiresome. He took a break. I'm not sure where he went during these time-outs but wherever it was, it must have been somewhere with vodka, because he'd return in a state of peaceful tranquility.

"Weekends should be our family time. With our kids!"

"Nicky is our kid."

My mother scoffed as if his words were outrageous. Hope hated everything Nicky represented: cheating, jealousy, and her own loneliness. Nicky was a direct representation of Sherri and what she meant for Hope. Someday I would look back at these moments, and I would see my mother as the only thing she really was at the time: *hurt*.

●●●●●

By the start of third grade, I had been in the disabilities class for over two years and continued to lag behind in every subject. My family was baffled. They couldn't agree on what, if anything, to do about the fact that I was nearly eight and reading at a kindergarten level. If my reading was bad, my math scores were worse, and I was often described as both a difficult student and a disturbance in the classroom.

"We didn't find anything that would cause any sort of obvious disability," the doctor explained.

It was one of the rare moments that both my parents were at an appointment. Stew's fingernails were black, caked with soot from a long day at work, which he'd left early for this. "So what do you suggest we do here?" my father asked.

My performance was so below average that the reading specialist at school suggested I be tested. My father wasn't overly concerned; he had never been a great student himself, and yet here he was, a functioning adult with a job. But, still, when the doctor confirmed that I did *not* have dyslexia, everyone seemed thoroughly disappointed.

"Look," the doctor said, "a lot of kids can't read proficiently. Her eyesight is great. Her hearing is great. There is no physical reason she would be behind. Some kids learn slower than others. She'll probably grow out of it."

"But she has no learning issues?"

The doctor looked at my mother as if the answer were obvious. "I don't see any evidence that she suffers from ADD, but clearly she has a tough time focusing on her school work. I'd advise leaving her in the disability class and hope that eventually she starts paying attention."

He thanked us for coming in and a receptionist saw us out. We walked through the dimly lit parking lot toward my father's beat-up Dodge pickup.

"Steph," my mom asked curiously, "you do pay attention in school, right?"

I opened my mouth to respond but paused when I realized the implications of whatever I said next. If I answered truthfully, which was yes, I tried very hard to sound out words but could not, then I must be stupid. But if I sided with this incompetent doctor and pretended I paid school no mind, then I was just lazy. Laziness could be changed. In later grades, academic laziness among classmates would even be considered cool. Someone who didn't care how they did on a test was a rebel. A rule breaker. But someone who was dumb, well, they were just dumb.

"It's just so boring," I finally said, and my mother looked horrified. "Who cares about *Charlotte's Web* anyway? She's a stupid pig."

"Charlotte is the spider, Steph."

●●●●●

After my sister Jenna was born there was a time when my family settled, and everyone appeared happy. But the honeymoon was brief. Only nine months after Jenna's arrival, my mother announced a new due date.

While I continued to perform at a below-average and altogether humiliating academic level, Hope prepared for a third child. By the time Lydia arrived, my father was twenty-eight years old, already once divorced from and remarried to my mother, and struggling to support four children. He worked long hours that were hard on his body for minimum wage. Having Lydia had been a reckless decision. Unlike the births I would one day witness on the Upper East Side, Lydia's was a somber occasion. The day she came home from the hospital there were no toys, flowers, or gifts. And there was definitely no doorman.

There are certain things in America that can suggest a person is either very wealthy or incredibly poor. Where I come from, a yard with dozens of cars in it screams poverty. The cars are mostly junk, being saved in the hope that one day they'll have a healthy part that can be salvaged or an engine to repurpose. But a person in East Hampton with a driveway full of automobiles has surely done well for themselves. At the very top of the list of wealth indicators is something far costlier than cars: *children.*

When a family on the Upper East Side has three kids, it's a sort of status symbol. It suggests to the world that they reside in one of the country's most expensive neighborhoods and they do so effortlessly. In a place where apartments are listed in the millions and school tuition can run close to a hundred thousand a year, they can not only afford to live there, they can afford to raise multiple dependents there. These individuals typically have children later in life, opting to first spend time on their education and careers, buying a home, and seeing other parts of the world. When an Upper East Side mother has a third child, there is no question as to why: *she wanted three kids, and she could afford three kids.*

Where my parents came from, multiple children typically occurred at a much younger age and suggested something entirely different: *a couple of high school sweethearts liked to shag and played fast and loose with the condoms.*

"What do you mean he didn't want this baby?" Gram asked. My family was sitting in the hospital waiting room. Papa was bouncing my sister Jenna on one leg while my mom was in labor. She was a handful. I was eight and very rude.

Aunt Patty sighed. "He has three kids he can't afford already."

"But my daughter only has two," Gram said pointedly.

"Well, you know what, Maureen?" Patty shot back. "Maybe Hope shouldn't have tricked him into having another baby."

It wasn't surprising the two sides clashed. Gram had been a single mother to three kids and had worked hard to stay off government assistance, and while she never directly said it, I always knew she saw the Kisers as beneath her. It was in the middle of this argument that I noticed the vending machines. *Oh, Doritos.* I walked over and stood right between the two women and their standoff.

"Can I get some chips?" I asked hopefully.

No one responded, so I began an unsuccessful attempt to reach my arm through the door and grab a snack out for free. Behind me the argument raged. It's not that I didn't mind the fighting; it's just that yelling in our home was so frequent it was like white noise to me. Our family rarely managed a weekend, event, or even a holiday without a brawl. In Sasha's Fifth Avenue home, I never once heard an adult yell, but raised voices were as much a part of my family's routine as brushing our teeth (which we did only in the mornings because my mother felt nighttime brushing was a conspiracy created by Crest to drum up more business). I had six cavities by the time I reached high school.

"Patty," Gram began, "it is still his child. He has a responsibility. There's nothing more beautiful in this world than creating a life." My grandmother was noble for defending her daughter, but even she knew her case was weak. Hope was manipulative when it came to Stew.

My parents had only just had Jenna when my mother began begging Stew to consider a third baby. Over and over again he'd say, "Hope, we don't have a pot to piss in with just these two. What do you want to go and add another mouth to feed for?"

"Because I love being a mother." What she meant was that she loved solidifying the bond between her and my father with the one weapon in her arsenal: shared offspring. Plus, motherhood gave her a purpose; it was how she filled her days. Sometimes it's easier to take care of others than it is to take care of yourself. "Just think about it," she begged, and he did, but the answer remained no.

In Manhattan, I'd met couples who froze their eggs for a more convenient time, then hired surrogates to gestate their babies for them just to keep their physique in check. The financial cost of a dependent did not matter before or after the child was born. But for my father, more children were a joy not quite worth the price of personal bankruptcy. He wasn't considering the cost of paying a baby nurse. He was contemplating if he could afford formula.

Eventually, Hope took matters into her own hands. She wanted three children regardless of whether she could handle or afford them. There was a pink pack of birth control pills which she left exposed on her nightstand. Though I was too young to understand the details of birth control, I knew she was no longer taking it. Each night she would pull out a single pill, walk into the kitchen, and promptly throw it in the trash can. The day she held up a stick with two blue lines, she swore it was a miracle.

"The only miracle around here," my dad sighed, "is going to be however we manage to get by."

9

TINY WOMAN

I WAS DRIBBLING A BASKETBALL on the basement floor while my mother threw onesies into the washing machine. My father had taken me to Walmart to pick out a hoop, which we set up by the street, and while I was proving to have very little natural talent, I had grown fond of having a Spalding in my hands. By now, most of the adults in my life had come to regard me as underachieving and ill-tempered. I did poorly in school, often required disciplinary action, and showed very little regard for authority, but the ball seemed to help. It gave me a purpose and something to do. I'd stand outside all afternoon and just shoot and shoot and shoot. I hardly ever scored but I didn't care.

That day, as I played inside, enjoying the cool cellar during the summer heat, Hope rushed about, desperate to finish her chores quickly. She had only a few minutes until my sisters would wake from a rare nap. Hope was folding the last of the laundry when I grew tired of dribbling and began one of my favorite pastimes of finding loose change often forgotten in the pockets of grown-ups. That was how I found it.

"What is this?"

"What's what?" my mother asked.

I had been searching my dad's dresser drawers. I did not know why my father's bureau was kept in an otherwise unfurnished basement, but I also wasn't an expert in home design. As I ran my hand along the wooden bottom, searching for coins, I felt something glossy. I took the item out and examined it. A photograph of a woman, rather large and not particularly attractive. I turned the photo over and sounded out the words that had been scribbled on the back, *To my love.*

"Hey!" I said, "Who is this super fat lady?"

I giggled, up until the moment my mom ripped the photo from my hand. Her tears, initially slow and quiet, turned heavy and uncontrollable. I knew immediately I'd done something wrong; I just wasn't sure what.

Later that night, as my dad packed his things, Lydia cried from her bassinet, and Jenna waddled around the living room. I had made a mistake, and because of it Hope was about to be a single mother, again. My grandparents feared for my mother, who was devastated by yet another breakup and was growing alarmingly depressed.

"I hate leaving here," I overheard my grandmother say to Papa one evening. "I'm so afraid that when I come back… I don't know. I just worry she'll have hurt herself."

They came over daily, helped my mother clean, and took my

sisters for outings, but still, it took Hope a long time to recover. I was furious with my mother. I didn't understand why Stew's unfaithfulness mattered so much. My father had not lived with us for most of my life, and we had always been fine. Why should it be any different this time? At nine, I could not understand why my father had so much power over my mother's happiness.

A few years later, my Papa left my grandmother for another woman, and my aunt's husband became schizophrenic. In each case I watched women I thought were strong morph into shells of themselves, and the lessons I took from all this were complicated: you could not trust a man to be there indefinitely, and you couldn't allow yourself to need one. My grandmother was the strongest woman I had known until a man took her money, her pride, and her heart.

The thing I would later come to realize is that women needing validation from men is a universal problem that affects every class. I'd see this as often on the Upper East Side as I had in the suburbs of Rhode Island. I had a friend in Boston whose parents, both doctors, had been happily married for twenty-five years. Yet, when my friend disclosed that her mother had never farted in front of her father because she never wanted him to find her unappealing, I scratched my head in confusion. Years later, in New York, I would have a friend whose father had been a big name in the film industry. When his girls were in high school, he cheated on his now ex-wife, and it was still all the women of the family could talk about. It was as if their whole lives ended the day the man of the house became unfaithful.

It seemed that women, regardless of their age, race, or tax bracket, were overshadowed by the men they were associated with.

Whether it was a stay-at-home mother watching the children from dawn to dusk or one with a master's and a job at the UN, when the weekends came the story remained the same. These women would busy themselves cooking, cleaning, and caring for the children, while the men carried on with their lives. The fact was, Americans supported working wives, so long as the women still did all the things they'd done when they didn't work. By the time I was an adult on the Upper East Side, I'd find that the evidence spoke for itself. Women in America were fucked. Poor, minority, and uneducated women in America were doubly fucked.

My mother hardly had any friends, and the few she did have she turned away in the aftermath of my father's departure. Within months, she had stopped eating altogether and began limiting our food to extreme rations. She grew thin enough that you could count every rib in her chest, and she kept everyone she was able to control on a strict eating schedule. Jenna, in the YMCA daycare, would watch as other kids unpacked colorful fruits and buttery cookies, while her brown paper bag contained scraps in comparison. She would reach in and slowly unwrap the one item my mother had packed her: two slices of white bread with a smear of reduced fat mayo in between. We knew better than to ask for more food, so my sisters and I became masters of snack stealing.

We'd wait until my mother was in the shower, then run to the kitchen, devouring as many food items as we could without getting caught. We'd stuff wrappers in drawers and cupboards, afraid the evidence might give our scheme away. Some days, when my mother had hit a particular low, the cupboards were bare and there was no food to steal. I'd beg my friends at school for food or talk the lunch ladies into giving me another free lunch. By the end of the school year, I'd racked up forty dollars in unpaid lunch fees. Hope was furious.

We limped along that way for the next three years, my mom never giving up on the idea of getting Stew back. By the time I was thirteen, she had succeeded in her quest, and my parents had reconciled once again. When it comes to marriage, everyone knows, third (or fourth) time's the charm. My parents bought a house with Gram's help, the first time either had ever owned anything that big, and on move-in day we were overjoyed.

My father had worked hard over the last decade, making up for his lack of education by polishing his handyman skills. He transitioned from the janitorial staff to a management position. He worked overtime on nights and weekends and often did the jobs nobody else wanted to do. Some weeks he'd start work at the manufacturing plant at five thirty a.m., only to have a boiler break down right before his shift ended at six p.m. He'd work all night, knowing he could not leave until it was running again. His responsibilities there never ended. After a snowstorm, he'd plow the parking lot. When the lights went out, he'd get the generator going. Once, the place even caught on fire, and until the firefighters arrived, he sprayed what he could with an extinguisher. The owner of the factory rewarded his brave efforts with a fifty-dollar Olive Garden gift card.

After eight years of this, he was offered a job overseeing the maintenance department at a Target warehouse. He did so well that they paid for him to take night classes at a local college when his shifts ended, and when he completed them, they promoted him to distribution manager. My father had done what many dream of doing. He'd jumped social classes. At least that's how it appeared on the surface.

As a Bob's Discount Furniture truck unloaded what was the grandest furniture I had ever seen, my mother whispered to Gram what should go where in our new house. Hope didn't like speaking to strangers. She often asked one of us to order her coffee or to ask a salesclerk how much an unmarked item was because she suffered from severe social anxiety.

"That new bed is for Lydia," my mom whispered. "And that dresser. And the bean bag. Oh, and all the new bedding is Lydia's."

In the distance, Jenna and Lydia chased one another around a small tree in the front yard. The girls, Irish twins, should have been equals in my mother's eyes. Two little round balls of energy with freckled faces and our dad's light hair, they easily passed for identical. But for some reason my mother had gravitated to, bonded with, and formed a primal instinct to protect Lydia. There was nothing Jenna ever could have done. My mother just loved Lydia more.

"Okay," Gram said carefully, "is anything in this order for Jenna?" She didn't bother asking if anything was for me. Gram was always the one who took care of my needs, so if any of the furniture had been marked for me, she'd have been the one to purchase it.

"Yeah, of course," Hope said as a delivery man added a rocking horse to Lydia's pile. "There should be another bed somewhere in there too." Over the years, this trend would continue, and my mother's love for her youngest would only intensify. But Jenna would grow older and become aware of and eventually resent their bond.

10

OH, BABY, BABY

"THE BABY WAS BORN RIGHT before we went to sleep!" Ruby announces when I come in. "Daddy called to tell us, and then me and Hunter had a dance party with Geepa and Gigi!"

Charmed by Ruby's enthusiasm, I feign surprise, though I already knew that Sasha had gone into labor from the birth announcement I received in my email earlier that morning. It is the first I've ever heard of such a thing: an online notification of a person's entrance into the world, and I am taken aback by the number of recipients on the chain. It turns out that I am just one of hundreds of people awaiting the news. Apparently, this newborn knows more people at one day old than I know as a grown woman. Just hours after the email goes out, family, friends, and acquaintances begin sending congratulatory gifts.

"What should I do with all the things coming in?" I ask Sasha's mother, Gigi.

Together, we survey the pile of lavish presents, until finally she shakes her head. "Let's just make room to walk but keep everything in the front hall until Sasha comes home."

In the coming weeks, I will discover that having a newborn requires skill in two main areas: functioning while exhausted, and completing activities in the dark. I will arrive in the mornings to find Sasha as she has always been. She'll have on a full face of makeup and her hair will be neatly combed. Sasha will have already made and served the children breakfast, changed them out of pajamas, and tidied up the house. I'll ask her how she is, and she will say great. But sometime during the day she will mention how frequently the baby woke in a fuss. I learn that in the wee hours, Sasha tiptoes around the unlit apartment, calming the deep sob of the hungry baby, while flipping the bottle heater on. Once the milk is warmed, she sneaks into the baby's room and feeds him until he's had enough. Then she changes the dirty diaper, puts on the sound machine, and rocks him gently. Only when he drifts off is she free to return to her own bed.

On a good night, I figure Sasha logs five hours of interrupted sleep.

Most Upper East Siders choose to put their wealth to good use and avoid the nuisance of sleepless nights. They hire a baby nurse, a woman whose sole purpose is to tend to the newborn's every need, day or night. Baby nurses work twenty-four hours a day seven days a week. A mother with a baby nurse will never need to change a diaper, clean a circumcision, or ease their baby's tummy troubles. The cost of this service is high—an experienced or certified baby nurse in New York City can put you out a thousand a day. Of course, Sasha's family could easily afford it; to them, the cost would hardly register. But Sasha loves motherhood. She never offloads her responsibilities as a mother, not even in the rawest, most difficult moments. I respect her for that. But I also *really* don't get it.

I think about what motherhood feels like for women who cannot afford nannies or baby nurses, housekeepers or tutors. If being a mom is this challenging for Sasha, whose wealth and resources far exceed the majority of Americans', what is it like for a teen or single mother? Even I, clocking on average only nine hours a day with the children, leave their house exhausted. How are moms with no partner, no financial resources, and no support managing such a heavy workload? It occurs to me that if I'd like an answer, I should start by asking my mother.

My sister Jenna was incredibly hyper as a child and hardly ever slept. She was so rowdy Aunt Patty referred to her as "hell on wheels." She was wild, destructive, and just when you'd finish cleaning up one mess, you'd find that Jenna had used your moment of distraction to run a permanent marker along the white kitchen wall. One December, she climbed onto a folding table on Christmas night, and it collapsed back onto her leg.

I remember vividly in the weeks that followed my mother wrapping her cast in plastic each night for a bath while she swaddled a screeching Lydia. As I watched my third episode of *Hey Arnold!*, she'd yell over for me to start my homework. By the time she coaxed Lydia to sleep it was nine, but Lydia would need two feedings before dawn. Hope would do both of them and then wake up with Jenna, who started her days around five. The next day there might be fatigue, but there would certainly be no babysitters or nannies to help keep her going.

I feel a flash of shame at how easily I focused on my mother's faults, never recognizing her strengths.

Somewhere around two p.m., as I am filling the fridge with bottles of congratulatory wine, Elissa calls and asks if I want to bring the kids over to Katherine's. We've been trapped in the apartment all day, and I welcome the idea of a break. I bundle the kids in their thickest coats, wrap their necks in scarves, and tuck their fingers into mittens. They walk stiffly to the elevator, the weight of their winter gear heavy on their tiny bodies, and I ask them to give me just a second. Something is jammed. There are so many presents by then, I can't get the door closed.

We finally get downstairs, and the doorman escorts us to a waiting cab, which zooms toward Katherine's new luxury building in the East 80s.

Luxury buildings can't offer the sort of prestige that comes with a Park or Fifth Avenue address, so they make up for it with amenities. In a city where addresses mean everything, the distinction between the two kinds of apartments is telling. Many luxury residences, some fifty floors high, offer things like panoramic city views, arcades, and movie theaters. Katherine's building features a state-of-the-art playroom: a blessing for any parent with time to kill or a toddler who refuses to sit still. Luxury buildings are often inhabited by younger or more progressive families, but everyone knows that a Park Ave prewar building is the old money part of town. Luxury buildings are where the new money lives.

I text Elissa from the cab when we are close, and she is waiting for us at the door when we arrive.

"Congratulations, Stephania!" Elissa beams.

Ruby and Hunter run to their friends as I settle in.

Immediately, other nannies join Elissa in offering me their best wishes on the new addition.

"Thanks." I smile, though their congratulations feel misplaced. This new baby isn't mine. He and I aren't even related. I'm just his nanny.

"Do you have a picture?" an older Chinese nanny asks.

There is one in the birth announcement email on my phone. I hold it open. The women gush with excitement, and I look again to ensure we are seeing the same thing. Sure enough, there on the screen is the purplish figure, an alien of sorts. With eyes shut tightly, the smallest bit of a face is visible, tucked warmly within a knit hat. Admittedly, I know very little about newborns, so perhaps these women know something that I do not.

Elissa begins recalling memories of Katherine's first days. Her face beams with pride as she speaks. Elissa is a career nanny, and these children aren't her job: they are her life. She insists that eventually I will love this baby as much as I do his siblings, and I imagine that she is right. Still, I remain skeptical, the baby's sudden existence reminding me of something I have nearly forgotten: that I'm not very qualified to be doing this.

Each night I return home to my shabby apartment and listen as Lila discusses visas her firm is trying to get approved and cases that end in upsets. I have nothing comparable to say, but I feel good when

I successfully navigate a day with Sasha's children. I know that Lila's job is more admirable, but I almost think mine is harder. Some days, I love being with the children so much, I nearly forget the dreams I'm abandoning.

"Ah, Katherine's mom has something for the baby," Elissa says and then disappears for a moment. When she returns, her hands are full of bundles. *More fucking monogrammed pacifiers*, I think, but I assure her Sasha will love them.

The next hour I am occupied with rounds of freeze tag and requests for more Pirate's Booty. The other nannies are not inclined toward runaround play, so the children rely on me for any active pastime. I don't mind. I spent all of high school and most of college playing in sports games or practices. Elissa and the other nannies occasionally join in, but most of them have forty years on me. When it comes to this part of nannying, the physical aspect, I am a star, and the oldies are the scrubs. It's the only area where I can outshine them.

"Do you have any Goldfish, Stephanie?" Hunter asks. We are sitting at a kid-sized table by the windows.

"Sorry, bud. You already ate them all."

Elissa offers Hunter some hummus, but he swiftly declines.

I peer into the now nearly empty tote bag I had earlier filled with food. "How about bunny fruit snacks?" I ask. He agrees then tears open the bag.

Katherine looks at Elissa with wide, pleading eyes. "Can I have a bunny fruit snack?"

Katherine isn't allowed sweets. Her parents employ a full-time chef, who they stole from the kitchen of a Momofuku restaurant, after having what they called "the most delightful bao buns of our lifetime." They offered him a salary no one could refuse, and so now he makes the family three square meals a day and cooks Katherine only lean proteins and vegetables, cutting up each item into bite-sized pieces, all while keeping to exact ratios. I've often glanced at Katherine's meals and thought, *I've seen cats eat more appealing entrees.*

"Please?" Katherine asks, hopeful.

Elissa is neurotic about following her boss's wishes, having been subjected to enough berating to know she must tread lightly. She's worked for Katherine's family for fifteen years, more than half my life, but is terrified to bend even a single rule. Agencies often phrase job descriptions with "looking for a team player/someone who can fade into the background." This is what most traditional nannies do: they work quietly, they're hardly seen, and never heard. In one agency, a nanny was refused an interview with a family when the recruiter found her personality was "too big." These nannies take direction and orders without opinion but with discretion. I wonder how a seventy-year-old adult can possibly be content working in a home where she too is treated like a child.

"Oh, no, my dear," Elissa says, regretfully, "we have cucumber slices and the melon. How about the carrots? They are very good."

Katherine and Elissa smile at one another, but the exchange is somber. Elissa once told me that at her third birthday party, Katherine anxiously awaited her cake, only to find that it was organic, lemon, and sugar-free. Katherine didn't complain. But only one of the eighteen children in attendance would eat it. That one kid was her.

The kids are still eating when the door swings open and Lily waddles in. Lily is a twenty-month-old trust fund baby and a regular in the playroom. Her parents employ two nannies, a chauffeur, and four housekeepers for their family of three. Lily comes dressed in Armani dresses and fur vests. I once saw the tag of her onesie sticking out with the word VERSACE written clear across the fabric. Later that day, Lily opened a grape juice box, took a gulp, and immediately spilled the rest all over herself, destroying her outfit in six seconds flat.

"Hi, Steph!" Lily's mom waves enthusiastically. "I didn't know you guys were coming here today!"

"Elissa invited us over last minute. The kids were getting bored at home, so thank God she did," I laugh.

Lily's mom is Swedish and beautiful. She speaks in a crisp accent, has fabulous outfits, and has taken an immediate liking to me. We've met only a handful of times, but she loves to compliment me on my childcare skills. It's as if she thinks I am the only nanny in the world who has mastered the art of hide-and-seek. I brush off her kind words, my face burning pink, but I secretly adore the attention. I never set out to be a talented nanny. But here is this beautiful, foreign, incredibly wealthy woman telling me that *I* am good at something. It's a constant tug-of-war between being ashamed to be doing this job at all and feeling pride in doing it well. I wake up each day, underwhelmed with the idea of changing diapers once again, only to find myself delighted by a single compliment. Lily's mother holds no significance in my life. *So then why can't I shy away from her praise?*

We chat for five or so minutes before I return to the nanny side of the room. All of the children are back to playing by then, and the vibe among the nannies has shifted. A darkness has descended upon the normally joyful group. I wonder what I have missed.

"Lily's mom could talk forever," I say as I sit down.

Everyone is silent, except for one nanny who snickers. No one meets my gaze. Even Elissa, never at a loss for words, says nothing. "What?" I ask, confused.

When everyone stays quiet, I repeat myself, this time directing my question to Elissa.

"Stephania, Lily's mom is not that chatty." She sighs.

"What do you mean? She just spent three straight minutes telling me about the new SoulCycle on 83rd Street," I argue. "Wait, do you guys know Laurie Cole? She's an instructor there, and she sometimes works out Hillary Clinton!" They do not know Laurie, and I'm fairly certain none of them knows of SoulCycle either. My enthusiasm dies. Elissa carries on.

"Have you ever seen Lily's mom talk to any of us?"

I pause. I don't think that I have, and I tell her as much. Elissa nods. "She doesn't talk to any nanny but you."

I laugh out loud at the absurdity of the claim. "Elissa, why would I be the only nanny she talks to?"

This time Elissa looks directly at me, and her response is firm. "She talks to you because you are white."

For weeks after that incident, I subtly observe Lily's mother. On countless occasions, I watch her interact with other moms, grandparents, and me. I can't help but replay Elissa's words day after day.

After this moment, I begin to see it everywhere I look. No one asks me for identification when I present a family membership at the Bronx Zoo, but an employee calls Katherine's family to make sure Elissa has permission to be there. When I drive us thirty minutes to the Botanical Garden in my boss's BMW SUV, I don't think twice about it until Elissa discloses she is not allowed to drive the children.

"You don't drive?" I ask.

"I do," she says quietly. "But Katherine's father worries we learn to drive dangerously in my country."

I wanted to believe that my white privilege was not giving me a leg up on nannies who were more qualified, experienced, and better equipped for raising children. But I never found any evidence to disprove Elissa's claim.

Lily's mom remained an active member of the playroom. I saw her dozens of times in the years to come. Still always talking. To people who looked just like her.

11

PALM BEACH

I STEP OFF A SIX fifteen flight from JFK to Palm Beach and still have a thirty-minute Uber ride to go. It is now nine a.m., and I am already sipping my way through my third Starbucks. Still drowsy, my eyes adjust to the brightness of the Sunshine State as the driver speeds down a wide highway. I don't recognize any of it. Outside of Orlando, I have never been anywhere in Florida, and I have certainly never heard of the tiny island off of Palm Beach. Sasha mentioned that her family had a house there. When Sasha asked me to join them, I couldn't say yes fast enough. It was exactly the sort of opportunity that Elissa had urged me to take full advantage of.

"Here you are, miss," the driver says as we arrive.

He pulls into a single driveway leading to two massive houses. There's a smaller opening farther down, also meant for cars, with a sign that says "service." I later learn that all the estates here have them, and it's essentially parking for the help. One of the houses is slightly larger, though they're equally elegant, and I cannot make out numbers on either of them. I ask the man which one is mine.

"What do you mean?" he asks in a thick Haitian accent.

"Like, which house is number 638?"

He squints in confusion. "Both of them." Then he points to the smaller one. "That's the guest house."

"Oh, yeah. Thanks," I mumble as I begin to drag my suitcase along the rocky path.

The residence I arrive at is a nine-bedroom, eleven-bathroom estate. It's a single-family home large enough to house twenty people comfortably. The house sits in front of an ocean with an average water temperature of 78 degrees. The property is massive and surrounded by thick, bright lawns. There are palm trees and a running trail, plus golf carts to get you from one part of the yard to another. There's a putting green to practice your golf swing. A hot tub by the pool. Just below that, a private beach. Up until this point I thought I comprehended wealth, but I realize now there is a difference between being wealthy and being *rich*. Having money can get you things, but being rich allows you anything.

I inhale the humid air while listening to waves crash onto the rocks of the beach. A large marble fountain gently sprays water from a concrete fish's mouth. I think back to the vacations I can recall from my childhood: the Howard Johnsons and the beachside motels in the dead of winter, the only time my family could score an affordable rate. Once, when I was in high school, we went to a basketball tournament in Pennsylvania. We had so little money for the five-day trip that we ate at Taco Bell every single night. I played three games a day running on Supreme Crunch Wraps and Mountain Dew. The hotel was so gnarly that my mother developed impetigo from the "hot tub," and I played the last two days with strep throat. The entire trip for our family of five came in just under our four-hundred-dollar budget.

"Stephanie, hi!"

I turn to find Sasha's father, George, returning from what I assume has been an early round of golf. He places his bag of clubs on the ground. "How was the flight?"

I know George and his wife Gigi, though our interactions have always been brief. Rarely have I spent more than fifteen minutes in a room with either of them, and I am nervous to spend an entire week in what is technically their home.

A vacation with Sasha and the kids is one thing, but one with her entire extended family is something altogether different, especially in this secluded location. It's uncomfortable to spend every second of the day in a home that is not yours with people you hardly know. Privacy becomes a distant memory. You don't want to be overheard on the phone, being loud, or, worst of all, *pooping.* You become reliant on your employers for food and coffee and rides. And God forbid your period surprises you and you're forced to ask your boss to get you tampons.

"It was good. No delays or anything."

Suddenly, the wheel of my suitcase finds itself caught in a mound of dirt. I jerk back and my backpack slips off my shoulder.

"Oh, here. Let me get the suitcase."

I assure him that I am fine, but he insists and eventually takes it off my hands. Before retiring, George worked on Wall Street. He'd spent a lifetime spinning deals and making fat paychecks, donating libraries, and purchasing penthouses. He owns many homes. Multiple luxury cars. He even hired the New York City Ballet to perform live at his oldest daughter's birthday party.

Some of the more gossipy moms I know talk about George like he is some sort of Big Bank royalty. On the Upper East Side, he seems to be a household name. But on this sunny Monday morning, he's just a man offering to carry a suitcase for his grandkids' nanny. It is through this unexpected act of kindness that I suddenly understand Sasha's humility. Her family is not extraordinary in any way—they are simply decent people—but on the Upper East Side, that sort of normalcy is so rare they become extraordinary.

We are only a few feet away from the main entrance when the front door swings open.

"Stephanie!" Ruby and Hunter scream.

They rush toward me with their arms open wide. It has only been five days since I've seen them, but they act as if we've been apart forever. Time is different for children. It moves unreasonably fast or painfully slow, but rarely do they feel it as it actually is.

"The kids have been waiting for you to get here," I hear Sasha say, but my view of her is blocked by the children.

"We made pictures for you!" Hunter exclaims.

Ruby grabs my hand and pulls me up to the front door, where poster boards display scribbled handwriting. The words express joy for my arrival: *Welcum Stefane*. Sasha and I exchange a quick smile, and I tell Ruby that it's amazing.

Sasha begins to introduce me to more of her family when we finally get inside. I catch just a glance of her nephews as they rush by, passing a football between them. I recognize them only from their mother's public Instagram account. Gigi says a quick hello, and somewhere in the third living room I hear the baby fussing. I'm aware of every interaction—I even participate in them—but I'm distracted by my surroundings.

The home is spacious beyond comprehension. It's more lavish than a celebrity bachelor pad. Everywhere I turn, I spot landscapers and pool boys, cleaners and personal swim instructors. This place requires an entire team of people to remain functional. The concept is so foreign that I cannot move past the outlandishness.

"Let me show you your room," Sasha says, and as we enter I see that my suitcase is already there.

Sasha apologizes profusely, explaining that they had planned to give me the guest house, but her brother's family needed more space. I tell her that it's not a problem, which it isn't, considering the guest room I am given is twice the size of my bedroom back in New York.

We are still discussing the room when another door opens, and I hear the footsteps of more guests entering the home. "Oh, my brother and his wife just got back. Let me introduce you to them."

A hit HBO show is airing its sixth or so season. Everyone I know is watching it, or has watched it, and my friends cannot believe that I'm going to spend a week with one of its stars. Neither can I. Sasha's brother is a lot like her when I meet him. Quiet, reserved, seemingly kind. But his celebrity wife is not what I had anticipated. In a pair of lounge pants and black-framed reading glasses, with her hair tossed up in a bun, she introduces herself as if she needs an introduction. I am prepared for her to be arrogant, self-interested, even rude, but instead she is warm and friendly. She has a couple of Golden Globes and a net worth of millions, yet she goes out of her way to shake *my* hand.

Many of the wealthy people I've encountered have been predictably self-important, impatient, and lacking empathy. Others, like Sasha, stay humble. Very few land somewhere in the middle, but Sasha's sister-in-law is another reminder of what all the wealth in this elite world tends to disguise: underneath the exotic cars, vacation homes, and private jets, when you're this close up to them, privileged people are still just people.

The trip is a merry-go-round of contradictions. As we arrive at the Island Club for lunch, I notice an unsettling lack of diversity, and I'm once again haunted by Elissa's remarks. It was not the first time that I had considered that my whiteness could be giving me an advantage, but it was the first time I'd been able to confirm it. Now, weeks later, in this beachy oasis, the clientele appears to be a singular demographic: old and *white*. The only color I see exists in the background—individuals who move in swift silence and appear only when necessary: busboys, cooks, a maintenance man. While Sasha's sister-in-law has only just humanized this lavish world, the club pollutes it, creating an overwhelming sense of confusion that I cannot sort through.

Homes on the island range between two and sixty million, with the average price landing around ten million. The town has a permanent population of eight hundred, as most homeowners spend no more than a few months of the year here. It is the second most expensive small town in the U.S. Burt Reynolds called the island the "best place in the world."

As far as I can tell, the club is the heart of the island. The people who live here, and whose names are prominent enough to award them membership in the club, rely on the establishment for every part of their day. It is the only commercial property on the entire island, and it has its own stores and coffee shops, plus a town hall. It offers restaurants, both formal and informal, and bars to enjoy a midday drink. There are pools and tennis courts and camps and play structures for children. Of course, the big draw is the beach. But this isn't *just* a country club. It's one of the most expensive private clubs in the world, and the members know it.

A woman walks by with her nutritionist alongside her. The nutritionist is explaining the calories of every last vegetable in the woman's Cobb salad. I imagine that any one of these rich people could clear my student loans with a flick of the wrist. With that thought comes a rush of resentment. It is the first time I take a look at my luxurious surroundings and feel anything other than awe. I'm surrounded by families with more money than they could ever need, and they're being served by people who are likely just as capable as them but who simply weren't fortunate enough to inherit millions at birth.

I'm starting to question if I'll ever be a writer or, better yet, if I'm good enough to be anything of significance. Growing up, people were always referring to my family as white trash, and here I begin to wonder if that's all we are. What I am. If I had been born to parents who could afford a college education, I wouldn't be here. I wouldn't *need* to be a nanny. But I was an undisciplined and uninterested student, so maybe this would have been my destiny regardless? I get caught up in the question of whether I didn't work hard enough or if my hard work got me as far as it could, given my circumstances. I'm not sure of the answer.

Sasha asks me what I want to eat, and I choose grilled cheese. The temperature is nearly 80 degrees, but she wears the baby in a Björn, subjecting herself to his body heat, in hopes that he'll nap comfortably. Her husband waits for the food while Ruby explains the ice cream system to me.

"So when we finish, we can go up to that window and get ANY two flavors we want AND toppings!"

I ask her what flavors she'll choose, and it's more with the mint chocolate chip. Ruby has a serious sweet tooth, and we laugh about the dessert I make her back home: whipped cream mixed with Hershey's syrup and approximately seventy sprinkles.

●●●●●

The baby is not yet sleeping through the night, and Sasha's mornings often begin before sunrise. Between feeding the baby and waking with Ruby and Hunter, she appears to be a robotic superhuman. Even on vacation her duties as a mother never stop. She spends afternoons swimming with Hunter, mornings taking Ruby to tennis lessons, and in-between moments pumping for the baby's next feed. There is a certain weight to motherhood, and I wonder how heavy it must have felt to my mother at such a young age.

"OUUUUUUCHHHHYY!" Hunter screams out in pain.

He had been cheerfully engaged in superhero pretend play before he misjudged the space between the couch and the floor. He lands with a thud into the coffee table. I do my best to soothe him, but he wants his mother. In moments of extreme stress, Hunter always wants his mother. It's a feeling I wish I could identify with.

Sasha comes in as soon as she hears the commotion, Ruby following close behind.

"Oh, no, what happened, sweet boy?" Sasha asks.

"I bump my head!" Hunter wails.

Sasha looks to me for confirmation and I nod.

"Mom! I said I want to show you my drawing!" Ruby screams.

"I know, Ruby. I can't wait to see it. Can you just give me a few minutes because your brother is really sad?"

Ruby throws her head back. It's the first hint of a tantrum brewing. Just then Sasha's husband enters with the baby, who is also crying.

"Hey, Sash. I can't get him to take a bottle. Can you do it?"

Sasha is still dealing with Hunter and asks for a second. Her husband says he can't wait. *The baby is too upset.* Just then Ruby starts yelling. I offer to take a look at her art, but that only escalates her fury. Now all of them are crying.

Minutes pass before Sasha is able to tame the situation. It takes patience, love, and more hands than one human has. I watch from a corner of the living room as Sasha feeds the baby the last of his milk. She bounces lightly across the room and soft words of a lullaby pass through her lips. In the days since the vacation began, I have watched as the other adults enjoy lazy mornings by the pool and tanning on the beach. I've seen Sasha's husband scroll through his phone and her parents leave to shop. But I have yet to see Sasha manage more than a brief moment to herself. I realize then that Sasha's type of motherhood requires a selflessness that I fear I don't possess. It makes me think that perhaps the responsibility of having a child is not for everyone.

●●●●●

Ruby and I spend the next few days out on the beach. In the mornings we are home, and later we eat lunches at the country club, but our afternoons are by the water. Each day around three o'clock we make our way down the stone path to a private sandy beach. We bring buckets and shovels and spend hours collecting interesting shells. Later we take them back to the house and wash them off to get a better look. I find comfort not just in the waves and ocean breeze but in Ruby's company.

We are sitting just close enough for our toes to touch the water when Ruby has an idea. She wants to open a salon and asks me to build a chair in the sand. As I sit on a pile of tiny rocks, she twists my hair into painful ponytails. Her fingers are caked in sunblock and seaweed. She is the worst hairdresser anyone has ever had.

"Okay, but what's the best ride at Disney World?" she asks for the third time.

"I told you. I really like Space Mountain, but Haunted Mansion is okay, too."

"I'm never going on Haunted Mansion," Ruby says. "Too scary."

"But Space Mountain is a roller coaster in the dark," I remind her.

She pauses to think but then answers assertively, "Eh, that's no biggie."

Her comment makes me laugh, but lately I find joy in everything Ruby says.

It is here on this beach that I find myself more deeply attached to this job than I ever thought possible. Nannying had been a means to an end. A way to make money to pay down loans I never wanted in the first place. But while Ruby flips through strands of my hair I am lost in a tornado of memories. We've spent nearly two years together *but how has she grown so much?*

I think back to the days before she could tie her shoelaces, and now I listen as she spells out the letters of her name. I've watched her mom dedicate every waking minute of every day to her children while never asking for anything but their happiness in return. The more I see of Sasha's mothering, the more intensely I begin to resent my own childhood. Her devotion and attention far outweigh any-thing my mother had been able to offer, and, as a result, Ruby is all the things I was not: well mannered, good natured, polite, and respectful.

As the sun begins to set, an orange glaze falls across the ocean. Ruby and I carry our buckets of shells home while watching the seagulls. I can feel a patch of sunburn behind my neck growing warm, but I'm engrossed in more pressing thoughts. When I worked at the PR firm, I'd leave for the day, and I wouldn't think about my job again until the next morning. If a project crossed my mind, it would be a fleeting thought. But here, seaside with Ruby, I realize that this job is not a job. It's a person. A little being whom you learn to nurture, protect, and *love*. People say not to love your job too much because a job can't love you back, and that's why this is different. My job does love me back, but being so emotionally invested is dangerous.

I overheard a conversation between Sasha and her mother that morning. They were discussing Hunter and Ruby's summer plans. Ruby will go to camp a full day, just like she will do in elementary school next year. Hunter will go half the day, an easy way to prepare him for a longer day at preschool, Sasha says. With the two big kids soon out of the house for most of the day, there will be just the baby, and Sasha is the most hands-on mother I know. No one has said it yet, but I know their need for me is about to decrease.

There's also one more thing. The more time I have spent with Elissa, the larger my nanny network has become, and I listened one day as a career nanny told Elissa about her new job.

"The hours are long. Seven to seven," the woman says, "and I have to do all the cooking and light housekeeping. But the agency I work with negotiated my salary based on my experience, and it's the best contract I've ever had."

"What is your pay?" Elissa asks.

"One hundred thousand a year with full medical. Plus a bonus at Christmas."

I had been unaware that a full-charge nanny in Manhattan could make a higher salary than most suburban management workers. It's shocking and absurd, and the information stayed tucked away in my mind.

On a whim I decided to send my resume to a downtown agency. They emailed me back immediately, eager to speak to a candidate with both a college education and Fifth Avenue experience. "Our open current positions range from seventy-five to a hundred thousand a year," a woman had said when she called me days later. "We'd love for you to come in and discuss these opportunities with us."

I had told her that I would, but I was torn. *If I'm going to do a job that I never intended to do in the first place,* I think, *then I should do it in whatever way I get the most out of it.* Ruby runs off toward the house, and I'm only a few steps behind her. "Come on, Stephanie! Let's go home."

Then I run past her. I watch as her little legs fight to catch up, and I think of all the things that I have learned about Ruby: that she loves mint chocolate chip ice cream and eats peppermint bark even in the summer. She spends most of her time doing art projects, and she's never very successful when using an Easy-Bake Oven. Her best friend is a blond girl named Caroline, and on group playdates, out of all the children, Ruby is always the best behaved. She likes gymnastics but not soccer. Her favorite entree is Perdue chicken nuggets. She hates peanut butter. Thinks it's *the absolute worst,* in fact. It takes her an unreasonably long time to fall asleep at night, and even when you think she's finally down, you'll find that she's only been resting her eyes. She's six and smart and kind. I am not related to Ruby. I'm not her aunt or even a family friend, but I love her as if I were.

I know that I am approaching the time to move on, because even if I love my job, it is ultimately just that. Leaving this job and these children that I've grown so fond of would be the smart decision. The right decision.

Wouldn't it?

12

HARD CHOICES

HUNTER AND I ARE WAITING at the 68th Street playground
for a playdate who is running late. It's been a few weeks since we've
returned from Florida, and the weather in New York City is just
beginning to turn. The trees of Central Park are no longer bare, and
I watch the tourists stand under the cherry blossom trees, straining
for the perfect Instagram post.

"Stephanie, I'm hungry," Hunter complains.

"I know, buddy. Priscilla's nearly here." Priscilla is four and
mean, but her father is a good friend of Hunter's uncle, so we have no
choice but to continue waiting, despite the thirty-minute tardiness.
"Look, there she is." I point Hunter in her direction and am relieved
when they run off to the slide together. I sit down on a bench, light-
headed. I reach down and push against my stomach, which has been
bothering me for days, feeling like a hangover that won't quit. I pull
out my phone and text Lila.

You still feel sick? she asks. My complaints have been relentless. Horrible, I answer.

She tells me I should look into getting an appointment tomorrow, but I have to work. I tell her I'll go to the walk-in if it continues throughout the weekend. I put down my phone, heave myself up off the bench, and pretend for Hunter that everything is fine.

Before Grandma Kiser married Grandpa Larry, she had been engaged to another man, Dale Oder. They were best friends, Dale and Larry, though as you might imagine, in the end they weren't. My grandmother was sixteen at the time of her first engagement. Having dropped out of school four years earlier, she hardly seemed young for marriage. She had become pregnant before the engagement began. They were set to wed prior to the baby's due date, but one hot July evening Grandma Kiser and Dale had a fight so loud and tense that three different neighbors called the police. Before they arrived, Dale exploded, punching my grandmother hard in the mouth. She left that night.

The following week, her mother took her to a woman's house. Grandma Kiser slipped through a side door and down to a concrete basement. When she returned to her mother's car, there was no more baby, and there was certainly no more engagement.

I am thinking of this when a nurse gives me an apple juice. Strange that that's what I remember most, the juice. The nausea I'd texted Lila about hadn't gone away, even through a weekend partying with friends, drinking cranberry vodkas, and dancing in an overcrowded downtown nightclub. So I'd spent a day getting blood work and scans that ended with a middle-aged man I had never seen before telling me I'm pregnant.

Everyone wants me to know my options, but I just want them to stop talking.

"There is, of course, always adoption. There are lots of loving couples looking for a child of their own," an older nurse mentions. As she scurries away I notice a small gold cross around her neck and I understand her play. It is the same cross my grandmother always wore. Like any good Catholic, Gram did not believe in abortion, but she did believe in praying to the Blessed Mother for forgiveness. It was something I was about to need a lot of. I sip the juice and listen to the discharge instructions. Or at least I try to. I had taken a sick day from work, texted Sasha that I was ill, which wasn't entirely a lie. It was the sickest I'd ever felt.

Someone passes by and asks if I want some crackers. I say I don't. They tell me to rest some more.

"How are you doing? Do you need a little more time?"

I look up at another nurse, who smiles sympathetically. There are other women in the office, and as I look around, I wonder if they are all as conflicted as me.

"I'm good," I say and get up slowly to leave. "Do you have a trash can?"

"Of course, right over here."

I toss the empty carton in the garbage on my way out.

When I get outside I call my mom. Gram is overtly religious, my sisters are still too young to deal with such a complicated issue, and this isn't the sort of thing you call your father about. Hope feels like the most logical choice, and when she first answers I'm relieved. I cry my way through most of the conversation, barely managing to get out what I want to say.

When I finish, I'm sobbing so heavily I can barely breathe, and I sit down on a bench to recover.

"Do you need me to come to New York?"

I assumed this would be a given, but the hesitation in her voice suggests otherwise. I pause, unsure what to say next, but hold on to the hope that of course she'll arrive by morning.

"If you can…but if it's too hard, you don't have to."

"All right," she says and then there is more hesitation. "Why don't you go get some sleep, and I'll check in later today."

"Yeah, sure," I say and my throat feels thick as I hang up.

I walk back to my apartment with no idea of what to do next or how to move forward. I feel impossibly alone. Lila won't be up yet; it's too early in the morning after a night clubbing downtown. I spend the rest of the day alone.

The next time I see my mother is three months later, when I go home to Rhode Island for a visit. By that point I wasn't even sure who I was anymore.

●●●●●

I don't talk about the abortion all that much at first. I imagine so many versions of it that it becomes difficult to recall the actual truth. I tell close friends, the ones who knew me well enough to sense something is wrong, that I had a miscarriage. It feels easier than what is real, which is that I've made a choice that I don't particularly like and that I am deeply ashamed of. I never see the therapist my ob-gyn recommends. Instead, I lock the experience away, trying to pretend it never happened by waking up each morning, going to work, and caring for a baby that is not my own.

Most of my friends understood my decision but some couldn't help but ask invasive questions like "Do you ever regret it?" The father and I didn't know each other very well. We'd only been on a few dates, but we'd been equal partners in this outcome. Yet, no one ever brought him up. It was as if he had no responsibility in the matter. As far I could tell, the only one who would be judged by God was me and me alone. I didn't even know if I believed in God, but I knew that there was no punishment he could give a woman for this that would be worse than the one they gave themselves.

I ignored the pain until the memory faded enough to seem like a dream. But every weekday morning, I'd return to Sasha's East Side apartment *and there was a baby*. Just someone else's.

A feeling of overwhelming guilt began to consume me. Instead of dealing with it, I grew resentful and angry, difficult, and demanding. I knew logically, perhaps better than anyone, the repercussions of bringing a child into the world before you're ready. Maturity, stability, and desire are key. I had none of those things, but my job was to raise children. If I'd had a child, I would have relied on the government for help with housing or food or childcare. I could have continued nannying to pay for shelter, but then who would watch my kid? If I gave up nannying, I could care for the baby myself, but then I would not have income. As a nanny, I wasn't even entitled to parental leave. The situation was impossible, but still, I asked myself, *How can I care for someone else's baby when I chose to abort my own?*

It was a month later that Sasha brought up the inevitable.

"With both big kids being in camp and school full time, we really won't need you as much."

I had prepared to dread this moment. Yes, I want the opportunity to find something higher paying. Yes, I know that a job with more benefits exists. But, no, it is for none of these reasons that I am suddenly ready to leave. I have become comfortable working in this home, with these people, doing this job, but all I want now is to get away from things that remind me of the past.

"We could maybe have you part-time, though? Just reduce your hours a bit," Sasha continued, but I stopped her.

"I love your kids so much, but you need someone part-time, and I need something full," I said, and Sasha agreed. It was time for me to move on.

I was in the midst of a full-blown personal crisis. I claimed to want to do better than my family, but I'd just made the exact same mistake my parents had. Only, unlike them, I was a coward. I didn't face my mistake. I'd just eliminated it. My time on Fifth Avenue, as enriching as some of it had been, left me questioning my place in the world. Was I *the help* or just someone who *needed help*? Was this as good as I would ever do for myself? Had I peaked here, changing diapers in someone else's multimillion-dollar home, or did better things await me? Was it my own mother who had stumbled throughout motherhood? Or was a bad mother the one too selfish to even give her child life?

Two weeks later I leave Sasha's Fifth Avenue apartment for the last time. In order to make the separation as easy for the children as possible, Sasha does not tell them I am leaving. Instead, she spins a story that I am simply going away for the summer:

"Stephanie's going to have a summer vacation. Like we go to the Hamptons. She's going to her summer house, and then we will see her again when we get back to the city."

Only I don't have a summer house. Lila and I do have a new apartment, since I made enough money with Sasha's family to finally leave East Harlem, but my closet-sized bedroom in Hell's Kitchen is so humid in the summer that I can hardly breathe; the irony in my neighborhood's name is not lost on me. Lila's room is across the living room, but there's a strain in our relationship now. It's like I've become unreachable since the abortion. At first, she tries to comfort me, but it doesn't help. I scream at her when we're together, call her an awful friend, a spoiled brat. I sink as low as to tell her she's just like her mother. The smallest things set me off. She changes course and tries to give me space, but I hate that too, so she gives up and I grow bitter. On top of all of this, I don't have the luxury of enjoying the summer or going unemployed for very long. I have bills to pay, and I know that I'll need to lock in a new position soon.

Sure, I'd come back to visit Ruby and Hunter, but it will never be the same.

On my very last day, I took the kids for ice cream. As I looked over the flavors displayed on the counter, I reported bad news to Ruby.

"They're out of mint chocolate chip."

"Oh, that's okay," she says, and I am surprised.

"Really?"

"Yeah, I'm over mint chocolate chip. I've moved on to vanilla now."

●●●●●

I submit my resume to all of New York's premier household staffing agencies. It's late June, three weeks since I left Sasha's, when one calls me in for an interview.

"Can you do Monday?" the woman on the other side of the line asks.

"Sure, Monday's great."

"Perfect," she exclaims. "I was so excited to get your resume! We have a West Village family looking for your qualifications exactly! They want a college-educated nanny who can drive and swim. Oh, and they have the two sweetest little kids. I think you'll love them!"

"I'm sure, too," I tell her, but I say it half-heartedly. I do love two sweet little kids, but they live seventy blocks north of the West Village, and they rarely venture downtown. I miss Ruby and Hunter greatly, but I still know that I need to move on in order to make the most out of nannying.

Otherwise, I am derailing my life for nothing.

I say I'll see her Monday and hang up, only to find an email from Sasha.

I lean my back up against the air conditioner and skim through the message with heart-wrenching interest. Sasha mentions that the baby has begun crawling and Hunter has started taking swim lessons. I laugh when she describes Hunter's new favorite pastime of blowing "fart bubbles" in the water. Sasha says that he likes the pool, but he much prefers lounging in the hot tub.

Ruby's report, however, is denser and detailed with actual news. She has just spent her first week at the summer camp her premier all-girls school requires students to participate in before the academic year begins. It's a way for the children to get adjusted to the idea of a full day before actually having to start it. The idea is brilliant, though somewhat coddling, and Sasha says that Ruby adored every minute of her week there.

In Manhattan's infamously cutthroat world of school admissions, Ruby has it easy. Parents donate thousands of dollars to get their five-year-old into a top-tier school. Even then, the applicant pool is deep and overflowing with the children of legacies and wealth, hailing from families whose names don't require introductions.

The application process takes both parent and child months to complete. Preschoolers are asked to sit for hour-long interviews and participate in academic testing and are observed socializing with other children. Their moms write long essays about their child and what makes them unique, but it can be difficult to pinpoint what makes one four-year-old better than another. Especially since most of them can't spell so much as a three-letter word and they eat their own boogers in addition to their breakfast.

Most wealthy city kids apply to six or seven elite private schools and are lucky if they get into three or four. The Dalton School, on the Upper East Side, sends 31 percent of its students to Ivy League universities. Parents will spend a full year donating, networking, and all but begging their child's way in. But with an acceptance rate of just 14 percent, Dalton is nearly as selective as Dartmouth.

This insane process is designed to secure one coveted prize: entrance into an elementary school that charges more than most colleges. In New York City, $45,000 a year for a third-grade education is considered the norm, and parents are happy to pay it. But Ruby is a rarity. Her mom had gone to the Spence School, as had both of her aunts and all of her cousins. Sasha had applied to two schools for her daughter, one being a safety, but Ruby was destined for Spence.

At the end of the email, Sasha has inserted a photo of Ruby, beaming, her little navy skirt falling just below her knees. It takes a moment, but then I see it, and the resemblance is uncanny. Quickly, I begin searching through old photos on my Facebook page. I scroll through hundreds of pictures, years' worth, until my profile transports me back to the year 2007, and then there it is. Fifteen-year-old me, on my first day at an all-girls school. A different all-girls school, of course, though there were some similarities. I put the photos side by side. I see two hopeful students in matching uniform skirts; we *almost* seem alike.

It strikes me that education was how I ended up here. Everything about my life today can be traced back to one pivotal moment: the day I set foot in a private high school.

13

LYNX

LINCOLN SCHOOL FOR GIRLS HAD agreed to accept me for the 2007–2008 academic school year under one condition: I repeat the tenth grade.

Somewhere between seventh and eighth grade I lost twenty pounds, gained five inches, and practiced free throws outside in the snow until my fingers bled. I *finally* had a skill one could be proud of. My father, maybe seeing a bit of himself in me, put what little we had into sending me to a summer basketball camp run by Lincoln's head coach.

Stew had been a high school hockey star, making all-state as a goalie. He learned to skate on a frozen pond in Johnston, at first using sticks he found in the woods and makeshift nets to practice swinging. His father would show up to his games drunk, screaming at the "goddamn stupid blind as a motherfucking bat" referees until he was finally ejected from the game. Grandma Kiser would come out when the game was over and smack Grandpa Larry on the head, her face beaming because her son, the star goalie, had another shut-out. This sliver of recognition never left my father, and now he saw potential in me, so I was being taught by some of the best coaches in the state.

When the Lincoln coach at camp proposed the idea of my transferring to the school, it had seemed just that, *an idea*, and a bad one.

"The athletic director will be on campus tomorrow and is going to stop by to watch you," the coach warned me. "Be ready."

Shortly after lunch, Vivien, no taller than five feet, showed up. She stood well dressed and serious, like a stiff model in a Ralph Lauren catalog. As she lingered on the sidelines, I played a series of one-on-ones. I beat one opponent. Then another and another. I hadn't been looking to impress Vivien because I cared about her school. In fact, on that first day she watched me, I didn't even know what private education really was. At that point, I was so delighted to finally be good at something, I loved nothing more than an audience.

Vivien did not speak to me that day, but by my sixth win, she had left the gym, and by the following day, I was enrolled at Lincoln.

Lincoln was a single-sex school with a rigorous academic program and a graduation rate of 100 percent. I was a C student who had failed algebra twice and had no intention of nailing it the third time around. Lincoln's website proudly stated that all of its graduating students went on to attend university. The tuition wasn't much less than my dad's yearly salary, but they awarded me a financial aid package that all but covered my entire tuition. *What business did I have at a place like that?*

At North Providence High, I'd been one of 951 students. We'd report to a homeroom, where the teacher might remember your name, but if they didn't, that was probably a good thing. I'd routinely complete just enough work to skate by, which was admittedly very little, but the school had low standards, and at home my family didn't value education. Why would they? My father had a trade skill, and that's what had saved his life. Nothing more.

I frequented detention, retained absolutely nothing in math, and went to summer school twice. Once, in fourth grade, I walked the half mile home from school overwhelmed by my academic performance that quarter. Though the winter chill stung my hands, I kept them exposed, too impressed by the report card I was holding to put it in my backpack. Upon arrival, I presented it to my mother proudly and waited for her applause. She glanced curiously over the sheet of paper and then stared at me blankly.

"Pretty good," I asked, "right?"

"Steph, you got two Cs and a D."

"But I also got two A's!"

"In gym and health…" she said, shaking her head in disbelief before she carried on pretending to sweep the floor.

I wasn't engaged in school, and from what my grades suggested, I wasn't very good at it. There had never been any reason for me to take an interest in academics. Not one that I could see, anyway.

But now I was beginning tenth grade at Lincoln School for Girls, where my graduating class would be made up of only thirty-three students.

"Where do I go?" I asked my dad on my first day.

He shrugged his shoulders. "How should I know?"

I was sitting in the passenger seat of his PT Cruiser. It was the first recent-model vehicle he had ever purchased, and our family admired it as one might a Lamborghini. But as I looked around at the cars dropping off other students, I saw that we stood out. My father's little red Cruiser was charming, but the other girls were arriving in Mercedes, Range Rovers, and Escalades. These cars reminded me of something that had occurred only two days earlier.

"Come on, Jenna. Move over!" Lydia had said.

"I can't! There's no room!"

"Shhh, you idiots!" my mother hissed.

The four of us sat huddled in my bedroom closet. My dad stood leaning against the door. It was too dark to make out any of their faces, but I imagine we all looked equally petrified. From the driveway I could hear the clicking and clacking of the man just doing his job.

"Is he gone?" Hope finally whispered.

"Let's check," I said and then we all tiptoed out.

Our family, rather sad and lost in my younger years, had grown into ourselves. We were now more of a circus and less of a depressing teen drama. Each of us went by our initials. Even outsiders referred to us as SK, HK, LK, JK—except for my father, who we nicknamed FB—for fat bastard. And I had gone from being a disobedient child to a wild and classless teenager. My father was funny but inappropriate, and while he had made far more of himself than anyone anticipated, he had spent the first 90 percent of his life on government block cheese, counting pennies, and it still showed.

Jumping classes is one thing: navigating the new one is something entirely different.

In hindsight, it is unclear why my family chose to hide in a closet while someone repossessed our old Saturn. It could not have come as a shock. My mother had been open and honest about her decision to stop making payments on the vehicle.

"This car is junk, Stewy," Hope cried. "I hate it!"

"Well then let the fucking repo man come and get it," my dad had said, and so, some twenty-two weeks later, *the fucking repo man* did just that. But now I, a girl who hid with her family in closets, and whose water intake consisted entirely of whatever amount was found in Diet Coke, was walking into a school where the students wore lululemon on a lazy day and who had been operating juice presses since elementary school. As I looked at the school's front door, my stomach turned sour. *What had I gotten myself into?*

A few days from then, my parents would accompany me to my first after-school event. It would be a welcoming ceremony, where the teachers would have us sit at round tables, and the headmistress would ask that we each decorate our own reusable lunch plate, in the interest of sustainability. My parents would stare in horror as teenage girls used Crayola markers to doodle flowers and hearts on something they would later eat off of. I didn't mind the exercise, seeing as how the most incredible part of Lincoln so far was the lunch program. There was no treat greater to me than a buffet without my mother's watchful eye. Unlike public school lunches, which had always been small portions of chicken nuggets with cartons of chocolate milk, Lincoln offered free and diverse meals to all of its students. In their lunchroom, which they called the Dining Room, I wasn't picking from two or three unappetizing entrees. This cafeteria provided infinite options, like grilled kielbasa, chef salads, and desserts, and you could have as many rounds as you'd like.

Afterward, while moms in Lilly Pulitzer dresses embraced other parents whom they hadn't seen all summer, my mother would sit silently in oversized sweatpants and one of my father's Reebok hoodies. There, at that moment, I didn't think much of it. Sweatpants were all I knew, worn to any and all occasions, so if anyone seemed out of place, it was the moms dressed in wallpaper. But as I gained exposure to the finer things in life, my perception of my family's wardrobe changed, too, and soon I'd find myself embarrassed every time I opened my closet.

When we drove home from the event, my dad announced that Lincoln was "quite literally the gayest place" he had ever been. I laughed along at his joke, but secretly I was terrified. I knew that I would be an outcast there long before anyone else did. But on that very first day, trying to force myself out of my father's car, I didn't understand just how hard fitting in would be.

Girls with pencil thin legs and Lacoste polos pranced up to the entrance like queens returning to their castle. They had hemmed their kilts to well above the knee. I looked down at my own kilt, the one and only my mom had bought on account of how expensive they were. "Don't stain it," she'd said as she reluctantly paid the cashier fifty dollars of my grandmother's money. But no one had mentioned anything about hemming the uniform. It was one thing to be the new girl. It was another to be new, poor, and looking like I belonged in *Little House on the Prairie.*

"Could you walk in with me?" I blurted.

My father stared at me blankly in response. This was his version of no. My family would not fit in here, but unlike me, they didn't have to try. This place, where students were encouraged to address teachers by their first names and where parents donated annually in the thousands, made little sense to my parents.

I kept my head down as I made the short walk from my dad's car to the two great big red doors. "I'm looking for my homeroom," I said to the receptionist when I made it inside.

She pointed behind her to what looked like an original sitting room from George Washington's estate. I mumbled a thank you and scurried inside. There were thirty or so girls in the room spread out among couches, chairs, and the floor. Small groups of girls sat around one larger group who dominated the center. It was immediately clear that the center group was what could only be defined as the cool kids. This middle group included some of the prettiest and wealthiest girls in the room. They referred to themselves as the Fine Nine, though of course I didn't know this just yet.

"Good morning, girls."

A studious-looking young woman named Ms. Fran was trying but failing to command the room. As she began to take attendance, random bursts of laughter erupted from teenage girls who were high on first-day-of-school enthusiasm. I listened carefully to her roll-call a list of names that all seemed weirdly similar: *Lacey, Stacy, Kelsey.* I realized that if I were to ever fit in here, I would need two things. The first was approximately $500,000. The second was to legally change my name to *Steph-acy*.

"Stephanie Kiser?" Ms. Fran called.

Then it was quiet. In a room full of girls who had been classmates for their entire young lives, a new name on the attendance sheet was enough to hush the whole group. I felt my face grow hot as I half raised an unsure hand.

Ms. Fran spoke to me sympathetically. "Stephanie, we're delighted to have you join us."

"Thank you," I said, barely audibly.

Lincoln School enrolled many girls who had always been, as far as they knew, someone important. One junior was the daughter of the man who wrote *The Polar Express*. A girl in the class above her was the daughter of a New England Patriots linebacker. And sitting next to me during attendance was Alex. Her mom had recently launched a small jewelry line under the name Alex and Ani. By the time we graduated, you could find those bangles everywhere.

Ms. Fran dismissed us, and I gathered my things while trying to remember my locker number. I was nearly out the door when a girl from the middle circle stopped me.

Kelsey was five foot ten, frightfully thin, and had pesticides where her soul should have been. She stood in front of me, with two of her Fine Niners. One of them was Lila, whom I recognized from the summer basketball camp. I remembered her because she had been particularly unskilled. She had full features, looked more mature than the rest of us, and was perhaps simply too pretty to be good at free throws. Now, Lila and I exchanged our first official hello, then she told her friends she needed to get to class. As she left, so did any kindness in the room, and I shifted uncomfortably. Kelsey and I glared at one another for what felt like an inappropriate amount of time before she finally spoke.

"Are those, like, fake Birkenstocks?"

I looked down at my feet. The truth was that I had no idea. I didn't even know what Birkenstocks were. I was wearing the shoe the school had instructed me to purchase.

"I'm not sure," I said. "I think so?"

Kelsey and her friend laughed. I wasn't sure what they were laughing at but assumed I must have said something funny and felt relieved.

"So where are you from?" Kelsey asked.

"North Providence," I said.

"Oh, God," she responded.

I knew she was being condescending, but I was pathetically desperate to stay in everyone's good graces, and so I asked, "Where are you from?"

"*Not* North Providence." She laughed.

Suddenly, any interest I had in her approval vanished, and I felt nothing but fury. I wanted to retaliate with something equally offensive, but my brain couldn't think fast enough. Kelsey grabbed the Burberry scarf around her neck before nodding to her friend to move out.

"This scarf," she whispered as she brushed past me, "probably cost more than your entire life."

Saying this to a peer at my old school would have been a simple way to ensure a beating. My instinct was to fight back, to prove that I was tough, but I was somewhere else now, somewhere entirely different from anywhere I had ever been before. I didn't know how to react to such an insult. Grandma Kiser would have punched Kelsey square in the mouth, but I said nothing at all. Instead, I did something that I had not been groomed to do. Something that would become so habitual over the next decade that it would turn a once mouthy and unruly kid passive: *I bit my tongue.*

●●●●●

The old white colonial was massive, but it wasn't the size that intrigued me most. It was the red door. It was the sort of door a child might fantasize led to magical places, and in a way this one did. Lila's house was the first home I'd ever been in that had a separate dining room apart from the actual kitchen, and the place was so clean you could have eaten off the floor. As I made my way through the first floor, each room amazed me more than the last. Even the checkered tiling in the foyer was exquisite.

"Do you want to see my room?" Lila asked.

I said yes, and we had to travel very far, as it was one million stairs and several antique vases away from the front hall. My eyes darted from room to room, not wanting to miss a thing. After all, I wasn't sure I'd ever be back. It had been a complete shock when Lila had asked, "Do you want to come over after school, since we don't have basketball practice until four?"

Lila was extraordinarily kind, but she was also beautiful, wealthy, and a member of the dreadful Fine Nine. My being there, should it get back to the heinous Kelsey, wouldn't go over big. Lila was popular, and I was a peasant. Over the course of my first few months as a Lincoln student, I had become notorious for three things: not doing homework, supporting my local Walmart, and shooting a mean free throw. Lila's befriending me would send her social currency plunging. I knew that and, I imagine, so did she.

Everything in the home was so dramatic and beautiful, each room seemed to tell a new story. Lila's bedroom had faint clouds painted on the ceiling, and an autographed picture of Britney Spears sat on a mantle. There were framed illustrations of funny bears dancing in tutus that her grandfather had painted himself and a reading nook that overlooked a peaceful backyard. I had only ever seen more books in a library.

"My mom went shopping today," Lila said when she saw me glance at a pile of clothes on the bed.

"Did she get them for your birthday or something?" I asked. I had never known someone to receive half a new wardrobe randomly. My sisters and I got new clothes on holidays or once a year before school, but never just because.

"Oh, no. My birthday isn't until November first," she said. It turned out that we were born a day apart in the same hospital.

Lila's mother, Joie, called us downstairs about half an hour before she had to drive us back to school. The smell of chocolate chip cookies wafted through the room. A tall blond in diamond jewelry and a Burberry sweater but with tattoos covering each arm removed her baking apron and entertained us with her antics. I laughed as she sprinkled unexpected words like *dude* and *fucking loser* throughout her stories. She appeared to have it all. That afternoon Lila's mother seemed a happy woman living a brilliant life. She was cool, edgy, talented, wealthy, and attractive. She had two beautiful children and a terrific husband, but Joie would turn out to be the least fulfilled person I have ever met. Lila's mother was my first piece of definitive proof: money cannot fix everything.

Lila and I became the Odd Couple of friendship. I'd waltz into Lila's house in sweaty basketball shorts, eat pasta in her kitchen, and use my sweatshirt sleeve as a napkin. I had not yet mastered the art of small talk and could be counted on to say no more than hello. Lila's grandmother could not believe how ill-mannered I was, but at home my father reassured me.

"It's these liberals," he told me, "a bunch of pompous asses."

While I could not accurately define a liberal at age fifteen, I did know that I hated them. At school, members of the Young Politicians club wore sweatshirts that suggested their affiliation. I would have never joined such a club, but I remember seeing the girls with a printed donkey on their back and feeling disgusted. My family hardly got by as it was, yet here was a group of people who wanted to take even more from my dad's paycheck. And *for what?* To help people not even permitted in this country?

"Also, Lila's dad used two different forks at dinner," I later said. "Like one for each item. What was that about?"

"Oh, who knows. He's a stuffed shirt."

"Stiff as a board." I agreed.

Lila's house was like a foreign land to me, but the culture shock on her end was just as great.

"Where are we going?" I yelled from the back of the minivan.

The whole car was screaming, so I had to strain to be heard. I'm not sure what everyone was arguing about, but if I had to guess, it was insignificant.

"I told you, Papa Gino's."

"I hate Papa Gino's," Jenna cried.

"Then don't eat!"

Next to me, in the third row, Lila sat quietly. The noise of my family put her on high alert, as did their vulgarity and frequent insults. She sat silently through dinner as we discussed what we always did: basketball. Though Lila was on the team, she didn't have a single competitive bone in her body. She was content on the bench and found our family insane for taking a game so seriously. But as my talent began to soar, basketball became the entire family's hobby. It was something to do, and it was something to talk about. Basketball unified us in a way nothing else ever had.

Every game was followed by a two-hour play-by-play analysis. Unless I'd played poorly. In that case, no one spoke at all.

"Then Renee missed that layup and screwed the game," my dad said.

"She should have just taken the jump shot," I agreed.

"Ah, but her pull-ups suck."

"Well, I think she was probably trying to draw the foul," my mom piped in, and then my dad and I tormented her.

"We got the big reporter over here," I joked.

"This idiot. She doesn't know her ass from her elbow."

Hope, offended, began pleading her case that as a devoted Celtics fan she knew basketball. She watched every single one of their games and knew just as much as us. We laughed more, then told her she was a loser.

Lila slept over that night and came out of the bathroom wearing two sweatshirts. Our boiler was, once again, broken, and we didn't have any sort of heat. She had a perpetual runny nose at my house, and nearly everything she asked got her roasted.

"Do you have any water, by chance?" she said.

That one always landed us in hysterics. "No, but there are four different kinds of diet soda," one of my sisters would mention.

Lila and I had shared a nursery room in the same hospital on a cold day in November. We were born at the same time in the same place. We'd both grow to be around five foot eight with hazel eyes and long dark hair. The homes that awaited us on our first days of life were about ten miles apart. Just ten miles, but entirely different worlds.

Lila would be a straight A student and a member of a youth group. She was an incredible artist like her mother, never knew a summer without a vacation home in Vermont, and would see eight different countries before age ten. I adored Taco Bell, knew that going to the movies was a luxury, and at five broke my jaw, but went to such a negligent pediatrician that the fracture wouldn't be discovered until six years later. I would not know of international travel until middle school and had no idea that America had never had a black president until Obama had already won. Lila had her first kiss in high school. I snuck a boy into our basement at twelve, where my four-year-old sister walked in on him fingering me under a Scooby Doo blanket. When I was in middle school, my mother went to a psychic whose only advice to her was to keep an eye on me or I'd be pregnant within a year. Neither of us could disagree.

Lila and I were kids from two parallel universes whose worlds crossed in an unexpected way. Until Lincoln, I had only ever had friends like me, and Lila had only known girls like her. Our friendship was the first time I saw a life that I was jealous of and the person living it wasn't an actress or musician. She was someone real and tangible and right there in front of me all the time. I knew that perhaps, maybe, I could have a life like this someday too, but I didn't know how to get it.

Some ten years later, Lila and I would be walking down Lexington Avenue reminiscing.

"You know what's crazy?"

"What?" I asked.

"The first time I went to your house…" She paused. "It was the first time I realized my family had money."

14

THE INTERVIEWER

AN AGENCY HAS ME INTERVIEWING with a family on Fifth Avenue in ten minutes. Each agency I meet with seems to have the same universal set of questions and standards. "How many years of full-time experience do you have?" "Do you have a four-year college degree?" "Can you drive and swim?" The agency announces that they adore me and quickly send me out to their clients in need. It takes me two days to set up five interviews, and today is my first. My cell service on the subway ride uptown is spotty, and the incoming texts are delayed. Still, my fingers type furiously, my argument with Lila distracting me from the interview that I should be preparing for.

Steph, I don't want to live together anymore that's why I'm moving out. We don't even have fun together at this point. We literally don't get along, a text from her reads.

She's right. Over these last months, I have become perpetually miserable. My current state of unhappiness didn't emerge suddenly.

It is the result of a gradual building up as my life became increasingly fragmented. I am running in circles, chasing after a new life, only to find that my climbing the social ladder is costing me far more happiness than it is bringing. I have alienated my family, steamrolled past personal trauma, and feel unfulfilled by my work. The only thing that still matters is proving myself, but I'm not even sure what that means anymore. I don't write anymore. I probably never will.

Recently, I have even lost interest in the things I once enjoyed. I now find nights at the club infuriating, the alcohol I drink there venomous, and I've gained ten pounds in the last few months alone. My arguments with Lila roll over and carry on, like a war more than a battle. We grew up together but now we've grown apart. The best thing would be to get space from one another, but the thought of creating more distance in my most reliable friendship when the rest of my life is in limbo is so unimaginable that I argue against the suggestion, even though I agree with it.

We do get along! You just need to have your boyfriend move out. How long have I been telling you that? You pretend you understand and then just keep doing whatever you want and it's SO annoying. I say this, plus much more, but even as I send the text, I know that it will only make matters worse.

In high school, Lila and I had spent lazy summer days on Rhode Island's beaches, shopping in the state's only real mall, and going to movies. In college, we'd gone to bars, sometimes three or four nights a week. We'd danced until a bartender turned the lights on and herded us out, then stopped at 7-Eleven for taquitos to eat on the walk back to our dorm. When my childhood crush gave me a curable yet discouraging STD, it was Lila who accompanied me to the doctor's appointment. I came out mortified and sickly, but Lila smiled when she saw me. "Bet that was a doozy," she said, and despite how depleted I felt, I laughed.

That's what I remember most from growing up together. We were always laughing. But now our friendship is nothing but a toxic, diluted version of what it once was, reduced to snide remarks and spiteful insults, and there is nothing to say that can fix it. *I hate her. I hate her. I hate her*, I think as I type. No, I hate myself, but in Lila I see my reflection. I want to shatter it. I cannot escape the grief of my abortion and half expected Lila to pull me through it. Because that's what I'd always done in times of stress: I'd reached for my best friend's hand, and she had led me through the chaos. But this time it wasn't working. The attempts she did make only made me angrier, more aggressive. I'd lash out at her in ways I didn't know myself capable of, and then hated myself even more. Lila's life was no easier than mine, but I envied the freedom and privilege I *thought* she had. If I reflected on Lila's life in its simplest form, it seemed as if she'd always had things handed to her. My jealousy flourished. Our situations were very different, but both of our lives were imploding and so was our friendship.

As I arrive at 985 Park Avenue, I focus my attention on the interview, reminding myself that the issues between Lila and me will, unfortunately, still be there when it concludes. I tell the doorman, who is forced to wear a suit and gloves even on this 80-degree day, what apartment I am going to. He dials up and then directs me to the penthouse. I take a deep breath and head toward the elevator, thankful for this brief distraction. After all, what could be better to take my mind off things than another ridiculously wealthy New Yorker?

An assistant keeps me waiting in a study for twenty-five minutes before Mr. and Mrs. Robertson finally arrive. I stand up to shake their hands but feel startled, their appearance far different from what I was expecting. Mrs. Robertson is a large woman, something that is nearly unheard of within the clique of Upper East Side moms, and she looks nothing like the picture that had popped up on Google when I'd searched her earlier that day. Her husband, however, is even more surprising. The once-handsome CEO of a major credit card corporation is now old and frail, nearly eighty, and barely verbal.

They sit, and a staff member hurries in behind them, placing down a tray that holds a massive bowl of soup.

"Do you mind if I eat?" Mrs. Robertson asks.

"No, of course not," I say, though I find the request odd.

"Where are you from?" Mrs. Robertson asks, and I tell her. "And where did you go to school?"

"Emerson," I say.

I explain that I'd originally landed a sports scholarship to a junior college but was desperate to study writing and worked my grades up to a transfer. I do not mention that I now consider that move a mistake.

"What did you study?"

"Writing for Film and Television."

Her husband lets out a phlegmy cough that makes him sound very close to death, which, frankly, I believe he is. "Childcare is a far cry from entertainment," he manages.

No shit, Grandpa.

"And who do you work for now?" she asks.

"Well, I actually just finished up with them, but they live just a few blocks up from here," I say, and I describe Sasha's family. Suddenly my stomach turns at the thought of Sasha's children and having to start over with new ones. I push aside that feeling too and focus back on the questions.

"I know them!" she exclaims. "I wouldn't know them by first name, or face really, but I attended their wedding!"

"Oh!" I say, interested though confused. "How do you know the Ross family?"

"I worked with the groom's mother for a while. Wait, wait, no." She pauses to think. "Okay, no, the bride's father it was! George. I worked with George!"

It is moments like this that prove how different things are in the world of the 1 percent. You can go anywhere. Celebrate anyone. Even if you can't place their face or their name, you're part of the same club. It's when we establish this commonality that Mrs. Robertson's tone changes. I suddenly seem worthy of her time and apparently am now an interesting candidate for this position. On the Upper East Side, the two most important pieces of information won't be listed on a resume. Recruiters in this industry direct you to list past employers anonymously, for their privacy. My resume vaguely lists Sasha and her husband as "High Networth Family," but the anonymity is for show. More important than how you performed at your job is who you performed it for.

"How much of this job did the agency explain?"

"They only summarized."

"Okay, well, listen," she says, and then I hear soft snores from beside her. Her elderly husband has fallen asleep, but I ignore this oddity and continue listening. "If you work here, you are to be my eyes and ears, that's our deal. Nothing should happen that I don't know about. I want you to know exactly what this is and what I will expect of you. My son has recently started to rebel. He doesn't think he needs nannies anymore. He does not want them…"

"Oh, no," I say. "How old is he?"

"Frederick is seventeen."

I stare at her blankly, unsure of what to respond or even what to think.

Seventeen? As in a year away from legal adulthood? It seems to me that a young woman nannying a boy only seven years her junior should be criminal and is, at the very least, highly inappropriate. The idea is unorthodox if not downright creepy.

Suddenly, I want to leave the interview, this nine-million-dollar apartment, and whatever sort of position they are offering. It is exactly this sort of family that would have the audacity to call *mine* crazy.

"But he does still need a nanny, I'm afraid. So this is the deal. We have one to two nannies on at all times. You will work five days on, two days off. The five days on will be live-in. We have staff quarters on the third floor. Now, while on duty, you will need to wake Frederick at six thirty a.m. Watch to be sure he has brushed his teeth, packed his backpack, and applied deodorant. The chef has his breakfast out at seven, and he must finish the entire thing. He needs the nutrients for his busy day. Once he has finished you will escort him to school, then our driver will drop you back here around nine. From there you will organize his room, check on his grades, order any clothing or toiletries he needs. At two o'clock, you pick him up and supervise his after-school activities. He has tutors between three and five. I like him to eat a light snack on the ride to Asphalt Green, where he will have his two-hour tennis lesson. He will need to be home from his last tutor no later than seven thirty, which will then be followed by a brief shower and dinner, and you will tuck him in for lights out at ten sharp."

There is silence, during which time Mrs. Robertson takes a very large gulp of Pepsi. The old man continues to snore, and I cautiously think of a simple follow-up question.

"So, the workday ends around ten?" I ask.

"Oh, no, no. Frederick should be in bed by ten. Once he's settled in bed, you and I meet to discuss his day. You should be taking notes throughout it so you can keep me up to speed on his moods, any issues, concerns. It's all about communication. In a few months, he's going to start thinking about his college applications, Ivy Leagues only, and we're aiming for zero rejections. We need to keep him on the right track here; do you know what I mean?"

In fact, I do not know what Mrs. Robertson means.

My senior year of high school had consisted of nights at the mall with friends and sleeping through my alarm on weekends. No one checked to see if I had done my homework, although if they had, maybe I would have viewed it as a necessity instead of a light suggestion. All the things this boy was doing, everything Stanford and MIT would see on his application, they weren't *really* him. They were things that he did because his family could afford coaches and tutors and nannies and chefs. Perhaps the most noteworthy thing about him was that someone still skinned his apple slices.

Teenagers were meant to push boundaries and test freedom. Not be micromanaged and put to bed like toddlers. It was no wonder the agency had been so vague about details.

"Has anyone discussed salary with you yet?"

"No, not yet," I say.

Some sort of home aide pops in to prepare the old husband for bed. I count her as the sixth staff member to make an appearance during our strange interview. The aide gently rouses Mr. Robertson before helping him stand. Mrs. Robertson stands to kiss her love goodnight, and it is all quite disgusting. "We're offering ninety thousand a year with full benefits."

It wasn't actually that much considering the number of hours I'd be working. I had interviews for live-out positions on the horizon that offered higher wages. All of the nanny jobs listed by the elite agencies came with salaries between sixty-five and a hundred and fifty thousand a year.

"In addition," she says, "I offer a $25,000 cash bonus."

"Wow," I say, because this sort of high bonus is something I have never heard of before. Not even from my nanny friends in Elissa's circle, who spoke of all sorts of job perks from vacations to cars, had I ever heard of a nontaxed bonus of such a sum.

"But there is a catch. You only receive the bonus after completing two full years with us."

"I assume most people make it two years?"

Mrs. Robertson begins to laugh, a sort of unpleasant, overprivileged laugh. "No, no, they do not. As I've said, my son doesn't exactly welcome his caregivers. He can be somewhat, say, *hostile* with them. But that's why I implemented the bonus system. A sort of 'survivors prize,' if you will."

Mrs. Robertson asks for permission for her assistant to check my references, and I agree. I have no intention of taking the job, but I don't want to be rude. A week later the agency calls to tell me Mrs. Robertson has decided not to offer me the position after all. The more she thought about it, they say, the more I just didn't seem like the right fit.

The next two weeks are filled with interviews and trials, reference permissions and background checks. I interview with families all over Manhattan, each one somehow crazier than the last. I begin to see just how lucky I had been to find Sasha. With the Ross family, I made slightly less than I will with new families of similar means, but the job was relaxed and enjoyable. Sasha was normal and actively participated in parenting. Her children were sweet and well-mannered. I begin to wonder if it's even possible to find that sort of balance again.

In one nanny audition a judge, who the internet insists bought his way on to the bench, has two toddlers and an unpleasant wife. The wife stays at home and spends most of her day mentioning that she told her husband she does not want a nanny for the children, and so she does not know why I am there. The children's clothes must be washed immediately after they undress, neither has ever been on a playdate, and their three-year-old daughter has never once had a cold. The children take personal gymnastic classes so that they won't be exposed to germs by kids in the group lessons. A chef makes the judge a hot lunch every morning and then a chauffeur drives the food forty minutes across town to the courthouse. The position requires me to work holidays, except for Christmas Day, though I will need to agree to a red-eye to their residence in Hawaii that night. I trial with them for three days from six thirty a.m. to six thirty p.m. When the mother asks me to please sneeze outside the apartment, I decide to move on.

The next family invites me to work in the Hamptons for a weekend. A Google search identifies the eighteen-month-old boy's father, Mr. Boyston, as one of one hundred and five billionaires in New York. He's overweight and arrogant and employs fifty-eight staff members throughout his four residences. The position has no set hours. The live-in nannies, who rotate four days on and four days off, are on all twenty-four hours of their shift. My day starts when the boy wakes around five and it ends long after he is asleep. Only once every diaper pail has been emptied and every surface has been sanitized do I retire to bed. I sleep in a tiny room adjacent to the boy's, a baby monitor beside me, and I listen for any cries throughout the night.

On the last day, the boy and I are attempting to catch butterflies in the yard when Mr. Boyston joins us. Both tall and obese, he waddles across the yard, then asks the boy if he wants to go over to their docked yacht, a five-minute walk away. The boy shrieks with excitement, and then the father calls out, "Felipe!"

Within seconds a small man with tanned skin and broken English appears. "Yes, Mr. Boyston?"

Mr. Boyston directs the staffer to bring a golf cart around. Felipe disappears, then suddenly zooms up and loads Mr. Boyston and the boy onto the cart.

"The boat's down there," he says to me. "You just follow the path to the water. Just run behind and meet us there."

"Like, chase after the golf cart?" I ask, because I imagine that I *must* be misunderstanding the request.

"Yes, so that you get there just a little after us. I can't watch him while I'm on the boat. I'm going to fish."

I am sixty seconds into running after a fat billionaire and his baby when I decide that today is the last day I will ever see these people. On my final day at Mr. Boyston's Hamptons estate, a black car service, hired to transport the nannies to and from the city in the summer months, takes me back to Hell's Kitchen. During the two-hour drive, I skim through job listings in my field, wanting more than ever to return to a normal job. There are lots of entry-level jobs in PR or social media that I know I would qualify for. But the pay remains inadequate. My New York rent is fifteen hundred dollars a month, my loans are eleven hundred, and sometimes it's nice to eat. As tempting as a professional nine-to-six job may be, the thought is delusional, and I have no options. I think of my friends whose parents provide safety nets that saved them from this instability, and in this moment of uncertainty, I hate them for it.

I lean my head back and fight off tears. Your twenties tend to be a selfish period, and I'm under the impression my current predicament is unique to me. But all over the country, twentysomethings are returning home to their parents' basements after graduating,

forfeiting both their pride and their independence. They're searching for jobs, taking ones they never intended to, and wondering if
they'll ever again be debt-free.

I thought going to a good college was going to make my life
easier and open more doors for me, but the reality is much more
complicated. I need to clothe, feed, house, and support myself, all
while paying back the amount of money some might borrow to buy
a three-bedroom home. I had been under the impression that in
America college was for anyone, but student debt was nothing more
than tax on the poor. I had no problem with the idea that I needed to
pay back what I'd borrowed, but I'd been paying a thousand a month
on my loan for years now and most of that went to interest. I'd hardly
paid down any of the amount I'd borrowed because the bank's 4.5
percent interest rate wouldn't allow any actual progress—a modern
way of blocking upward mobility. Out in the real world, I saw who
college was truly for: those who could afford it. I feel trapped, hopeless, and ashamed. I have turned on this luxurious world that I was
once grateful for and awestruck by. Despite how much I loved the
children I've cared for, I've grown resentful of them. Resentful of the
opportunities they have to become anyone they aspire to be. They'll
never need to choose a university based on the financial aid package
or sacrifice their passions for a livable salary. They'll be able to take
unpaid summer internships that impress future employers instead
of working minimum wage jobs to save for the year ahead. These
things won't matter. They can afford to be anyone they want to be.

As we exit the highway and reenter the city on East 32nd Street, I
find myself desperate for someone to talk to. We drive through busy

Manhattan streets, and though I'm surrounded by people, I feel more alone than ever. I think of Lila first, as I always have, but her advice is no longer mine to seek, and I decide it's better to make peace with that than force another unwanted conversation. For a brief moment, I consider breaking the silence and calling my mother. But then I think back to the last time I saw her and again I am bitter.

"Are you really going to eat another slice of pizza?" my mother had asked from across the table.

By then my mother's anorexia was at its worst. She was five foot eleven and one hundred and three pounds. After decades of eliminating foods from her diet, she had finally found the perfect recipe for remaining alarmingly thin. At first it was about portion control, but soon foods she had loved vanished from her diet altogether. She gave up dressing on her salads. Now she was a practicing vegetarian and consumed only two pieces of bread and a slice of pizza a day. She worked out for an hour each morning and afternoon, walked her dogs three miles each night, and never drank alcohol. In all this time, I had never once heard another adult in her life suggest she consider treatment for her disease.

Perhaps it was because of my mother's issues that food had become such a comfort in the midst of my identity crisis. Growing up, my mother had made food so scarce that obtaining extra was an achievement. I'd go to sleepovers at friends' houses, and their parents would find me in the pantry stuffing my shirt with cookies. At pizza parties I would eat not a slice but a pie. What should have been a source of survival was instead a weapon, and it was now one I used against myself.

"Yes," I told my mother. "Sorry I can't starve myself like you do."

Despite this, and every other issue we'd ever had, the truth was that right now I missed her.

I slide my phone into my backpack as the car pulls up in front of my shabby building on West 46th Street. There is no one to call. Nothing to do. No choices to make. I made the decision to go to college so that I would not find myself like my parents: uneducated, broke, and out of options, but I was just as trapped as they ever were. Our debts were proportionate to the money we earned, but I was no better off than they had ever been. In order to pay each bill, to simply survive, I had to make a lot of money. In New York City, working for the rich was the quickest way to do it.

I cannot afford to be anything other than a nanny. This is the only way at this particular moment in time that I can thrive—I hate this, *but I know this*—and so I take out my computer and respond to the last agency to contact me.

Stefany is Jewish, which she mentions several times, and her husband is Middle Eastern and very busy. He works long hours in his family's Soho art gallery, and he travels frequently throughout the year. They have a five-year-old boy, Digby, who is aloof and shows no interest in my existence but who Stefany swears will come around. Their new baby, Sampson, will be mine to watch between the hours of seven and seven, though, like Sasha, Stefany spends most of her time at home. She describes parenting in a way that reminds me of my former boss. It is the first thing that convinces me that I have found a decent fit.

"I will tell you, I like to be with my kids, and there are going to be days where I'm going to want to be around all day," Stefany says.

"My last boss was like that, so I get it," I say.

On the final day of my trial, we're sitting outside by their salt-water pool. They live in Tribeca, a welcome break from the Upper East Side. Their house is custom built, upscale, and modern but not as over the top as the residences in my most recent interviews. Stefany and her life, though of course still extravagant, appear more grounded.

Stefany finishes feeding Sampson and asks if I want to hold him. He's three months old and fragile, his little head fidgeting under a sun hat. I rest him on my lap while Stefany and I continue chatting.

"Are you comfortable doing errands in a Porsche?" she asks. "They're the only kind of cars we have."

I admit that I've never driven a Porsche, but that I'd be happy to do so. Just then Digby walks by and mutters, "Stupid ugly baby," under his breath. His mother doesn't reply, and I assume she must not have heard him.

"I'm also sort of a neat freak. If you haven't noticed," Stefany laughs, but I have noticed. She has already directed me to pick multiple crumbs off the floor, but her desire to keep the house sterile seems to be her only negative, and one I'm confident I can cooperate with. With a full-time housekeeper on staff, I imagine her homes rarely find themselves dirty, anyway.

"So the hours will be seven to seven, Monday through Friday, for a twelve hundred-dollar-a-week take home. I'm not sure what that looks like before taxes. My accountant will have to look into it, but anyhow, that's the offer."

Though the hours are long, the pay is fine, and I'm more than willing to throw myself into work. Plus, it's a job that pays on the books, which isn't common in the nannying world, and I need a pay stub to qualify for things like credit cards and apartment leases. The hours that I'm with Stefany's boys will keep me busy and distracted, and I find myself grateful for the promise of such a long workweek.

Stefany gives me a contract that I read only briefly before signing. We decide that I will move into their East Hampton home for the summer the following Monday. In five weeks, when they return to the city, so will I. It's rushed and sudden, like a relationship you should probably be more cautious getting into, but I need the job. As I leave, Stefany says she will see me next week, and I thank her for everything. Digby glares at me from a chair in the living room while I wave goodbye. Next to him, his baby brother sleeps. I think one more time about working with a newborn. *Should I do this again?* I shrug off the thought, but there's a part of me that keeps wondering, *Isn't working with a baby why you're a mess in the first place?*

"We're really happy we found you," Stefany says as I leave. "I know it's particular, but you know, we just really wanted someone who went to college," she says.

Oh, yes, I think to myself. *Thank goodness for that college education. This is exactly what I was hoping to use it for.*

I climb the four flights of stairs to my apartment in a zombie-like trance. Things were looking up when Stefany had hired me earlier that day. Sure, I didn't feel any sort of instant connection to her or her children, nothing like the day I met my beloved Ruby and Hunter, but it was easily the best of the options I'd been presented with. That much I was sure of. But nannying made me feel like a failure. All I wanted was to take pride in a career, and this hardly seemed a real job. I had felt a brief relief when Stefany had hired me, but now, back in my own gloomy reality, I just feel lost.

I pull out my computer and turn on a show. I choose something I've seen a dozen times, a story that I know the ending to, something predictable. Aside from the theme song of *Law & Order*, the apartment is silent. I'm left with nothing but disappointment.

15

CHARITY CASE

BY MY JUNIOR YEAR OF high school, I'd become something of a curiosity at Lincoln. Not so different from a Chucky doll, I had become both interesting *and* frightening to people. Lincoln's basketball team had undergone a complete transformation. The coach had lured in a few more scholarship kids, and now a team that had won only one game two seasons ago was on track to win the entire division. The local papers were covering our games, and there was talk that I'd be the first athlete in the school's history to score a thousand points. But I also had a reputation for being a bad sport, hot tempered, and a bit of a bitch on the court. I may have been in a place of high class, but I brought my classless roots with me.

School administrators worked hard to curb my attitude, and some days it worked, but by night I'd be home and back to my old ways again. When I was in the gym at Lincoln, I was an unpleasant star. The next day I'd be back in the classroom, and suddenly an overachiever was the last thing I seemed to be.

●●●●●

"All right, Stephanie. Let's hear it," my father said.

I was nearing the end of my senior year, and tensions in our house were high. "Hear what?" I asked, but I knew, and so did everyone else.

Stew and I had been caught in the same heated debate for weeks. I was about to be the first person in our family to go to college, but there were no celebrations. Talking to my parents about where I wanted to go to school was harder than swallowing eight razor blades smeared in organic peanut butter.

"I want to check out Assumption," I said.

"Division three. No athletic scholarships." Stew scowled. "It's out."

"But I don't like any of the schools looking at me for basketball."

It was the same line I had been repeating for weeks. I had no interest in Pace, or Merrimack, or any school that sounded like it was named after a pioneer woman. I also no longer wanted to play basketball, which was perhaps the bigger issue. Once everyone else in my class started receiving their acceptance letters, it hit me. I had just spent three years squandering my opportunity at a private high school education by producing half-baked schoolwork and basking in my athletic glory.

"You think you're going to get anywhere without basketball? With your grades?" Stew argued. "Come on."

"I'll take out loans and focus on schoolwork and get good grades. That's the point of school anyway, right? To do well in class?"

"Well, you've certainly never shined academically before," he laughed. "Why would it be different now?"

I bit one side of my lip until I tasted blood. I was furious with the conversation and tired of his snide remarks, but there was a truth to them that I could not deny. By the time my senior year rolled around, Lincoln's gymnasium had raised four championship sports banners. Three of them were mine. But my grades were those of someone barely skating by.

"Hey, dumb ass," my dad would say, "did you do your homework?"

I would have arrived home at seven and promptly turned on the television. By eight my backpack sat on the floor untouched. *No*, I clearly had not done any homework.

"Look, I don't want to get any more calls from this Mr. Shoefell. Guy's calling me two, three times a week bitching. I don't have time to be playing grab ass with him all time. Do your shit."

"Yeah, yeah," I muttered. That was that.

●●●●●

"Basketball is my entire life. It's all I do. I practice, and I play in games, and I practice more. And it got me here, but now I want more, and I don't want to base the rest of my life on a game that will end in four years."

"Well maybe you should have thought about that before you flunked physics three times. You should go where they give you money to shoot a ball into a basket, or you shouldn't go at all," my father said.

My guidance counselor had explained my options. He also mentioned that my parents had been the only ones in my entire class to not come in for a college guidance meeting and that I had chosen to only take the SATs once. Of the thirty-some girls in my class, I appeared to be the least engaged with the process, she said.

I nodded, embarrassed and unsure how I could force my parents to take an interest in higher learning.

"Stephanie," the counselor sighed, "most of your classmates saw an SAT tutor twice a week since junior year. You didn't even purchase the prep book I suggested. It shows a complete lack of proactivity."

Despite his hard work, it had been the toughest winter my father had faced financially since I was a kid. I knew how expensive the SAT book was. When the school year began, my classmates arrived with the eight hundred dollars' worth of new textbooks needed for their course load. Meanwhile, my mother drove me to town hall, where they would loan out whichever of the books they had available and in stock to students whose families paid town taxes. Lincoln covered tuition for scholarship students, but they often overlooked the other supplies a student would need to succeed. If a student couldn't afford the tuition, chances were they couldn't afford the two-hundred-dollar calculator. Giving a student a scholarship doesn't even the playing field; it simply puts them in the same arena.

I left the meeting fighting back tears. *Maybe I wasn't meant for college*, I thought, but then I remembered the message echoed to me throughout the last few years: *if you don't go to a good college, you'll never get a good job.* I'd have to figure this out. I couldn't help but be angry that I was going to leave this place the same way I'd come in: as a reject.

On graduation day, we wore white dresses and held hand-picked daisies. Sweat from my hands rubbed against the sheet of paper I clenched tightly. When it was finally time for me to speak and I reached the podium, my whole body trembled with nerves. I thought my parents would be proud when an anonymous group picked my speech for commencement.

"They picked your speech?" my dad asked.

No one was more shocked than me.

"I didn't know you wrote things," Lydia added. It wasn't something I had broadcast, but I'd grown fond of writing and was doing so in most of my free time. A creative writing class I had picked up as an easy elective had piqued my interest. I loved reading my work out loud and hearing my classmates laugh as I rehearsed what were often outrageous lines. It provided a rush that I had only ever felt playing sports, but with sports came adrenaline, whereas writing was simply emotions. Basketball left me wild. Writing kept me grounded.

Three weeks after graduation, my school's monthly magazine arrived in our mailbox for the very last time. On the back page was a letter written by the headmistress. It talked about my speech, then me as a student, and how I represented everything Lincoln hoped to achieve. The letter spoke of how I'd arrived at their school as a seed, but at the moment in which I addressed the crowd at graduation, my teachers watched as I transformed into a flower. I proved that in the right environment, and with proper encouragement, any student could thrive. I must have read the words fifteen times over. They *had* to be worth something.

I brought the letter inside, summoned my family into the kitchen, and read the letter out loud. At the end, everyone wore wide-eyed faces, looking stunned. I thought, *this is it, this is the moment they're all impressed.* It turned out that after three long years, that's not quite what they were thinking.

"That headmistress..." My dad shook his head. "I mean, she's really a gayblade."

My private school education forever altered my trajectory. It was the first place that exposed me to the possibility of more. I was surrounded by successful adults who had important careers and significant resources. I was not part of their circle, but maybe I could be. I made long-lasting and complex friendships that would grow and encourage me throughout my life. I met Lila, with whom I'd share a history and bond that would forever go unmatched. Lincoln was a new beginning, but it taught me more than just the value of hard work or real friendship. It provided me with the most valuable lesson I'd need when I entered the world of elite Manhattan: the art of being the poorest person in a wealthy room.

16

OTHER STEFANY

"DIGBY, WE HAVE TO LEAVE for camp in five minutes. Can you please put your shoes on?"

"Don't talk to me!" Digby screams. "I hate you! Dumb, fat, Stephanie!"

In just a few weeks, finding myself uncomfortable living in a near-stranger's home, I have lost most of the weight that I had gained earlier that year. So, while I know that I am not currently fat, I do wish that Digby would stop suggesting it.

Each morning, around six fifty, I walk upstairs to begin my shift, and each morning, five-year-old Digby announces that fat Stephanie has arrived. His insults vary as he enjoys a variety of unkind commentary. He throws around words like *stupid* and *foolish*, though his favorite label for me appears to be original: *non-use.*

"Can I have a cookie?" he asks.

"You're not allowed sugar," I say, as he is not permitted desserts, and he already knows the answer.

"Ugh. You're such non-use, Stephanie."

The first time I mention this to my new boss, Other Stefany laughs. "He's just testing out new words," she tells me. But slowly her real reasoning for not addressing his behavior is revealed. Stefany takes a progressive, modern approach to parenting: "My philosophy is no discipline. Digby is a good boy; he needs guidance, not regulation," she says.

"Okay." I pause just to make sure I fully understand what it is she is telling me. "So, like, he's allowed to keep calling me fat Stephanie then?"

"I think it's better to just suggest he use different words. Why don't you try reminding him that *fat* is unkind," Stefany says. But Digby doesn't mind being unkind. What Digby minds is me.

When we arrive at camp drop-off that morning, Stefany asks me to stroll the baby in the air-conditioned hall while she seeks out Digby's counselor.

Hampton Country Day, the Ritz-Carlton of children's summer camps, features pools, ziplines, rock-climbing walls, private sports lessons, and high-quality organic lunches. The camp should be every child's summer dream, but Digby finds the dining options subpar, and yesterday he told his mother as much.

"The whole wheat pasta primavera was disgusting," he said.

Other Stefany gasps. "That's terrible, Dig. What was the alternative?"

"Salmon. But it was overcooked. I couldn't even eat it."

With that, Stefany decides that she has no choice but to speak to a camp staff member. "I mean, I have to," she explains to me. "This is a two-thousand-dollar-a-week day camp. At the very least, they should be offering to cook the fish to his liking."

I nod in agreement, *totally*, but really I am just wondering what pasta primavera is.

As Stefany and Digby disappear, I push a sleeping Sampson around the bustling hall. Campers drop in with their Dominican nannies or their Botox-frozen mothers, who wear gorgeous long, white dresses paired with round straw hats. All of them look like Gwyneth Paltrow, or are trying to look like her at least, and I think back to a time when these sorts of women fascinated me. Now it's so played out, I find myself just bored.

"Really, though, that's what Spirit's counselor told me," a woman whispers.

I turn to my left to sneak a peek at the two mothers conversing next to me. I don't know either of them, but Stefany has mentioned them before, saying that the shorter of the two is a member of the Tisch family. At the time, I don't know the name, and so it holds no significance to me. Only later do I learn that the woman's family has a net worth of over twenty billion dollars and that everything from hospitals to art galleries to donated libraries bears their name. To me, she appears like all the other women here, draped in Dolce but otherwise average.

"But what did her counselor mean?" the Tisch woman asks.

"She was just saying that we pay thousands of dollars to send them here, right? Like, it's crazy. But the counselors only make three hundred dollars a week!"

I'm shocked to learn that counselors working sometimes

ten-hour days are earning less than minimum wage and wonder what legal loophole makes this possible. Perhaps the room and board the camp provides them with is considered part of their pay? But still. The Tisch woman seems lost in her friend's story, and I wonder if she's as surprised as I am. She stares at her blankly. "So… is three hundred dollars a week a lot or a little?"

There's a pause in which her friend appears briefly bothered, but it passes too quickly. "Oh, you're awful!" the friend laughs. "It's a little. They're paying the help very little is my point."

Suddenly, I hear my name. I see Other Stefany by the front door and roll the baby toward her. I think to tell her about the conversation I just overheard but decide against it. Other Stefany isn't Sasha, and had she participated in this conversation, she would surely have been equally offensive. I'm starting to fear that perhaps I've made a mistake and might be working for a woman I'll grow to genuinely dislike.

"It's all set," she says. "I talked to Digby's group leader. They're going to have him sit down with the chef today to discuss his preferences on meats and whatnot. Such a relief, isn't it?"

"Definitely," I say.

Such a relief.

●●●●●

"The pizza should be here in ten minutes. Can you set up plates, waters, and a charcuterie board on the patio for five o'clock?"

"Of course," I say before immediately googling what the fuck a charcuterie board is.

Other Stefany seems to be feeling slightly unhinged today, the pressure of hosting her first Hamptons playdate too much to bear and the panic of possibly being rejected by the other mothers so immediate. There are four local Tribeca children coming over, and a Super Soccer Stars coach has been hired to give them a lesson. Stefany's spacious backyard is littered with soccer balls and nets plus cones and other pieces of equipment that surely aren't necessary but have been purchased for show. The saltwater in-ground pool has been covered as a precaution, and the many pieces of patio furniture have been wiped clean. This two-hour event has taken weeks to plan, and no detail has gone unaddressed.

Stefany is trying on many long and impractical dresses for an afternoon in her home. When it's just Stefany and me, I find her company fine, oftentimes even enjoyable. At her core, I believe she is a good person, but her desire to be regarded as a great mom by her privileged peers brings out unpleasant qualities. Around other mothers, her personality takes on a new form. Poor before marrying into her husband's rich family, Stefany speaks openly and often of her wealth now, taking every opportunity to mention something they own or a vacation they have gone on. It's obnoxious and arrogant, and if it were not for Digby, perhaps the most irritating part of my job.

As people begin to arrive, Stefany barks orders at me. "Don't let anyone use the main bathrooms, please. Only the one by the kitchen because I don't want people tracking footprints throughout the house. Actually, no children in the house at all. It'll make a mess, but of course, the mothers might want a tour of my home since it's so unique. You can let them in." I nod to her demands while cutting a cucumber into slices. "Sure thing," I tell her.

"Stephanie!" she shouts so loudly I nearly jump, "what are you doing! Those slices are way too thick. Do you want the children to choke?"

She rips the knife from my hand before I can respond.

"What's wrong with you?" she sneers. "It's like you've never used a knife before."

The first hour of Other Stefany's soccer party proceeds without incident. The children are invested in their soccer lesson, kicking the balls into tiny nets, following the coach, and playing along with his silly games. He tells them to pretend to be soccer ducks and they quack. Later, he asks them to collect the balls by balancing them on their heads. However, while most of the kids listen and giggle and eagerly participate, Digby lies in the grass, tossing his shoes up in the air.

I walk out to the patio and begin setting the table when I hear Stefany talking to the other moms. They sit on outdoor couches and sip rosé while discussing things like green juices and goat milk soaps.

"Oh, gosh, look at my Digby," Stefany laughs. "Dig, honey. What are you doing? Put your shoes back on, little goose!" Then she turns to the other moms. "You know, we keep trying to gently push the sports because he's just so naturally athletic. But he's just got that creative, independent mind, you know?"

"Oh, for sure," a mom says, sitting with a fifteen-thousand-dollar Hermès Birkin bag on her lap but dressed in athletic shorts "I mean, you can see it."

I look over to the strange boy in the grass and wonder if this mom really agrees or if she's just practicing good manners. Digby is allowed only lean protein, fruits, and vegetables. He's extremely thin, uncoordinated, and perhaps the least athletic child I have ever observed. Digby, at nearly six, is not a bad kid, but he's being raised in a world where there are no rules or consequences. Having a "no discipline" philosophy has taught him that being cruel is acceptable. Stefany teaches him strict religious values, doesn't allow screen time, and bans books like Harry Potter and most things by Dr. Seuss. Too many rules and too much sheltering have resulted in a socially inept child.

Surely these mothers, whose children are interacting and playing normally, must see that too.

"Steph," Other Stefany snaps, "has dinner been prepared?"

"Everything's all set."

"Great. Here, will you just take Sampson?" she asks. "I need to join the dinner table. But keep him outside so he feels a part of everything. But in the shade so he doesn't get hot."

There is very little shade in the backyard at five p.m., so Sampson and I sit in a corner by the grills. The children dig into their food and wave goodbye to the soccer coach. Stefany slips him two hundred dollars for his hour-long service and makes a show of thanking him. I'm bouncing Sampson on my lap when Stefany begins calling for Digby.

"Digby, come on over with your friends for dinner."

"They're not my friends. I don't even know these people!" he screams from across the yard by the firepit.

He's not wrong. He did just meet these children, but still, he is the only one of the group unable to socialize.

"Sweetheart, please. You've been working so hard, you must be starving. Come eat."

"No! I'm doing a concert!" he says, and then, unfortunately, he does.

For the past few weeks, I have listened to Digby shout lyrics to his favorite song for hours at a time. Now, in the middle of dinner, a group of unfamiliar children and mothers get to witness the same performance. Stefany jokes about her son's quirky behavior, as she calls it, and the other moms laugh along.

I don't practice Santeria! I ain't got no crystal ball. Well, I had a million dollars but I, I'd, spend it all!!!!

I imagine that if anyone here once enjoyed the music of Sublime, they don't anymore. *If I could find that Heina, and that Sancho that she's found. Well I'd pop a cap in Sancho and I'd slap her down!!* I listen to the lyrics carefully and then ask myself how it can be that while *The Cat in the Hat* is prohibited in Other Stefany's home, a song about a jealous ex-boyfriend taking revenge on the man who stole his girl has made the cut.

The concert continues, and by the time Stefany coaxes the boy to the table, Sampson is fussing. Digby makes a stink about joining the other children as he walks across the yard. As Sampson and I head for the house, I catch one more glimpse of the playdate. It's just enough time to watch Digby slap a boy on his way to the table.

17

NO GYMS FOR THE HELP

STEFANY REQUIRES MY ASSISTANCE DURING all of the children's waking hours, leaving very little time for myself. Most days that summer I am on the clock between the hours of six forty-five a.m. and seven thirty p.m. While the money is good, the hours are brutal, and I realize my work-life balance is not so different from what my father's was when he worked at the mill.

With her husband back in the city for work, the two children together outnumber her, and Stefany says she cannot handle both of them on her own. For me, the work is a welcome distraction, though exhausting, and most of my waking hours revolve around someone else's needs.

By the time my shift ends and I've showered, the time is eight p.m. I retire to my room in the basement and open up my computer, then sift through dozens of ROOMMATE WANTED ads. The process is stressful. Finding housing in New York City, specifically reasonably priced housing, can be nearly impossible. But Lila and I can no longer coexist. In fact, we haven't spoken all summer. She's hung back in our Hell's Kitchen apartment while I've sorted out my job search in the Hamptons. We've decided not to renew our lease, and Lila will be gone by the time I return. Although I've toyed with the idea of finding a replacement roommate for our apartment, I decide a fresh start will do me good, so I make the decision to find a new place.

When an interesting listing catches my eye, I reply with a brief introduction of myself. I tell them what I do for work and how old I am. All dull facts that people share as if they can really help determine roommate compatibility. I'm in the middle of writing one of these emails when my chest begins to hurt. It's a new phenomenon. The first time this happened I thought I was having a heart attack.

You're too young, I told myself. After an hour of feeling as if a fifty-pound weight was stuck on top of my body and struggling to catch what felt like any air at all, the pain subsided and so did any worry. But days later it happened again. Eventually I went to the doctor.

For months after my abortion, I had been telling my doctor that I wasn't feeling myself. "I just don't feel right," I had said. So my doctor would refer me to a different doctor, who would tell me I was fine and then send me to another, who would diagnose me with seasonal affective disorder, and then finally I'd be off to a third, who would dryly say it sounded like I had a case of "the millennials." That's the thing about mental health. When you have strep throat, they run a test and you get a firm diagnosis. Mental health is, in some ways, a guessing game, and there's no lab in the world that can guarantee you a correct diagnosis.

None of these doctors could offer me any concrete answers, but they did all offer me prescriptions. Some suggested that these pills were the best way to deal with the aftereffects of an abortion. I was young and had no reliable adults to lean on, and so without thinking, I tried them all. But they didn't help. I wanted to feel like myself again; instead, these medications made me feel nothing at all. I longed for the days when I found humor in everything, a time when I felt empathy for everyone, and hope could be found on even the gloomiest days. All these pills did was allow me to feel numb. Not happy. Not sad. Just empty.

I thought back to the other women throughout my life who had found themselves a weak opponent to depression or anxiety. Lila's mother had been fortunate enough to afford the most expensive rehabs, but they failed her repeatedly. Then there was my sister Jenna, who had endured two long stays in a state mental ward. Wanting help was one thing, but finding quality help, affording it, and pushing yourself through it was another. It seemed the mental health system was flawed, no matter what sort of patient was seeking treatment. I knew that if I wanted to rise above this, it wouldn't come from a three-hundred-dollar-an-hour therapist alone, if only for the simple fact I couldn't afford it long term. There was no easy fix, and no one was coming to save me. I had to save myself.

That night I reply to one final ad. The listing is for a third roommate in a doorman building in Chelsea. The rent is more than I would like, eighteen hundred a month, but I am taking home twelve hundred dollars a week after taxes. With my loans and other bills, I will have just enough to afford it. That's the good thing about working more than half the hours in a twenty-four-hour day. I have more money than ever before and absolutely no time to spend it.

I lie down on the king-sized bed in an otherwise unfurnished room created specifically for the house's help and realize I am coming to a crossroads. The reason I had been a great nanny to Ruby and Hunter wasn't because I had been intrigued by their world of privilege or because I'd made so much money. Sure, the pay was the reason I needed to do this job, but it wasn't why I had been successful in it. I had been a good nanny because I had chosen to focus on the positives of my work and because I had wholeheartedly loved the children that I cared for. But I was never again going to be able to find joy in this work if I continued resenting it. And I couldn't stop feeling resentful until I faced my own personal demons.

●●●●●

I end up living in the doorman building in Chelsea. The luxury of the building is a signal to me that I'm getting closer to success. When I'd moved to New York, this sort of amenity-heavy residence had seemed so far out of reach, a place reserved for only the city's finest. It's a real taste of that marvelous life I had been striving for when I arrived here. Plus, I'm going to have new friends and a fresh start. I get an opportunity to stop feeling sorry for myself, to appreciate what I do have, and to stop focusing on the negatives. My behavior has been self-sabotaging, and before I can admit it to anyone else, I need to admit it to myself. So I do. The only way over pain is through it. I stop relying on things that momentarily numb my emotions, and I face them head-on. This feels awful, later difficult, and then eventually so simple, I wish I had the sense to have done it this way all along.

I am twenty-five years old, and I still have a chance to become the person I had wanted to be the day I arrived in New York. It takes every last bit of my hope for me to reach this conclusion, and I am not sure where the inner voice comes from, telling me I need to pick myself back up. It feels like a supernatural phenomenon, this sudden clarity, but maybe there is nothing miraculous about it. Maybe this is what growing up without safety nets creates: someone scrappy. Just like I had seen my father do repeatedly throughout my childhood, I get knocked down and then get back up. My childhood was a how-to guide on ways to keep going. The one thing I had that most of the children on the Upper East Side would never have was grit.

The week before I move to Chelsea, I wake early and pull my computer out once more. I research Cavalier King Charles spaniel breeders and find two reputable ones. One of them has a litter available now. I scroll through the pictures until I come to the very last dog. Later that day, I ask the owner why that puppy is a bit cheaper than his brothers and sisters.

"He's a runt," the man sighed, "and he's got a birthmark on his lip. He's got good blood but he's a reject. He'll never be able to be a show dog."

I put a deposit down on him on the spot.

That night, after the kids are asleep and I am free to go, I walk down to the beach. I sit by the water and toss uneaten pieces of a sandwich to the famished seagulls. I am not yet ready to talk to my mother, but I know that I miss my sisters. It has been months since I've spoken to either of them. I throw the last piece of bread and then pick up my phone and dial.

"Hello?" my dad says.

The first few minutes of our conversation are difficult, awkward to an unsettling degree, to the point that I think we both consider just hanging up. But slowly it improves. I tell him that I am going through a hard time, but he already knows.

Thanks to Obamacare, I am still on his insurance, though in a few months I'll be ineligible, and he'd seen that I'd been to a therapist.

"Did it help?" he asked.

I tell him that I don't think so.

I have friends who swear by therapy. They say it changed their lives and helped them achieve a higher-functioning version of themselves. I believe them, but for me, telling a stranger my feelings doesn't help. In fact, it only seems to deepen my resentment and self-doubt. I need to sort through my emotions in other ways.

"But you were usually happy. An idiot, of course, but still happy," my dad says. "I just don't know, like, what set this all off?"

"It's just been a hard time," I say, but for the first time I go a little further. I tell him the whole story.

"Well, I'm glad you called," he said at the end of the phone call. "You know, I know we've had our problems..." he paused. The words seemed caught in his throat, like something he wanted to say but wasn't sure he should. I understood that feeling.

"It's fine," I said.

"No," he finally continued, "it's not. But we're family, and at the end of the day we're going to be here for you. I know we haven't always done a good job of that, but we are. We're here for you."

This is the first step to making peace with my parents. It is a critical moment. I both realize and accept here in this conversation that I can't change who they are or where I came from. I can't be angry with them for not having more than they did. They are different from me, and we don't share the same values or beliefs, but those things are okay as long as we respect and attempt to understand one another.

My family will watch from afar, yet closer than before, as I rebuild my life. I replay my dad's words a few more times before responding.

We're here for you.

"I know," I said and felt my face burn hot with tears. My dad's love has always had its limits, and our relationship was often flawed, but it doesn't matter. His words are enough to give me hope.

●●●●●

The summer comes to an end with little excitement, and we return permanently to New York City from the Hamptons on Labor Day weekend. That Saturday, three of my oldest friends travel into the city to help me move into my new home. I don't own much furniture, just a bed and a television, and there are only a few boxes of clothes and shoes. It takes us just an hour to lug everything from the top of the fifth-floor walk-up down to the rented U-Haul. When my friend Jess takes down the very last box, Olivia asks if I am ready.

I am standing in the emptiness that was once Lila's and my living room. I clutch my new puppy tight against my chest. "Just give me a minute," I tell Olivia, then hand her the dog. I listen to her footsteps disappear down the long staircase until it is silent. *How lucky am I to have a friend like her*, I think in the quiet.

Looking around the bare apartment, I recognize fully all the damage I caused myself this last year. Resentment is such an ugly thing, and I had allowed it to dictate so many aspects of my life. It is a miserable moment, but I suddenly see hope in every beaten corner of the room. I look around at the cracking paint and exposed pipes and think, *This apartment was sort of shit.* Leaving it gives me reasons to be sad, but it is also a symbol of my opportunity to start fresh. As I gather my purse, I look into Lila's old room. From the window behind where her bed had been, midday sunlight slithers in. There is so much good that lies ahead; I can see that now. I'm sure of it.

The following Tuesday, I return to work, this time at Stefany's Tribeca loft. It isn't as spacious as their Hamptons sanctuary, but it is just as handsome. I share the elevator ride up with Lo Bosworth from the '00s MTV hit *The Hills*, who pauses by the trash to dump some Valentino shoes, which I scoop up later that day. They don't fit, but I sell them online. I bet Lo has never even heard of Poshmark.

"Good morning, Digby," I say.

"Shut up," he responds.

Seconds later Stefany enters the kitchen and hands the baby off to me. "I need to get dressed, but tell me, how was the move?"

"It was good! Super easy. And I really love the new building. It has a terrace and a gym." I smile at the thought. "I think I'm going to be really happy there."

"A gym, huh?" Stefany says.

There is a hostility in her voice that I have heard her use with others—waitstaff or secretaries, people with whom she has only brief interactions and whom she decides are less than her. Last time I'd overheard this tone was in late August, when a worker remodeling their second kitchen had asked to use the bathroom, and she had declined. "I'm sorry; would you mind driving into town to use the bathroom? There's a Starbucks there. It's only ten minutes away." I was aware that Stefany could be curt with others, but she had never been so with me.

"We didn't even have a gym until a few years ago. You're starting to live like us. Makes me think maybe we're paying you too much." She laughs.

18

PLEASE CLEAN THE UNDERWEAR

DIGBY IS FIVE YEARS OLD and shits his pants nearly every day. Not accidentally, but spitefully, on purpose. He has been potty-trained for three years, uses the toilet when convenient, and is fully aware that this behavior is unacceptable. But still, he keeps doing it, and his mother keeps making me hand-wash his soiled underpants.

"He just is so smart," Stefany sighs as I carry a pair of briefs caked with poop into the laundry room. "He can't stop whatever he's doing to go. That's what it is. He was so focused on his LEGO creation that he literally couldn't pause to go to the bathroom."

Unbeknownst to Stefany, I have been interviewing for new positions all week, and I am working for her only until a better offer comes along. I no longer respond to her wildly inaccurate observations of her son.

"Can I just throw this pair out?" I ask. I look down at the white undies that are filled, not with the poop of a baby or toddler but of a full-grown child.

"Absolutely not. These are linen boxers; do you know how much they cost per pair? Put them in the sink and scrape it."

I sigh but do as I am told. If I am going to continue accepting a paycheck each week, I need to adhere to my boss's demands, however outrageous. I don't understand why a woman who recently bragged that her entire shoe collection is Chanel can't afford to purchase her son new linen undergarments. But I am also acutely aware that Other Stefany does not give a fuck what I do or do not understand.

"Mom! I need more bath crystals," Digby screams from the tub.

Stefany goes sprinting in her son's direction to get him some. When she returns, I am rubbing the two sides of the underwear together under the sink. Digby had sat in the poop for some time, and parts had hardened onto the cloth, but I'm hoping the friction will loosen it.

"What are you doing?" Stefany screams at me.

I pause, puzzled. "Cleaning the underwear?"

"Okay, yeah, so that's not how to clean underwear. My goodness, Steph, you need to learn to do these things correctly."

Stefany grabs the underwear and begins using her bare fingers to scrape the shit away. After a second she waves me off.

"Stop lingering and go get the baby. Like everything else around here, I'll just have to do this myself."

●●●●●

"Steph, I'd like you to bond with Digby. You've put in very little effort, and he hasn't taken to you, so this afternoon I'd like the two of you to go to lunch."

Stefany often speaks to me as if I am half-incompetent, half newborn baby. The conversations are awkward, and I believe the contrived dialogue is a result of her incessant desire to seem proper. It's like talking to Alexa, except Stefany has a body, cannot be unplugged, and refuses to lower her volume.

"Okay, sure. Where would you like me to take him?"

Digby overhears this from the other room and immediately shrieks in protest. I had dined with Ruby and Hunter dozens of times. They loved Shake Shack and McDonald's, pizza slices, and the corner bagel shop. Digby has a far stricter diet, but he is, after all, still five. I can only assume we'll be going somewhere similar, and I find the idea of daytime french fries appealing.

"I've made a reservation at Fig & Olive for twelve o'clock. You can leave in an hour."

Now—internally, of course—I scream too.

Fig & Olive, an uptown eatery frequented by professionals in suits and pencil skirts, describes itself as an upscale restaurant serving seasonal Mediterranean fare. With great confusion, the hostess seats Digby and me by a table of lawyers who discuss their defense strategy in a complicated case.

"Digby, do you want me to ask if they have a children's menu?" I ask.

My eyes scan entrees I am unable to identify. It seems highly unlikely that Digby, though he can read at a high level, will recognize his options.

"I already know what I want."

"Really," I say, surprised. "What are you getting?"

"I'm getting the kabocha squash risotto. It's good."

"Sounds very awesome," I say, thinking of all the times at his age that my family couldn't afford groceries. And my peers at public school who received free meals and who arrived an hour early to ensure they would have breakfast that day. Yet, here is a child so self-assured he doesn't even consider ordering off the children's menu. There is an arrogance and privilege to this that I haven't seen in most adults, never mind a five-year-old.

I am grateful when the food finally arrives. Having lunch with Digby is like spending an afternoon with a twisted Benjamin Button. In some ways, he is immature, the result of being overly sheltered. But he is also an old soul. He doesn't joke or giggle, and he is missing many childlike qualities altogether. I have no idea how to interact with him, and it doesn't help that he despises me.

"Steph," Digby asks, "will I die soon?"

I'm startled by the question. "What? Digby, no. You're only five."

"You can get cancer at five."

He's not wrong, but still, I pause. These sorts of topics with children, even the kids I'm securely bonded with, are difficult to navigate. Anything you say can be confused or misinterpreted in their delicate minds.

"That's true. But most of the time people live long lives. I don't think you should worry about this just yet."

Digby pauses, and I briefly mistake the silence for satisfaction, but then he continues.

"But if I eat too much sugar, my body will get weak, and I won't be able to fight off the bad germs. And mom says when we die there is no heaven, and then there'll be nowhere for me to go. But at Christmas, dad's mom, Grandma Irma, said that Jesus will be waiting for me in heaven." He sighs heavily, unlike the little boy he is. "I don't want to die."

There is no hope for Digby and me to form a deep relationship, but I feel bad for him, this oddly independent, scared little boy, shouldering fears instilled in him too early by an overprotective parent who's more concerned with seeming like the perfect mother than being one. Digby has no freedom to come into his own or form his own ideas. There is no "right" way to parent, but I think children need things in moderation. Without moderation, they are presented with too much or too little, and the outcome of this is *Digby*.

Later that day I give Stefany my notice. When I call the agency to confirm I am leaving, my agent sighs from the other end of the phone and says she's not surprised.

"Why?" I ask.

"The last nanny we placed with Stefany lasted even less time than you. One afternoon she went on a lunch break and just never returned. Stefany thought she might have been murdered or kidnapped, but the girl told us she was fine; she just couldn't spend a single moment longer working for that woman."

Madison Agency quickly schedules me for three interviews. The first one is a drag, the children all boring and unbathed. I know while speaking to the parents I have no interest in pursuing the position. If I am going to do this job again, I need to find the perfect family, one where the children and their parents are compatible with my personality and nannying style. It will be difficult, but not impossible, and patience will be key.

I head to the second interview, knocking on the door of a Park Avenue penthouse. The agency had prepared me for this interview, mentioning that the family was very famous. "Discretion is necessary," the agency staffer had said, "as these people are important public figures." I'm eager to see who they are.

A dark-haired, attractive man opens the door and greets me kindly. His wife, petite and neat, is meek but cordial. I have never seen these people in my life, and although their apartment looks like something from a magazine, I am unimpressed with the entire situation. I had daydreamed of an interview with Blake Lively and Ryan Reynolds, and now here I am, sitting on a plush vintage chair in just another rich person's home.

"So can I ask you something?" the dad said.

"Of course."

"You're not..." he stops to consider the right wording. "You aren't exactly like the other nannies we've interviewed for this position. Truthfully, I don't think you're the right fit. You seem terrific, but we really want someone who is more of a maid. Our kids are older, so we mainly need someone to make meals and clean up after all of them. But I'm just curious, why do you want to do this?"

I explain my situation to him. I speak of the student loans and the interest rates and how I fell into this line of work rather by accident, but I can't help but consider the absurdity. I have not yet mentioned that I don't typically cook or clean, but I don't have to. By simply looking at me, this man presumes that these are not tasks I am willing to do. I wonder what would happen if I was a young woman of the same age but a different race sitting here in this interview—would they consider me maid material then?

"But then I fell in love with the first kids I nannied. I was happy going to work every day. I guess I just found that I loved it."

On my way out, the parents and I chat mindlessly. They remind me of Sasha and her husband, surrounded by luxury but otherwise just regular people. As they lead me down a long hall back to the door, I spot a large family photo on the wall. I recognize a face in it, and the second I step outside, I pull out my phone to google it. I wouldn't have classified Jared Kushner's sister as a celebrity, but perhaps the agency was just being careful. Either way, I am irritated with myself. I had actually liked them.

I take the train downtown for my final interview of the day. It's late afternoon, nearly sunset, and the cobblestone streets of Tribeca glow with a warm tint in the light. One magazine describes 443 Greenwich Street as the city's first "paparazzi-proof building." It is home to celebrities and the megarich. The family I am interviewing with is not famous, but their neighbors are. The lobby is dark and cozy, and the doormen are more attentive than even the most professional ones on Park Avenue. I suppose you have to be, when the people inside the building you guard are named Justin Timberlake and Jennifer Lawrence. "The Mr. and Mrs. aren't back yet," the doorman explains. "You can wait here until they arrive."

I sit in the dimly lit lobby for what feels like a very long time. It strikes me as odd that things considered trendy and cool in New

York City are almost always unlit. I check the time. My interview had been scheduled for four thirty p.m. It is now five fifteen. Had I been this late, it would have been an automatic rejection. Their tardiness worries me, the idea that before they even meet me, they view my time as expendable.

"Stephanie?" One of the doormen asks. "The Mrs. just called and said they're stuck in traffic on the FDR, but we're going to send you up. Their baby nurse, Rosa, is upstairs. She's going to have you FaceTime them for the interview."

It is odd, but I oblige, as there does not seem to be any alternative. I am escorted to an elevator, where a button is pushed for me, confirming that I will not accidentally wander off onto a random celebrity's floor.

Rosa, the weekend nanny, and the full-time housekeeper are kind and warm as I arrive to the apartment that Sunday evening. Rosa explains that Dr. Rowe and her husband had decided to take the two older boys to the Bronx Zoo and their driver hadn't been able to find a faster route back. The baby is home, and she says she'd be happy to introduce me as soon as my FaceTime concludes.

"Here you go," Rosa says and hands me the screen. "They'll call on this. It's my company phone."

Company phone? This is no Google headquarters. We are sitting in someone's five-thousand-square-foot apartment. But as I look around at all the individuals employed here, I think perhaps I was wrong. Keeping this home running is an operation, and this operation requires staff. It is one thing to employ a single person. It is another to employ ten.

By the time Dr. Rowe dials in, I am irritated and tired from a long day of interviews and most of all tired of speaking to strangers. I thought our call would be quick, but I'm surprised by how naturally the conversation flows. I take an immediate liking to Dr. Rowe, and she seems intrigued by me. "You're exactly the sort of nanny we've been looking for," she says shortly into our call. I answer her questions thoughtfully and crack jokes that land. It's the sort of immediate connection I rarely have with people, and I am excited when she asks me to come back to spend the day with them the following week.

I thank her and on my way out consider all we'd discussed. I liked Dr. Rowe, and our childcare philosophies were similar, that much is obvious. She and her husband both have big, important careers, and they are not exactly hands-on. She had been honest about having round-the-clock care and requiring a young, energetic nanny who could work core hours of seven a.m. to seven thirty p.m. daily. I would be required to travel, often internationally, and be in charge of managing all staff members related to the children. I know that I can do it, but I am coming straight out of a disastrous situation with Stefany, and I have reservations about taking another intense position. I am swiping my MetroCard to enter the subway station when my phone begins to ring.

"Stephanie!" a woman from the agency squeals. "Dr. Rowe adored you! She knows you had other interviews today, and she doesn't want you to get away, so she's called us with an offer she hopes you can't resist!"

"What is it?"

"One hundred and twenty-five thousand a year with full health and dental, time and a half for overtime, a monthly MetroCard, and an annual bonus. What do you think?"

I walk outside the subway station and back onto the street. I have an incredible six-figure offer in front of me, and I am not sure I want it. I have only recently managed some self-improvement, and I know that whatever choice I make now, whatever position and family I choose will have a lasting impact on where my life goes next. Here I am, face-to-face with what I always wanted from New York City: money. On paper, the offer is terrific. I would be at the top of the nanny food chain. I would have risen as high as one can in only a few years. I would have a big salary, promises of a large bonus, and benefits I'd never dreamed of. *So why doesn't it feel right?* I don't want to say no to the opportunity because I am unsure why I'm not ready to commit, so I say okay.

My new position with Dr. Rowe is set to begin in a week's time, but I remain wary of my choice, so I agree to one last interview uptown. I am primarily working with agencies, but I still check Care.com and recently connected with a family of two toddlers on the Upper East Side. Their post advertised for a young, active, and energetic full-time nanny. In theory, I am all of these things, though recently my back has been hurting and I really do love resting. I do not mention either of those in our messages.

The morning of the interview, I nearly cancel, deciding that it isn't possible that this family would offer me a better package than the Rowes had. But I keep putting off the call, afraid of any sort of confrontation, and eventually decide it will be easier to just go.

"Hi," Theo whispers when he answers the door. "The baby is sleeping. Come on into the living room."

Devon and Theo are younger than I expect: both in their thirties with few wrinkles and even some life left in their eyes. Theo wears a pair of Air Force 1s, Devon sports something I won't later remember, and I think of how dissimilar they are from the other Upper East Side parents I've known. I take in the views of the city from their high-rise apartment and watch bug-sized people move along the busy streets. In New York City, it's often easy to find yourself feeling small, but from up here, an entire metropolis seems tiny.

"And this is my little Barbie doll, Small Barb, and this is my big Barbie doll, Boss Barb," their three-year-old, Rei, explains.

She has been showing me an assortment of dolls, and I observe that Rei is an outgoing though serious child, intelligent but probably demanding. Whereas Ruby at three was curious but reserved, Rei is chatty, inquisitive, and, even while sitting, she never quite stays still. When her parents ask her to give the grown-ups time to talk, she protests but is quickly distracted by her toys and tunes out.

"We have to tell you, we are so excited to be meeting with you," they say, and it sounds like the start of all the interviews. The next twenty minutes pass in the typical fashion. I answer their questions with ease. I have interviewed with enough families by now to know how to respond, but it's more than just knowing how to pitch myself. Our time together is slightly awkward, as most first interviews are, but it's also comfortable. I think back to the last time

I felt so relaxed in a work setting, and it feels a lot like the day I met Sasha's family.

I thank Devon and Theo for taking the time to meet with me, and Rei asks if I'll come over again soon. We all laugh, and I tell her maybe, though some part of me has already decided that I will. On the Q train ride home, I think over the job description that I have just been given. The hours are still long, eight to seven, and Devon and Theo are both busy lawyers. Devon often travels for work, and they need someone with flexibility, especially when they're hoping to have a third child. Unlike the Rowe family, they don't employ a big staff, so it would be only the children and me. I am comfortable with the ages of three and one, but I've only ever worked with a stay-at-home mom or with support staff, and I wonder if I am competent enough to manage.

The next day I'm walking to meet a friend down by the World Trade Center when my phone rings. Devon offers me the job. The position pays well, but it doesn't include healthcare, and I am no longer eligible to be on my parents'. "I'm super appreciative," I tell her, "I just need a few days to think."

When I arrive downtown, I email the agency that had matched me with the Rowes:

I'm supposed to start in a few days, and I still haven't received the contract. I really need to review it before starting.

The agent writes back almost immediately, saying that she spoke to Dr. Rowe, but that she's extremely busy. She'll be happy to give me the contract after I start. I turn to my friend, report back the news, and tell her I don't like the sound of it.

I call Devon back a few days later and tell her I'm ready to start as soon as possible.

19

HOAX CHECK

MY FIRST FEW YEARS OUT of high school did not go as expected, not that I'd ever had a healthy relationship with plans. The summer after graduation my father got me a job at the Target distribution center that he managed. The hours were brutal for any teenager, seven a.m. to four p.m., but the job was even worse than the timecard.

"What do you think?" Stew asked, after my first shift.

"I think it's the worst place I've ever been," I told him, and he laughed. It was exactly why he'd sent me there, he said.

Each morning I was assigned to a twenty-foot-long row of supplies. A conveyor belt would hustle along a box, which I'd scan then fill with whatever medications had lit up along the wall. It was an incredibly tedious task and the only one I did for the entirety of my nine-hour shift. I made thirteen dollars an hour, and by the end of the week my paycheck came out to just under four hundred. As a teenager, I felt like a king, but as for the single parents and grandparents working there, well, who knows how they managed?

One day I looked around, and I realized that aside from the four summer college hires, everyone on that pick line had been working there *their entire adult lives*. Fifteen senior women smoked cigarettes on their break and complained of hip pain from being on their feet all day. Most lived in Woonsocket, the same town as the distribution center, where a third of the population is on food stamps and the median income for a household in 2009 was roughly $38,000. They were old, tired, and sad. I doubted their lives would ever get easier.

When I started at Dean College three months later, I got right to work. I was scared from the things I had seen on that pick line and from a truth we did not speak of at home: that this was exactly the sort of job that my father had started off in.

One semester into college I was an honor roll student with a near perfect GPA and told my parents, "I'm transferring. I'm applying to BU, UCLA, Chapman, and Emerson."

"You're on a basketball scholarship."

"At a junior college," I reminded them. "And Dean doesn't have the major or resources I need. I'm going to be a writer."

"You're going to be a dumb ass" is all Stew could say.

When the acceptance letters rolled in, I was overjoyed. I had done it. *I had really done it.* But while I popped champagne bottles, my parents discussed my lack of common sense. They still weren't sold, so we made a deal.

"You take a gap year, think hard about this *poor* decision, and work full time to save some money to support yourself up in Boston,"

Stew said. "If you still feel like you gotta do this at the end of the year, I'll sign your student loans."

Three hundred and sixty days later, after demonstrating my dedication from the cashier booth of a local grocery store, I applied to Emerson once more. I knew it was the school for me. I'd seen the campus once while visiting Lila at BU, just two miles north. There was a vibrance, a sense of creativity that fed my mind. I was dusty from working a shift in the store's bakery department when the acceptance letter once again arrived. I brought it to my father with more pride than I had the first time. He sighed but agreed that a deal was a deal. I was so naive at nineteen I could have never known that signing those loans was surrendering my freedom.

In Boston, Lila and I lived a few blocks apart off the Green Line. She shared a two-bedroom apartment with her friend Jules, and from Lila's bedroom window you could see the bright lights of Fenway Park. You'd always know when someone hit a home run by the cheers that drifted into the small kitchen. Because my budget was smaller, I shared a bedroom with a student at Berklee named Leeann, who did not enjoy showers and whom I'd met through Craigslist. I didn't bother spending money on a bed, so I slept on a rock-hard futon I'd scored from Walmart at a rollback price. I was overjoyed with my new life.

To fulfill my science requirement, my adviser put me in a class on climate change. The first thing the professor asked was for students to raise their hands if they believed in it. I didn't flinch but was shocked when I realized that mine was the only hand down in the entire room. The professor did not ask me why I didn't believe in climate change, but she did ask other students why they did.

"The U.S. contributes about 25 percent of the world's carbon dioxide," someone explained.

True idiots, I thought to myself.

I could not believe that none of these people had the information that I did, which was that Al Gore had made up the entire "hot globe" thing. My family had discussed it dozens of times, and we were all in agreement that there was absolutely nothing to worry about. The Earth had been around so many years, it was bound to go through changes. I spent an entire semester solidly maintaining my insular worldview—hearing facts, feeling disturbed by their content, and ultimately disbelieving them.

Here at this creative liberal arts school, where people dressed for class as their favorite Lord of the Rings character and concocted love potions in their dorm rooms, there was only one freak, and it was me with my conservative beliefs.

Perhaps it was because I wasn't growing the way that she had expected, or because I was not blending in, that Lila made a suggestion.

"I'm doing a student summer program in London," she said. "Why don't you apply too?"

I had never owned a passport, so my parents were baffled when I suddenly collected my IDs and headed for Boston's passport agency.

"What do you need to go over there for?" my father asked.

The truth was I did not *need* to go to London for a summer, but I wanted to.

It didn't matter that I had never been outside of the U.S., and it certainly did not matter that I didn't have any money, because I was so mystified by the currency exchange, I thought pounds were equivalent to pennies anyhow.

When it came to other cultures or countries, my knowledge was so limited that when Lila told me she had once seen the pyramids with her family, I assumed for ten years that she had been referring to Egypt. For that entire decade, I told people my girl had once snapped Polaroid pics outside King Tut's tomb, when in reality, she had just been on a day trip from Cancun.

I did not know what I would want to see in the UK. Besides Elton John, I wasn't entirely sure what was even there. Still, I packed a small suitcase, begged my grandmother for a few hundred dollars, and screamed *Au revoir, motherfuckers!* as my family scowled at me from the front steps.

When I boarded the red-eye from JFK to Heathrow, I pulled out a "bucket list" I'd written the night before.

TO DO:

Madame Tussaud's Wax Museum

Drink Tea

The Palace (YAY THE QUEEN :D)

Go to big TopShop

I peered over to the next seat, where Lila was examining her own list. It was three pages long and contained a small hand-drawn map of the National Gallery. It was then that I understood that the only indisputable fact in my world was that I knew absolutely nothing about anywhere.

●●●●●

The London program had placed us in internship positions with charities for the summer. To get to our respective charities, Lila and I had to take two tubes and a bus. Our commute was an hour and a half each way, which is pretty remarkable if you consider that we did these jobs for free. Lila was placed at a facility for people recovering from mental health conditions, where she met a very handsome but overly arrogant employee whom she quickly began dating. I was placed at a daycare center for severely disabled adults, where we spent half the day coloring and the other half explaining the birds and the bees. As usual, if Lila was the Princess Diana of the UK, then I was Simon Cowell, for I was pretty rude, and also no one was quite sure what qualified me to be there.

For the first few weeks of our stay, Lila and I did very little aside from fall asleep anywhere and everywhere. We were jetlagged, then simply exhausted, traveling so far for work only to spend our nights exploring the city. One weekend we took a day trip to Brighton, and we were both so tired and drunk, we have absolutely no recollection of the day, except that when we arrived there was a beach, and by the time we left the water had somehow disappeared. I returned to work the next day both unable and unwilling to participate in my duties. I hadn't been in more than an hour when I ventured outside for a quick break.

"You all right?"

Startled, I answered my supervisor, Rose.

"Oh, yeah, great. Sorry, I hadn't realized anyone was out here."

Like most days in London, it was cloudy and not as warm as it should have been. Rose flicked her cigarette, then put it out with a quick stomp of her foot.

"You read this?" She held up a book with a picture of Hillary Clinton on the front. I nearly threw up.

"Oh, no," I said. "Not a big fan."

"Really?" she asked, surprised. "I'd have thought a young woman from America would have been all over this memoir. It's top of the charts here."

If Rose was surprised I hadn't read *Hard Choices*, I was equally surprised she had. I knew that Obama was, unfortunately, the president of the U.S., but at the time I couldn't have told you who the vice president was. I had no clue who governed Rhode Island or what a House seat was. I certainly didn't know who the "president" of the UK was. It struck me as odd that someone in this country would have any interest at all in a politician from another.

"She's coming here, you know," Rose continued. "To Hatchard's over in Piccadilly. Doing a talk and signing. You should really read it. I'm nearly finished myself, could lend you my copy."

"Oh, I don't know," I laughed, but I could hear my uncle's words at a wedding in the mountains of New Hampshire a few years back. "Fucking half-brained lesbian. Wants to give this country over to Mexico, leaving nothing but crumbs for our people."

Rose returned inside, and I was happy for the conversation to conclude, but the next day I found the book on my desk. I took it, to be polite.

"You should at least read a chapter." Lila encouraged, but of course she did: she was "a crazy snowflake pushing her liberal propaganda," my father would have said.

"No way," I said, but every day Rose checked in to hear my thoughts, and eventually I became tired of not having any.

The afternoon that I finally opened the book on the tube ride home, it was an unusually quiet rush hour. I looked at the cover and my stomach soured. It felt like a betrayal to every living family member to so much as hold Hillary Clinton's book. I thought of all the jokes we shared at the expense of the Obamas. "Oh, he's a racist," my grandmother said, and I could not imagine a universe where her assertion might be wrong. The bottom line was this: liberal agendas put our family at risk because all they care to do is take from the rich and give to the poor. Much later I would wonder why it had never occurred to me that *we* were the poor we stood so firmly against.

I had only planned to read one chapter, but by the time I reached page 59, titled "China: Uncharted Waters," I realized that I had no idea how politics actually worked. Worse, I had no idea how the world worked. My opinions, so deep and impassioned, were based on hearsay. I had never once considered forming my own beliefs on politics because I had been given them from the start. I wasn't sure that I liked Hillary Clinton, but I could see now that I didn't understand her or the work that she did. I needed to know more.

For five hundred pages I carried that book around London,

Paris, Lisbon, and more. I read on trains, planes, red buses, and yellow trolleys, outside the Louvre, and while waiting for croissants by Tower Bridge. Each day, Lila saw the gears turning, my mind reading a passage then my hands googling a topic, but she never said a word. She had her opinions, and she let me decide mine. I finished the book on a rooftop in Porto, a glass of red sangria in my hand, a horrible straw fedora on my head. Lila was lying on a sun chair next to me, when I suddenly turned to her.

"I just finished the book," I said.

"Great."

"It was very long."

"Very," she answered.

"A lot of information in there."

"Indeed," she said, clearly becoming uncomfortable with the odd conversation.

I paused entirely too long as I reached a moment of clarity. "Lila," I announced, "I do not think I'm a Republican."

I wasn't sure whether I should be relieved or ashamed, but Lila burst out laughing and then so did I.

It was, in a way, exactly what I had been hoping to find on my trip abroad: *more.* I had wanted to learn more about myself and the world that existed beyond the tiny bubble in which I had grown up. And had the trip ended there, like that, it would have been a nice story. But people's stories are rarely simple and often *not* very nice. And my London story would end with a trip to the emergency room.

●●●●●

"Call an ambulance," I told Lila.

We were set to fly back to the states in a few hours when Lila rolled over; glanced at the clock, which read 4:50 a.m.; and tried to respond before I started screaming.

"What's wrong?" she asked nervously.

"I'm fucking unwell!" I cried. "What are you missing?!"

When we arrived at the hospital, Lila checked me in while I vomited somewhere between the front entrance and the toilet. They took my temperature and, surprised by the high fever, brought me right in. A nurse asked where the pain was, and I pointed to my left side.

"What are her other symptoms?" she asked Lila.

"I really don't know. She's been sweating and throwing up and yelling a lot about feeling sick."

Just then a doctor came in. He felt around my midsection and looked at my vitals. He said they needed to get me some morphine, which was the first piece of good news that I had heard, but then no one could find my vein. A nurse poked a needle around my arm for ten minutes before I heard the word suppository. I was about to ask what that was, but then Lila giggled, and the next thing I knew there was something up my ass. I was drowsy enough to forget the incident soon after, but then too out of it to comprehend what would come next.

"We're going to send you guys in an ambulance to another hospital," the doctor said.

"Wait, why?" Lila asked.

"She needs surgery. Her appendix is going to rupture. We can't do it here."

"Surgery?" Lila asked. "No, no. She can't have surgery today! We have a flight back to the U.S. tonight."

"You'll need to cancel that," he told her. "The EMTs are ready to transport you both now."

The next few hours were a blur. I have no idea what was said or done because I was completely doped up and happy to be so. Meanwhile, Lila spent hours on the phone with our program leader, who advised only one thing: to just leave me at the hospital.

"It'll be much cheaper than missing your flight and having to buy another."

Lila, irritated but nevertheless loyal, refused. "I can't leave her in London, where she doesn't know anyone, in a hospital to get surgery alone," she said.

"Then find a way to make it work," he advised.

Lila googled my symptoms one last time, as a nurse prepared me for surgery.

"She didn't have a CT scan at the other hospital," Lila told the attending. "It's possible it could be something else, right?"

The doctor, oddly, did not totally disagree. Lila demanded they do one before cutting me open. Half an hour later, in the early evening, the doctor returned. He apologized on behalf of two hospitals, and said it looked like the kidney stones had passed.

Lila and I made our flight by about ten minutes. I was prescribed some painkillers for the flight, and by the time we touched down in New York I felt as good as new. Lila's mom, living in New York at the time, picked us up from JFK, and we recounted our ridiculous day.

"That is so crazy," Joie gasped, but then she brought up something

I hadn't considered. "Thank God it was in the UK, though. Imagine how screwed you'd have been if it had happened her."

"What do you mean?" I asked.

The health emergency I'd had in London, while frightening, could have been far more catastrophic for me. I had needed a rescue, IV's, and scans, which in America could lead an uninsured patient to bankruptcy. When I arrived at the hospital that morning, no one had asked me for my insurance. *Luckily*, I later thought, because there, I did not have any.

My whole life I had heard my family debate universal healthcare. "You know who wants that? Welfare leeches. You want healthcare, you oughta work for it. Nothing in this country is free."

For years, I had echoed this rhetoric. Healthcare, my family had assured me, should be earned. But now all I could think was, *should it? What would happen if I walked into a hospital here with an emergency but no Blue Cross card? Would they take me? If they did, would I receive the same quality care as everyone else? And most importantly, would it be worth it to seek care, or would I rather die than pay the bill?*

After that, I promised myself I would never risk going without proper health coverage, but then I became a nanny, and I found myself doing exactly that because that is how domestic jobs often work. No insurance is just part of the package.

20

REI

"GIVE ME THAT, NOW!" REI screams, snatching the toy car from Russ's hand before he has the chance to object. It's a moot point anyway; the odds of Russ obediently handing something over are low. He's beelining for the terrible twos, but Rei, who is nearing four, is trickier to manage. I have been Rei and Russ's nanny for eleven hours a day, five days a week for two months now. So far, I would rate the experience zero stars.

Russ lets out an animalistic screech and lunges toward Rei. He is bulky and strong, while his sister is lanky and thin. Russ eats like a football player during preseason, and Rei hardly eats at all, but she's feisty and somehow always wins.

Bathwater sprays from the tub as they struggle, but I don't bother to duck. I'm already in hell. Why not be sad and damp?

"Look," I say and hold out an identical Hot Wheels. Russ accepts it, but within ten seconds neither child is playing with a car anyway.

"I have to poop!" Rei announces.

"Now?" I ask.

She doesn't bother to respond but hops out of the tub and onto the toilet. "Hey, Russ?"

"Whaaa, Rei?"

"Do you know I'm pooping right now?"

"Huh?"

"I'm pooping."

Russ looks up and asks her yet again to repeat herself. "I SAID I'M POOPING."

I ask Rei to watch her tone. She is having a difficult time finding kind ways to speak to people and to showcase good manners especially when she is not feeling her best. Rei is squeamish and doesn't yet wipe herself, so I make sure she's clean before returning her to the tub. I give both children a two-minute warning and begin gathering their towels when I notice Rei is making a peculiar face. I ask her if she's okay and she nods yes, but after a moment she calls for me.

"What?" I ask, and she moves her body slightly.

As the water turns murky she winces. "I thought it was just a toot!"

"Rei poop in tub!" Russ screams, and despite being covered in his sister's feces, he laughs uncontrollably. I move swiftly between the apartment's two bathrooms, desperately trying to get the children into clean water. It takes me a few minutes to complete the task and, once they're in the other tub, I get to work cleaning the dirty one. I drain it, then scoop the poop that didn't fit down the drain into cups and toss them into a garbage bag. My red manicure dulls under the brown water, and I'm hit with sudden déjà vu.

"My tummy really hurts," I'd told Hope.

"Just get your bag," she'd said.

It was July, and the gym smelled of sweaty feet and postpubescent boys.

Hope said goodbye as I sat down to change into sneakers. The first few hours of Rhode Island College's basketball camp went on as usual. I ran significantly slower than the other kids and missed 100 percent of the shots I attempted. I drank more Gatorade than needed and did a lot of "tying" my shoelaces. By midday, I was done and called my mom to pick me up.

"Steph, cut it out. You're fine. I'll see you at three," she said as I heard the phone click.

The counselors shuffled us across campus to the pool after lunch. My stomach was feeling pretty gnarly by this point, and I was unusually sweaty. *Maybe the pool will help*, I thought. The first gush of water felt good. It was crowded, but one of those Olympic-sized pools, so I found room to paddle along. There were other sports camps using the space that day too: tennis, football, whatever else husky suburban dads like their kids to play. I was swimming along the shallow end, avoiding a game of Marco Polo, when the stomach pains grew stronger. I felt my limbs begin to tremble. Even with my body surrounded by cool water, I grew hot.

I thought it could be gas. I swam to a less busy part of the pool and pushed. A few bubbles surfaced and the pain subsided. I assumed that must have been all and was relieved, both literally and figuratively. I floated still for a moment when I saw it. Right next to me, a little turd. I knew it had to be mine.

I jumped out of the pool and raced to the locker room, diarrhea spilling down my legs. By the time I got to the toilet, it was everywhere. Brown muck covered my body, the floor, the stall. I had never been so humiliated in all my life.

But here and now, Rei's eyes brim with tears of laughter. It turns out one kid's humiliation is another's entertainment.

Just then Rei calls for me again. "Steph, quick!"

I sigh dramatically, even though I know there is no one to hear me. On my own with the children all day, I now understand the lonely truth of being a stay-at-home mother. In my previous positions, I was constantly surrounded by other adults; whether it was my employers or their staff, I rarely spent more than a few hours alone. But Rei and Russ's parents leave for work the moment I arrive and do not return until I leave in the evening. The days are boring and hard and, above all, lonely. I wonder if this was how my young mother had felt. If this was, in fact, how all mothers felt, regardless of their social status, location, or race.

The children can be sweet and loveable, and they exude a sense of childish wonder I adore. But they're hyperactive, physical, and they frequently test boundaries. Rei, having been with her previous nanny for the entirety of her young life, rejects me. Integrating yourself into a family's life is a process, and I'm stuck in the middle of the most challenging phase.

"What is it?" I ask.

But when I enter the bathroom there's no need for an explanation. I look at Russ, who has found his father's shaving cream and decorated the entire room in white fluff. The children burst into more laughter, and I'm not sure whether to join in or cry. As it turns out I'm too tired to do either.

"All right, guys. Everyone out of the tub."

Now the laughing stops, and Rei flings her body backward.

"No!" she screams. It's the sort of sudden mood change that three-year-old children frequently bless their grown-ups with. "I will not listen to you! Do you hear me, Stephanie? I am NOT listening!"

The next ten minutes or so will be dedicated to Rei's and my ongoing power struggle. Up until now, I have had little experience with discipline. Sasha always took charge when rules needed enforcing, and since Other Stefany did not believe in consequences, there was never a need for me to police Digby. Here, as a full-charge nanny, I am encountering new obstacles, the result of not working *with* a mom but for one.

"I do not like you! You are mean!" Rei screams.

I tell her I understand why she might feel this way, and that only seems to infuriate her more. She throws a sock my way, and then a Barbie accessory bounces off my nose. I don't bother to react. I've become shockingly patient and relaxed over the last few months and just in time. It turns out these two qualities are most necessary in mastering motherhood.

"I think you need to take a moment, breathe, and go to your room to calm down," I instruct.

"I THINK YOU NEED TO TAKE A BREATH AND GO IN YOUR ROOM, STEPHANIE!"

21

THANK YOU, J. K. ROWLING

I'M HOLDING THE CREDIT CARD that Devon has given me to cover the cost of Russ's haircut. Devon has me pay for nothing in cash; in fact, she hardly carries it because, unlike my parents' credit card, her Chase Sapphire doesn't collect debts. It collects points.

My mother and I both qualified for Credit One this year but had to pay a seventy-dollar fee just to activate a card with an eight-hundred-dollar credit limit. You have to establish credit to qualify for it, but how can you establish something you're not approved for? Devon's card gets her free flights, cash rebates, and presales. My card's only bonus is an interest rate of 20 percent.

It's a Tuesday afternoon, and we are on the M103 bus to Russ's barber shop on Lexington Avenue. The shop has only four chairs, and it is colorless, dated, and small. As Russ's tiny toddler body settles into the adult-sized chair, I look at the pictures that line the wall, a showcase of the important men who use this salon. The haircut takes ten minutes and costs fifty-two dollars. Russ cries for the first half of it and watches kids' YouTube shows for the other. Tom Brokaw has the next appointment. He takes Russ's seat after I transfer Russ back to his stroller.

Soon after I pick Rei up from school, we take the elevator twelve floors down to the building's playroom. I hear shrieks and laughter before we even enter the aquatic-themed space. Children prance between walls hand-painted with fish and bubbles, smiling sharks, and bright coral. Parked in the middle of the room is a yellow submarine, which they take turns climbing up and sliding down. I look around and see that all the children here today appear happy. All the children except mine.

"I want to go back upstairs," Rei demands.

"No, Rei. We just got here. We're going to play here for a while."

"I said I WANT to go upstairs."

Rei and I have a rather long list of complaints with one another. My quest to bond with her is failing even more than my initial efforts with Hunter, although it's still better than what I'd had with Digby. But Rei prefers her old nanny and isn't shy about telling me as much.

"Mel would let me go upstairs."

"Well, I'm not Mel."

"No, you're worser! You're way worser!"

I rationally explain to her why that is untrue and unkind to say, but she is uninterested. The other nannies in the playroom, most of whom I don't know yet, look up from their iPhones to witness the commotion. One tries to weigh in, but Rei all but tells her to fuck off, and she too backs away carefully. As Rei's emotions peak, I feel my face grow hot and decide against my better judgment to bring her upstairs.

It's one thing being unable to control a child in private, but public meltdowns are an entirely different phenomenon. I remember waiting for an elevator at the 92nd Street Y community center with a tired Russ screeching from his stroller. I silently counted down the seconds until the elevator arrived, humiliated by the scene we were causing. *I'm so sorry,* I wanted to say to every person in the room. When a child is having a tantrum at a restaurant or a store, in a bus or on a plane, that child's caregiver is typically as mortified as the people around them are bothered. On the day of the elevator incident, an older woman approached me with a scowl.

"Excuse me? Isn't there something you can do to make him stop?"

"I'm sorry?" I asked.

"Can't you distract him with something? He's causing a ruckus, you know."

I apologized but explained that I could not make the two-year-old calm down, as he was screaming about his shoes being the color blue. They were the same shoes he had been wearing for the last three months of his life.

"I don't like you, Stephanie. You are MEAN," Rei cries when we arrive back upstairs.

"You don't mean that," I say, although I'm fairly certain that she does.

The next few minutes are a roller coaster of emotions. I leave her in her room and hope she'll take the moment to calm down. It's unlikely, but possible.

In the kitchen, I scan the fridge for a vegetable to serve with dinner, racking my brain for a way to connect with Rei. The things I've tried, the methods that worked with Ruby and Hunter, prove useless with Rei. She's a different kid. Rei runs wilder and tests limits in a way Ruby never did. She's not afraid to challenge authority and has a short fuse. It's going to take more than some arts and crafts to bond with her.

"Ste," Russ calls.

I glance over just in time to watch him pour an entire bowl of cat food onto the kitchen floor.

"I make mess," he says.

"I see that, buddy."

At the far end of the hall is a closet of household supplies. I'm bent down, rummaging for a roll of Bounty, when I spot it, the thick spine covered in dust. Rei is only three and I wonder if she is too young, but I'm desperate. Russ calls my name and I go to him, grabbing the book on my way.

At dinner I hold it up at the table. Rei's eyes look over the front cover with interest, and she asks, "Who is that?"

"Have you ever heard of wizards?" I ask her.

Rei smiles wide, and I continue, "How about the boy who lived?"

●●●●●

"Did you see the news of the day that Rei shared at school?"

I have not, so Devon holds the sheet up to me. There, in black Sharpie, for all to see, is Rei's big share: *Yesterday we played Harry Potter. Stephanie was Lord Voldemort. AGAIN!*

Two changes take place in the weeks that follow our descent into the wizarding world. For one, I no longer beg Rei to practice manners or use nice tones. Instead of asking that she behave, I simply mention that she is a real Slytherin.

"Stephanie!" she gasps in horror, "I'm a Gryffindor!"

"Then act like one," I say, and to my most pleasant surprise, she usually does.

On one afternoon, when my decision to ban lollipops before dinner incites a meltdown, I'm able to avoid a confrontation altogether. Instead of discussing Rei's feelings and getting absolutely nowhere, I ignore Rei's little body flailing against the hardwood floors and head to the household printer. I carry a Dumbledore quote to her room, tape it to the wall in front of her, and walk out. Her screaming stops, and the apartment goes silent.

Minutes later Rei appears in the kitchen with the paper. Her eyes, swollen and red, look to me with curiosity. "What does this say? I can't read, you know."

"It says, 'Happiness can be found in the darkest of times only if we remember to turn on the lights.'"

Rei stays quiet. I watch as her eyes scan the room, and she bites down softly on her bottom lip. I'm fairly certain she has no idea what this quote means, but she does calm down and also turns on every lamp in the house for the next several days.

The second change is less exciting, though arguably more significant. For the first few months of my transition, Rei's old nanny, Mel, drops by on a regular basis. Understandably, she misses the children. While the visits do not bother Russ, they confuse Rei and make my job a thousand times harder. Mel's drop-ins are usually less than ninety minutes but take me hours to recover from.

Hey! I'm in the neighborhood so I'm gonna stop by and take Rei for ice cream around 3:30, Mel texts on a sunny Thursday afternoon. I can't very well say no. After all, they aren't my children. They are simply mine to feed, bathe, nurture, love, and protect for twelve hours a day, five days a week.

Sure, I text, just have her back for dinner and bath.

"Mel got me chocolate ice cream with no sprinkles because she knows that's my favorite," Rei says upon her return. "Do you even know about ice cream, Stephanie?"

"Yes, actually. I know very much about ice cream."

"But do you know about me and ice cream?"

I honestly don't even know what that means, and I cannot believe as an adult woman I have to dignify it with a response. "Yes, I know you like chocolate ice cream."

She pauses, thinking of something both clever and hurtful to say, settling on, "Mel knows ice cream better. I love Mely."

Of all the reasons I was apprehensive about taking this position, after spending a week shadowing her, Mel was the biggest. In many ways, her nannying profile mirrors my own. She is young and energetic, though more physically fit. Unlike me, she wears workout leggings, not because they are the cousins of sweatpants, but because she actually exercises. However, despite our many commonalities, she takes a very strict approach to nannying.

Mel is a no-nonsense kind of nanny. The moment a child gets out of line there are consequences, which often include yelling. I had never raised my voice as a nanny and didn't plan to start now, but Rei has been conditioned to respond to this sort of discipline, and I worry it will be hard to break her of that.

During my training week, when Rei misbehaves, I attempt to discuss the incident with her. But when Mel is there, she simply picks Rei up and places her in her room for a time-out. Rei screams, and Mel screams right back. Admittedly, the approach is more effective than my own, but it makes me want to run away and hide.

"You go to your room and do not come out until you have calmed your body. Do you understand me?" Mel yells.

Rei, stubborn even in her weakest moment, stares Mel down until she continues. "Do you understand?"

"YES!"

"Then go to your room!"

Each time I witness this sort of exchange I feel uneasy. It instantly transports me back to my childhood, to my own family, where screaming was the normal manner of communication. Even a slightly noisy home now makes me anxious and stressed, causing knots in my stomach and initiating an instant flight or fight response. If I learned one thing growing up, it was the effect a chaotic environment could have on a person. Although the yelling here is far tamer than anything I had ever known, the lesson remained the same: fighting fire with fire won't put one out; *it'll set the whole damn house ablaze.*

22

JOHN CENA FAN

MY SISTER HAD NOT SHOWERED, eaten, or gone to school in three days. Her hair was thick with grease, her clothes the same ones she'd been wearing since the start of the week. I had just arrived home from my last semester of college when I noticed this.

"Mom," I called from the kitchen.

Hope dragged in wearing oversized sweatpants in the late May heat. "What?"

"Jenna hasn't been to school. She hasn't done anything but sit in the dark typing on her laptop." I lowered my voice on the off chance my sister was in earshot. "She even takes the computer with her to pee."

"I know," Hope sighed.

"What do you mean you know?"

Hope shuffled over to the fridge and cracked open a cold Diet Coke. She looked exhausted. "I told your father." She paused to take a gulp. "I said, 'Stewy, Jenna won't go to school. She hasn't been in, I don't know, two weeks.'"

"Two weeks? Are you going to make her?"

"I tried."

"She has to go to school. It's literally the law."

"Well, if the high school ever sends the truant officer, they'll tell her she has to go. I can't take another screaming match with that kid," she said before shuffling back to the other room.

"Okay," I called, "but what is she doing on that computer all day? She's fourteen."

"I don't know," Hope called back. "Why don't you find out?"

A few hours later Lila was at my front door. A cat who had lost a fight and had a large chunk of flesh exposed scurried over her feet, but she was accustomed to our many feral pets and so remained unbothered. "What's going on?" she asked. I explained. "So you want us to go through her computer and look for…?"

"I don't know what," I said. "Just…something."

From the living room, we could hear a war raging between Hope and Jenna.

Lila never did adjust to the screaming at my house. Her defense mechanism was the opposite, and she'd shut down her emotions when feeling threatened. She'd ignore someone almost effortlessly in times of distress, and I never once heard her raise her voice in an argument. I found her way of handling conflict both baffling and infuriating. In my home, loud brawls were so commonplace that for many years I found them almost exciting. The noise meant something interesting was happening, and even though the content was stressful, it provided an adrenaline rush. The highs and lows were toxic, destructive, and, worst of all, *completely exhilarating.*

When I was growing up, my parents had huge blowups, and, if these meltdowns occurred in the car, inevitably someone got so mad they'd exit the vehicle and make a big show of walking home. The other would drive slowly alongside, demanding they get back in, while my sisters and I howled in laughter from the back seat. Once, my father punched and cracked the car's windshield in a fit of rage.

At the moment, Hope was demanding Jenna take a shower, mostly so Lila and I would have time to search through her laptop.

"I don't want to take a shower!" Jenna shouted.

"Jenna, you stink! Get in there and use soap this time!"

"No!"

"Now!"

A door slammed, muffling my sister's final *fuck you*, followed by the shower turning on.

Lila and I set the computer on the kitchen table. "Go to her recent history," I instructed.

"I don't have to. She left her tabs open."

I scanned the Tumblr posts, emails, and chat rooms that flooded the page. "What are these?" I whispered.

Jenna had taken a liking to WWE wrestling during my final year of college. While I had found it peculiar, I hadn't thought much of it. Until now.

In her first Tumblr, Jenna was Nikki Bella, twin to Brie Bella, a famous WWE divas duo. Jenna (or Nikki) had exchanged hundreds of messages with another profile under the name of John Cena. In the messages it appeared that Jenna and this user had dated, married, and were now expecting their first child.

They had messaged every minute of every day for the last week.

We found two more chats that were very similar. Disturbing, though not necessarily alarming. There was no part of me that feared they might be dangerous. Jenna was just a teenager fantasizing, albeit in a less predictable way than your average high schooler.

"She'll be out soon," I told Lila. "Open that last tab."

Lila clicked open to a black web page. She scrolled down to Jenna's last post: a one paragraph cry for help.

Five sentences containing the words *cutting, bulimia, suicide*—a confession of Jenna's recent attempts at self-harm and her desire to take it further. The hair on the back of my neck stood up. *Was it real?* Teens could be dramatic, and there was so much pretending in what we had already found, I could not be sure of its sincerity. But something *felt* wrong. Lila and I exchanged worried glances.

"Mom?"

"What?" she said, her eyes glued to the television.

"Look at this." I placed the computer down as she changed the channel to the Celtics game, the crowd cheering as Paul Pierce hit a fading three.

She squinted as her eyes danced across the screen of the old Acer laptop.

The shower stopped. For this brief moment our house was quiet.

Three hours later, Jenna was admitted to the Hasbro Children's Hospital Psychiatric Ward.

"But what exactly is wrong with her?" Hope asked the doctor as they admitted her for the night.

"For starters," he said gently, "your daughter believes that she actually is a WWE wrestler."

That day the staff allowed us to say goodbye to Jenna but kept her in isolation otherwise. "Common procedure," they said.

The list of what troubled Jenna turned out to be long. Bulimia, cutting, and suicidal thoughts were just the tip of the iceberg.

Lila and I visited her often during that first stay in the mental ward. When she was released, I naively assumed the whole thing was over. Over the next few years her illness would shift and evolve. Just when she'd improve in one area, she'd become sick in another. There were years she threw up so often, her teeth were permanently damaged, and others that she overate so heavily, she'd be fifty pounds overweight. She feared driving so much that she never got a license, and she was so hard on her body that she'd had multiple organs removed by the time she was twenty-three.

During her senior year, Jenna struggled to make and maintain friends and did not excel academically or participate in extracurriculars. Instead of skipping class like most students would, Jenna, allergic to peanuts, smeared her arms in Jiffy, then stabbed herself with an epi pen. After her eighth ambulance ride that quarter, my parents were summoned to the ER, where a doctor explained that this was a hospital and they had real emergencies to take care of.

"Please tell your daughter to stop calling the EMTs every time she wants to skip geometry," he pleaded.

Still, in those few first days of her absence, following that very first diagnosis, our family seemed only sorrowful. That week there was no shouting or vulgarity, no insults or fits. It was the only time I remember us all as mellow.

On the day Jenna was released, we were called to the hospital for a mandatory family therapy session. As Jenna and her psychiatrist took the two middle seats, my parents, grandmother, Lydia, and I circled around them. My father had come from a family and a neighborhood that was plagued with substance abuse and mental illness, but these are the exact places where the subject is most taboo. In Manhattan, having a therapist is a mark of success, wealth, and awareness. In a poor neighborhood, it can mean only one thing: you're crazy.

My father shifted in his seat uncomfortably throughout the meeting. When he did speak it was awkward, timid almost. It was strange, to see a man never at a loss of words with nothing to say at all.

"This is your fault!" my mother screamed at Gram.

At the time, Gram was living in our basement and spent a fair amount of time with Jenna. This, of course, had nothing to do with Jenna's mental illness.

"I don't think so, Hope. Why do you think she spends so much time downstairs with me? Because you never bother with her."

"Maybe she's down there because you're the only one with heat in the house. You have that fireplace but what did you do when we asked to borrow money to fix our boiler? You let your grandkids freeze."

"Do you know how much money I've lent you over the years, Hope? Do you? I've bailed you out so many times."

Still, Gram blamed my mother's neglect; my mother blamed Gram's indulgence; and Jenna blamed Lydia, who had been noticeably favored throughout their childhood. I would have been interested to know who the psychiatrist blamed, but unfortunately the poor man couldn't get a word in edgewise.

A few days after Jenna came home, a U-Haul pulled into the driveway.

My mother and Gram, the two people I remembered as a team during my youngest years, didn't even say goodbye to one another. Stew told Hope not to end things that way. Not to let a woman who had gone above and beyond for her to move out without a word.

Over the next few years Gram sent Hope birthday cards and Mother's Day gifts, but none of these olive branches would ever be returned. Gram left late that afternoon, and they never spoke again.

23

THE TWO AMERICAS

MY FAMILY AND I REMAINED on rocky terms for most of 2016, a consequence of Jenna's mental health break and my own in the aftermath of my abortion. And, as the presidential election neared, our conversations got more and more combative.

"Let me ask you something," Stew said a few weeks before November 8. I was one day into a weekend visit and already regretting my decision to return home. "Hillary wants to let all these illegals in, right? Who do you think is going to pay for their medical? Their food?"

"Who do you think paid ours when we were on WIC?"

"Stephanie, I worked my ass off. These people can't work."

"Of course they can work," I shot back.

"They pay no taxes!"

"That's not entirely true. Sometimes they pay into taxes but can't get a return."

"Ouuuhhhh, okay," he laughed ironically. "Talk about some fake news. Look, if Hillary wins, they'll all get their way and get to stay, and the middle class will disappear just like the liberals want. Costs the American people a fortune to keep them here, but by all means, save the browns!"

I told him it would actually cost much more to deport them all, to which he impolitely asked me to fuck off. "The people hate Hillary Clinton."

On the surface, I could understand why he felt this way. Even Lila, the most politically engaged friend I had, saw Hillary's limitations. Lila consumed articles and podcasts like I consumed added preservatives. My infatuation with Hillary came from her book introducing me to a new way of thinking. "But don't be naive," Lila cautioned, "she is not popular."

As the big day neared, I began to see a clear divide on my Facebook feed.

My friend list split into two categories: friends from the small suburban town where I grew up and friends I'd made in college or New York City. My hometown friends became very aggressive in their posts. Drain the swamp. No more freebies. Kill Hill. What I could not understand was that, similar to my father, the people posting these things were the same ones who would have benefited most from Hillary's policies. I told my New York friends it made absolutely no sense to me, but that was a lie because just a few years earlier I would have been echoing them.

Lila and I had friends over to our apartment the night the results rolled in. I ordered two dozen cupcakes from Magnolia Bakery, but accidentally got elephants instead of donkeys. I worried this was a Freudian slip.

It wasn't long before our excitement dwindled as we watched counties roll in and the map start to turn red. What was supposed to be an all-night celebration ending with fireworks at the Javits Center turned into everyone gone and lights out by midnight. I didn't sleep much that night but never checked my phone for fear of the inevitable. I felt sick as I dressed for work the next morning. I swiped my MetroCard and took my usual train uptown. On the subway, no one made a sound.

I cried on and off for most of that day. Knowing I couldn't face them, Lila quietly disposed of cookies that had Hillary in a pantsuit printed on them. I wasn't sure what I was most sad about: feeling that sexism had just been validated or that my political awakening now felt silly. It was like switching to the losing team in the fourth quarter. Clearly, a majority of Americans disagreed with all that I had learned, but while I wallowed in self-pity, my family celebrated from afar.

Make America Great Again, my father texted the group chat that afternoon.

I snapped.

You have three, NO FOUR, daughters, I texted back, and you're celebrating that a womanizer is now in charge of the free world. You think his tax plan is going to help you? You're in for a rude fucking awakening BECAUSE YOU DON'T MAKE ANY REAL MONEY. You're disgusting for voting this way. Too stupid to stop voting against your own best interests.

This was the precise moment in which my parents' and my

differences were no longer avoidable. I resented everything they were, and they hated who I had become. To them, I was a traitor. A stuck-up city brat who had become too materialistic to remember where she came from. To me, they were closed-minded, unaware, and uninformed. Everything I was trying to run from. We were all right, and we were all wrong.

It was many months before any of us spoke again.

A few days before Thanksgiving, I came across another thread on Facebook. One of my Emerson friends, who lived in LA and whose wealthy parents were supporting him while he tried to break into the film industry, posted about the dumb middle Americans, whose voting had ruined our country. I scrolled through comments that generalized the very people who had raised me, noticing repeated words: *racist, stupid, incompetent, idiots*.

I was still reeling from the election myself, but as I read through these comments, I couldn't help but feel furious.

"They make us feel dumb," my father had said back in October. "Your people, they act like we're just so stupid. There will always be bad people on both sides, but most of us are just trying to vote what's right for us. But they make us feel like we're too beneath them to even deserve a vote."

My father's reasons for voting Republican, backward as they may have been, made sense to him. He had worked harder than anyone I had ever known to get where he did. The truth was my dad was not racist or dumb or evil. He was scared. He was scared of the government taking more of what little he had. Like me, he just was not fully clear on how it all worked.

24

NO MORE NEWBORNS

DEVON TELLS ME THAT MEL is moving to Philadelphia with her husband, and I could not be more overjoyed. When Rei sees less of Mel, she stops comparing me to her. We have a clean slate, and I seize my opportunity to restructure. I have fewer rules, more wiggle room, and, admittedly, less control than Mel had. But each day Rei laughs more and screams less. She expresses all the emotions of a child, and although she remains fickle, Rei appears to grow fonder of my company. But every step forward in my nanny journey still seems to come with one mile back, and Devon soon announces to me that she is pregnant. I know this is happy news, but it takes everything in my soul not to reply, "Congrats, best wishes, and also I quit!"

"Stephanie! Guess what?" Rei says before I can even get my coat off one morning.

"What?" I ask.

"Guess what kind of fourth birthday party I'm having?" Again, I ask what.

"HARRRRRYYY POOTTTERRRR," she screams, and before I can even congratulate her, she pulls out a wand and attempts an Avada Kedavra on me.

●●●●●

"Steph, do you know where the soil for the mandrake station is?" Devon asks.

"Did you check under the box of potions?"

"Oh, no. I'll look."

Devon and I have spent the last few weeks working tirelessly on every last detail of this extravagant party. We spend days discussing the music and activities. My expertise on the wizarding world proves more useful than I could have ever predicted. Devon rents the play-room in their building, hires Pinkberry to cater dessert, and sends each kid home with a gift bag that includes a copy of the first Harry Potter book. But it is me who explains the care of magical creatures and who comes up with a plan to include Buckbeak in the festivities.

"Do you have a boyfriend?" Devon asks one morning as we unpack party supplies.

I say that I'm dating someone. The night before, Alex, a guy I've been seeing for a few months now, and I had gone golfing at Chelsea Piers. He's short for my taste, but witty, comedic in the way the British often are. I tell her about him and the Mexican restaurant we meet at each weekend but mention that it's casual in the way New York dating can often be.

"Do you think it will last?"

"I don't know. I'm an awful dater." I laugh. "But he's wonderful, and I'm happy right now," I add.

"The next time you guys are out uptown, let me know," she says. "I want to meet him."

I assume she is only being nice and shrug off the comment. But planning Rei's muggle bash gives Devon and me an opportunity to bond, and I find myself having more in common with her than I anticipated. Maybe it's because our age gap is small or because her work allows her less time to submerge herself in the Upper East Side mom culture. Devon is always in the mood for a martini, laughs hard at inappropriate jokes (which are usually her own), and constantly wishes she was spending the night somewhere her children were not.

In time, I realize that Devon's interest in forming a friendship isn't really about our age or interests at all. She's a thirtysomething mother working eighty hours a week with limited free time and few opportunities to socialize. Her life is an ever-repetitive loop of writing briefs, then slicing PB&J sandwiches. Our friendship offers her a glimpse into everything motherhood has stolen from her: freedom from mom life.

Devon loves her children but isn't afraid to talk about how difficult motherhood is and how exhausting she finds it. "Theo and I have the same job, same credentials, same education. Everything about our professional workload is equal, but when it comes to the children, most of that lands on me." I nod in agreement because I know what she says is true. Every day that I have worked for a mother, I have watched this storyline play out.

Seeing the inequality in childcare responsibilities was different when I worked for stay-at-home mothers. While I knew that Sasha's husband had no idea when the deadline to enroll in soccer class was and that Other Stefany's husband had never once given their son a bath, the imbalance between partners made more sense. The stay-at-home mothers were the ones at home, and their job was taking care of the children and household. I hardly ever saw their husbands, who usually left for work before I arrived and came back after I left.

Even growing up, my parents never approached parenthood as an equal responsibility.

"No. That's why you work part-time," Stew said when Hope asked him to clean the tub one weekend. Until now, I'd always agreed with him. *Though should I have?*

Tending to a household never stops. The position requires 24/7 coverage, and in those periods when my parents were separated, Hope was the only employee. Here, in Devon and Theo's home, Devon works just as much as all the fathers I have known in New York City, and, in fact, she often works harder. She would try a case in London, work six straight days preparing witnesses, then catch a red-eye home. And the moment she walked through the door, Theo would welcome her back, then ask, "Hey, are we out of mayonnaise? I want to make a turkey sandwich. And I think the kids might be hungry too."

The most spectacular part of this kind of exchange was that Theo did not believe Devon should be in charge of the entire family's lunch. It just never crossed his mind that *he* should be responsible either. Devon's life, by definition, is what many might consider the American dream. *But if that's true, why does it appear so incredibly hard?*

"Stephanie! Can you get my Nimbus 2000 for the world cup game?" Rei calls. The kids are wearing red pinnies, and Theo is trying to get an electronic snitch to fly around.

On Rei's actual birthday, I arrived at work early to place a neatly wrapped broom outside her apartment door. When the bell rang, I hid, but I could still hear Devon read aloud the card I'd put with it. "To Rei. Thanks for being a fan. Happy Bday. Love, Lord Voldemort."

"Here," I tell Rei, as I hand her both the Nimbus and a bludger.

"Thanks," she says before turning to her best friend, Caroline. "It was a birthday present. From the dark lord, of course."

Devon and I glance at one another, amused by Rei's enthusiasm. As the quidditch games begin, I breathe a sigh of relief. It's a feeling I've felt before. I know that I have reached a milestone, made the transition into a new family when the kinks have been worked out. The hardest part is done. I have formed connections, not just with the kids but with their mother, and soon their extended family too. Of course, submerging yourself so deeply into another family's life comes with its own set of obstacles, but today I'm just pleased to be over this initial one.

Over the next nine months, the children and I fall into a routine. There are no longer surprises. I know what to expect of them, and they grow familiar with me. Some may say too familiar, in fact. Devon and I become friends. For Devon, I am an outlet to the outside world. Together with her now-husband since college, her life has become a constant cycle of work and mothering. My weekend escapades seem to give her life. She'll often describe to me the million-dollar lawsuits she has just filed while sanitizing a new shipment of sippy cups. I'll tell her about the one-night stand I had in the West Village. Once, during the party preparations, I even mention Lila, whose Instagram I still occasionally peek at.

"You know what I always thought when watching these movies?" Devon asks. "I thought about having friends like Ron and Hermione. Can you imagine having friends you love so much you literally would die for each other?"

I say I can't and sit with that fib for a few minutes.

"Actually, that's not true," I say, "I did have a friend like that. Once. But we had a monstrous falling out. I had an abortion and was so mad at her for not being there for me after it. She tried, but she was dealing with her own problems too. We started bickering about everything, and eventually we had a big blowout. I completely lied to her about something and was so angry with her at the time that I didn't even really show remorse."

"Do you miss being friends?"

Every day, every second, all the time, I think.

Devon asks how long it has been since we last spoke.

"I don't know. A year and a half?" I say.

"Oh, that's not that long," she tells me. "There's still time."

"Yeah, maybe," I say, though I doubt it.

"By the way, should we drive out to my parents' house and pick up Russ's old newborn clothes? Maybe Friday?"

Devon's maternity shirt barely covers her growing midsection and suddenly I remember just how pregnant she is. "Sure. Let's go Friday afternoon," I say, but I hope Devon forgets.

I have no interest in baby clothes. I am no longer troubled by the idea of having a baby around for the emotional reasons I had in the past. It's that I fully comprehend how much work and stress newborns are, and I'm not looking forward to the hassle.

Before I started this job, I'd always imagined myself having three or four kids. Now, I feel more like Stew did when he was awaiting his fourth baby: *children are nothing more than another mouth to feed.*

25

BOSS BABY (NURSE)

WHEN SASHA DELIVERED HER SON, it was four full days until I saw or heard from her again. Days more until I had a good glimpse of the baby. But the morning Devon is induced, she sends me a text from her hospital bed.

I told Jin to just give me the drugs. Literally all of them.

Jin is Devon's doctor. Devon had sent me an Instagram post from DJ Khaled's account the week before showing Jin high-fiving DJK moments after his son was born. But today, Jin will have no one but Theo to high-five postdelivery, which I imagine she will find underwhelming in comparison.

Good idea re: drugs. Don't you wish you could take some to go? Like doggy bag morphine? I reply.

Yeah, I might ask about that. I just don't feel like being reported to child services is all.

Two hours after Tate is delivered, I bring Rei and Russ to the hospital to meet him. In the waiting room, Devon's parents hug me, an entire extended family celebrates, and her brother documents it all with his Nikon D3500. "Steph, do you want to come into the room?" an aunt asks before she brings the kids in to see their mother.

"Oh, no, that's okay," I say.

Although Devon and I are close, I feel that seeing her so soon after her insides have been torn apart would be too much, and I'm relieved to be left in the waiting room. I sit back and open an old *People* magazine. I have only just started reading about the *Roseanne* reboot's cancellation when Theo's mother appears.

"Steph," Nana instructs, "let's go."

"Oh, no. Really, it's actually very okay," I say. But Nana is a gruff and no-nonsense kind of woman. When she says something, it is not a request. I look down at the *Roseanne* article one more time, thinking how disappointed my parents will be to lose one of their favorite shows, then, reluctantly, follow Nana to Devon's room. Here, I find myself, *once again*, in an inappropriate position: by the edge of Devon's hospital bed. I find everything about myself on this day vaguely uncomfortable, a paid outsider, witnessing a family's intimate moments.

By the time Tate arrives home a few days later, the house is prepared. The nursery has been decorated, sanitized, and organized. Gray polka dots have been painted around the room and they cling tightly to the Pottery Barn crib in the corner. There are blankets from Bloomingdale's and sheets with "Tate" stitched across them. That morning, I open the blackout curtains and from the rocking chair take in the views from this new baby's room. He is two days old with a twenty-sixth-story view of Manhattan's skyline.

"Hi, I'm Stephanie. Nice to meet you," I say when Esther, the baby nurse, arrives.

"Okay, and here is Nanny Stephanie," she says and then scribbles something down on her notepad.

Esther is older. Maybe sixty, but perhaps I'm being generous. I notice the creases in her forehead and bags under her eyes when she stands near. She tells me that she's from Trinidad, lives in Brooklyn when she's not working, and has taken care of over forty newborns. I find this statistic disturbing. I imagine this woman moving into a new stranger's home every few months. As a baby nurse, her job is to take care of a newborn twenty-four hours a day, seven days a week. Naturally, she becomes attached to the child. They eat, sleep, and spend all their waking hours together. But by the time a baby is sleeping through the night, her services are no longer needed, and so she'll begin the entire process over again.

"So after my three months is complete, Stephanie will watch Rei, Russ, and baby Tate?"

Esther asks this of Devon as if I am not even in the room.

"I think I'll probably be back to work full-time by then. So the short answer is, yes, assuming all goes well."

Esther jots more down and makes a disapproving click of her tongue but says nothing. She turns toward me once more and takes a hard look, attempting to size me up. "And how old are you, Stephanie?"

"Twenty-seven," I say.

"You have a baby face. But twenty-seven is better than I thought." She sighs. "Now, for the next few months there are some things we will need to go over. One, I do not believe in holding the baby all day. If you do so, the baby will get used to the hands, and we do not want a child used to the hands. Understand?"

Devon says she completely agrees, and then they both turn to me. I have never considered the pros and cons of holding newborns with my hands, but nevertheless I too accept the philosophy. From the room over, Russ and Rei begin fighting over a Hatchimal, and I pretend that I must go check out the commotion. But Devon, familiar with my aversion to new company, simply flicks a finger at me. A signal for me to sit down and cut the shit.

"In addition, the baby must be kept on his schedule. We will do feedings, naps, and tummy time at the same hour daily without deviation. I do not take kindly to schedule interruptions. Now, per my personal schedule, I require a three-hour break for myself from one to four p.m. daily. I will also need adequate time to shower in the mornings. Also, I do not like to eat dinner late. I will need my Seamless ordered by six p.m. at the latest each evening. Any questions?"

I glance over to Devon. She's a thirty-six-year-old woman making a run for partner in a place where women have to work twice as hard as men to reach that status. She's used to being in charge. I've heard her on the phone with junior associates hours before a big filing and have even been caught on the wrong side of her wrath on occasion. Devon is passive-aggressive but commanding, and I am sure that she will now tell this tyrannical baby nurse to get a grip.

But maybe because of the hormones or just because Esther is thirty years her senior, Devon simply nods.

"Okay then," Esther smiles. "Now, where will I be sleeping tonight?"

"Oh, a little issue is that the rollaway bed didn't come in yet," Devon says, then points to something folded in the corner of the nursery. "But we have this air mattress until it does. I thought we could just blow it up next to the baby's crib for now."

There is a long pause before Esther finally releases her furrowed brow. "I'm afraid an air mattress is not going to work. I will need the rollaway bed to arrive immediately if I'm going to get any sleep whatsoever."

"Of course, of course. You know what? Let me see if I can expedite it right now."

"Okay, that would be great," Esther says. "Oh, and Devon?"

Devon pops her head back in quickly. "Yes?"

"Once you're done with that, I'll be ready to order my dinner."

I stare at the baby nurse, stunned. In five years working in the homes of wealthy Manhattanites, this is the first time I've witnessed a member of the staff be this assertive. Esther is unimpressed and, more importantly, completely uninterested in her employers. She is the opposite of anything I've ever observed in the help: she isn't submissive. In fact, I'd go as far as to say she was *dismissive* of the folks paying her.

In the homes of the rich, I've always felt, to some extent, that I was privileged to be there, and my employers often reinforced this feeling. But Esther approaches it as if she's doing *them* the favor.

●●●●●

"So," Devon asks when I walk in Friday morning, "did you love it?"

My head is groggy, a result of the post-Broadway cocktails my friend and I had in Times Square the night before. *Do we have to do Times Square, of all places?* he'd scoffed.

Though most of the city's locals see it as a filthy, money-sucking tourist trap full of people in Elmo suits and naked men with guitars, I have always loved Times Square. The lights, the smell of halal food wafting from the food trucks—it is, on any given weekend, the ultimate melting pot and the most quintessential New York City attraction.

"I liked it so much better than I thought I would." Devon and Theo had gifted me two dead center tickets to the Broadway hit *Hamilton*. I was excited, but the only play I had ever seen was *A Christmas Carol* at Trinity Rep in Providence, and I wouldn't have considered myself blown away by the performance.

"Wait, did you have a really hot Burr?" Devon asks excitedly. "We had the hottest actor the night we went."

"Oh, no! I had a totally mediocre Burr!"

Over the summer Devon and I ran into Lin-Manuel Miranda himself. I was waiting outside a magazine-worthy barn with Russ while Devon dropped Rei off inside. She was spending a week at the Hamptons' premier horse camp. It was essentially pony rides at a 600 percent markup. Russ pointed to a donkey that was casually strolling by us.

"Doggie...bigggggg."

"Not a dog, silly. That's a donkey."

"Yeah!" He giggled before turning serious. "He happy?"

I looked over at the barnyard creature. *Was he happy?* I wasn't really sure, but he looked content, and wasn't that what we were all just hoping to be?

"Steph!" Devon whispered loudly. "Stephanie! Get over here."

"What?"

"In two seconds, Lin is going to come out the barn door."

"Who?"

"Lin-Manuel!"

She shoved her phone in my face to show me a zoomed-in photo of Lin. At the time, I had never heard of him, so my interest in the sighting was low. We were back and forth over if this could really be him when a man that looked very much like the picture she showed me stepped out. Both Devon and I stood up straight, our mouths zipped shut, eyes wide. He was a few feet away from us when he stopped by a barn window, peeked in, and began performing a strange but excellent dance for whoever was inside. Devon and I exchanged nods. It was Lin, but I still actually had no clue who Lin was. Later, I told my parents I'd seen him. "He wrote *Hamilton*."

"He wrote about hamsters?" Stew asked.

Hope jumped in, asking if he was related to the former NBA player, Rick Hamilton. That's when I gave up. If I hadn't known who he was, why would they?

But I didn't have a single friend in Manhattan that wasn't on the hunt for tickets to *Hamilton* at one time or another.

For that whole week, Devon asked Rei who she had played with at camp.

Rei never once mentioned Lin's son, Bodie, despite Devon's suggestions. "Oh, wow. Yeah, Annie sounds nice. But hey, Rei, what about Bodie? He seems SO fun. I don't know, should we, like, invite him over for a playdate after camp one day?"

"No thanks," Rei said.

I tell Devon I do have to report something embarrassing about my time at the play, and she braces herself. "So, I did like it. But at halftime…"

"Intermission," she corrects.

"Yeah, at intermission, I had to go to the bathroom and google if Alexander Hamilton was a real person."

Devon pauses for a long time, staring blankly at me. She has nothing to say to that.

Once Devon leaves for her morning workout and Rei is at school, I'm left with Russ and Esther. My main issue with Esther, aside from the fact that she is openly unimpressed with me, is that she is now always around. Her job is to care for a newborn, and we have just reached December first, when Christmas tourists and flu cases converge on New York City. It's not exactly a welcoming time for an older woman and a baby to leave the house, and so they don't. Esther is constantly in the common spaces, watching her iPad or making bottles and often eating not one but two tuna sandwiches. This proximity is a bit much for me, and so I make it my mission to keep myself and the big kids out as much as physically possible.

"Come on, Russ. We're going to go over to Little Axel's house."

Little Axel, not to be confused with Russ's other friend, Big Axel, lives across the street. His apartment is an easy commute. While Rei finishes up her morning at preschool, Russ and Little Axel spend hours playing with cars, trucks, and PJ Masks and requesting anywhere from two to twenty-two goldfish pouches.

Little Axel's nanny, Mina, at thirty-four, is close to me in age and, though our similarities begin and end there, we get along so well that I consider her something of a friend.

"Axel's mom is not happy with me this morning." Mina laughs.

"Oh, no." I ask though I already know: "Were you late again?"

"Only ten minutes this time. It is just so hard to wake up!"

Mina, who is from Tibet and practices Buddhism, loves Axel as much as I love Russ. She takes her job seriously but is struggling in her transition from Axel's babysitter to his full-time nanny. "When it is just me and him, Axel is fine. But the minute he sees Mommy it's: 'No Mina. I no like Mina! I no want to talk to you, Mina.'"

Hearing of a child's hostility being directed toward someone other than myself is oddly and inappropriately comforting. Still, I feel for what Mina is going through. "It's hard working with a stay-at-home mom," I say, thinking specifically of Other Stefany, not Sasha. But even as easygoing as Sasha was, there were times her presence made my job more difficult. If children have a choice of adults, they nearly always choose their mothers. "What does she need you for anyway?" I ask. "She doesn't work, right?"

"Oh, no. But she is very busy. She goes to the Equinox for the Pilates classes and to lunch with other moms. And next week she's going to Paris with her best friend. Just for a few days. They love the bread there, she said."

I nod along. "So how is Axel's mom when he acts like that with you? Does she say anything?"

"She is great. She says, 'Axi, that's not true, and that's not okay to say to Mina. You apologize.'" Mina shrugs. "But you know the kids. They are just so difficult."

"Oh, I know," I sigh.

At lunch, Russ opens what I have packed for him. The boys eat the same thing each day at 11:45. Russ: folded slices of turkey, yogurt, a second yogurt, a bag of veggie straws, and two cheese sticks peeled into octopuses. Little Axel: two hard boiled eggs and an English muffin smeared with peanut butter. Neither lunch ever deviates.

"Mina, can you ask Alexa to play a song?" Little Axel asks.

"Sure, buddy," Mina says and then she calls out one of his favorites. "Axi loves this one," she tells me. "His daddy always put it on for him."

I recognize it vaguely. I had only just recently heard it for the first time: the third song on the *Hamilton* soundtrack.

●●●●●

Esther's time with baby Tate is coming to a close. She's been here fourteen weeks, two longer than anticipated, but she can't stay any longer because a new position starts soon.

"I need to rest in between babies. Can't work this hard without some play," she tells me.

On this day, though, she says that she is using her break to interview for a future job, six months down the road.

"How do you find jobs to apply to?" I ask.

"Oh, it used to be difficult, but now it's all word of mouth. I worked for a person who has a friend who has a sister who has a neighbor, and they're all having a baby. I don't find them anymore; they find me."

I suppose it must be true. Devon had heard enough praise

about Esther that by the time she interviewed her, she was selling the gig as much as Esther was selling herself. There were no pay negotiations, no long-winded trial. Devon wanted *this* baby nurse, and perhaps that was the precise reason Esther could have *this* many demands.

"Who is the coolest person you ever worked for?" I ask.

It was my favorite question to ask people like Esther. I was always dying to know what movie star they had seen or politician they had cooked for. While my intrigue with the glitz and the glamour of wealthy Manhattan had died down over the last few years, my obsession with who was who, had not. Maybe because celebrity gossip, particularly among my New York friends, was always a hot topic of conversation, and nannies were always willing to spill it. Except, apparently, for Esther.

"Babies are babies. They're all the same." She shrugged.

"No, no, not the actual kids. The parents. Like what parent were you most excited to work for?"

She shrugged again. "They are also all the same."

For the next few days I wondered if perhaps Esther had just never worked for anyone of particularly great means, success, or influence. It was possible over her long career living in other people's penthouses that they had all been rather mediocre. But days after she leaves, I'm swaddling the wailing four-month-old Esther had left me with, when Devon jokes, "I bet you're missing Esther right about now."

I can hardly hear her over the screams but say that I sure do.

"Well, I doubt she misses us." Devon laughs, "She must have

thought this place was the pits after living in Vanna White's house twice, am I right?"

I stick a pacifier in Tate's mouth, shocked. *What was wrong with Esther?*

Over her few months here I had observed her with unwavering interest. Her confidence, her candor, her ability to demand respect and boundaries without hesitation. Initially, I believed the reason for Esther's arrogance was cliché: *she's just a bitch.* But after weeks of watching her, I come to the conclusion that Esther isn't a shrew at all. She sees her place in this world in a way I have yet to see myself. Esther might be hired to help, but she treats herself like an equal, and as a result, everyone else treats her that way too.

26

THE MOST MAGICAL PLACE
ON EARTH

THE FOUR SEASONS OF WALT Disney World has spas, adults-only pools, and rooftop restaurants. There is a gift shop, but it sells diamonds, and an ice cream shop, but it only serves gelato. The whole place is off-white. *Why is everything off-white?*

It is incredible but, like so many places I have encountered over the course of my time with the ultrawealthy, not particularly child friendly.

Despite being at a Disney World property, I spot only one reference to Disney during our first afternoon, a very small and discretely placed shrub that has been trimmed into the shape of a mouse.

Devon and Theo had pitched this trip to me as a fun opportunity to see Disney World, but I had already seen Disney World and did not fancy the idea of seeing it with two children, an infant, and their entire extended family. Sure, I have an eight-hundred-dollar-a-night room at the Four Seasons, but I'm sharing it with a roommate who requires an aspirator to clear boogers from his nose.

"Alrightttt my friendsssss, what should we do first?" Devon's brother asks. Arlo, an actor living out in LA, has the disposition of an untrained puppy. Rei and Russ view him as the world's best uncle, and in many ways he is, but his liveliness often riles up the children and gives the adults a headache.

"Why don't we start with lunch? It's already two o'clock," Theo suggests, but Devon's parents cut in.

"Oh, but we just checked out the pool and it's beautiful. There's a lazy river. Who wants to go on the lazy river? Russ? Come on, what do you think?" Papi asks.

"YAY!" the children cheer in unison.

"Guys, I do think they need to eat…" Theo continues, but no one is listening. Devon's mom has pulled out her iPhone and is busy filming the lobby, her family, and lots of other things.

"Rei, Russ," Papi yells while waving to the camera, "say hi to Susu." I catch a glance exchanged between Devon and Theo.

"Okay, you know what, there's a snack bar by the saltwater pool. Why don't we all go to our rooms and change and then plan to meet there in a half hour?" Devon says and the group nods obediently. "And, Mom, put the phone away. If there's actually something worth filming, fine, but no one is going to cherish footage of the hotel check-in desk."

Susu fumbles to quickly slip her phone into her pocket. She'll have it out again and be snagging pictures of the kids' chicken tenders by lunch.

•••••

The next day, it's eleven a.m. by the time our group makes it to the gates of Harry Potter World despite having left the hotel at nine. The Uber ride was only twenty minutes long, but our group has eleven people and is diverse, in the sense that most members are either too young or too old to walk on their own. The grandparents have bad knees, and the baby essentially has no knees at all and requires tote bags full of formula, diapers, small toys, goldfish, and changes of clothes. We rent scooters for the old ones, use a double stroller for the littles, and by the time we make it to our first ride, the baby is the least fussy of the bunch.

"Is he tall enough?"

The grown-ups are measuring Russ against the height requirements for Harry Potter and the Forbidden Journey. He is clearly too short, as is Rei, but Rei has been waiting months for this ride and a missing inch isn't going to stop Devon from sneaking her on. Russ cries real and hysterical tears when his family departs to find seats on the ride and he is left in the "family waiting area" with me and the infant. When they return, Theo buys him a wand from Ollivanders. He picks out Ron Weasley's.

"But, Steph, guess what happened then?" Rei tugs on my leg.

I shush her politely, afraid that she will wake the baby, who is sleeping comfortably against my chest in the BabyBjörn. I cradle his head with one hand while using the other to wipe the sweat dripping down my neck. It's 85 degrees in Orlando today. Probably 92 if you include the pudgy baby's additional body heat.

"What happened?" I ask.

"Then the dementor came down flying out of the air, and I said, AHHHH! But Steph, what do dementors do exactly?"

"They suck all the joy and happiness from your soul," I say. *Much like this trip*, I think.

Just then I witness an awkward exchange between Theo's mom and Devon's father regarding the schedule of the motorized scooter they're sharing. I'm unsure why they didn't just rent two, as clearly money is not an issue at play, and instead use the item in shifts. Still, it's uncomfortable being so close to family drama. Particularly when it's a family that you have no relation to.

"Well, then LUCKILY Harry came just in time. Harry always saves the day, Steph, doesn't he?"

I want to tell her no, in fact, Harry's a fool. If she wants to discuss real heroism, I'd be more inclined to mention Dumbledore, Snape, Hermione even. Instead, I nod in agreement, and Rei asks when we can go to "the dark part" of the park.

"Well, Diagon Alley is in the other park, so we'd have to take the Hogwarts Express over to it."

We have been at Universal a total of two hours, and already our group is falling apart. The kids are furious about the lines and heat. The elderly aren't feeling much better. The baby has woken up, and I need to purchase a bottle of water to mix his formula together. Devon quickly surveys her group and decides we should take the ride to the other side. "I don't know how much longer they'll last," she says, and she's right. By one thirty, everyone is so disenchanted with Universal Studios, Devon says we should go back to the hotel.

The one time my family had been able to afford a trip to Disney World, I'd just graduated from high school. Up until then, we'd never been on a real vacation all together.

Hope had her head dug deep into Lydia's arm. "Look at this idiot," my father sighed.

The plane climbed upward steadily, but Hope was still acting like a pilot in Pearl Harbor.

"Didn't she get a Xanax for the flight?"

"She wouldn't take it," Jenna replied. "She said they make her stomach hurt."

"She's probably just afraid the Xanax contains calories," one of us snickered. Just then Hope started to dry heave. My dad, Jenna, and I all quickly turned our heads as if we didn't know her, leaving poor Lydia to deal with the situation.

When we arrived at Disney's Port Orleans—French Quarter resort, we could not believe the luxury: the pool, the game room, the soft serve ice cream.

Our first three days truly were magical. We went to every Disney park, ate at Planet Hollywood, and purchased small souvenirs from end-of-the-ride gift shops. Even Jenna, who despises heat and crowds, was having a blast.

On Thursday, we ventured to Downtown Disney for a night we'd all been waiting for. The first *Hunger Games* movie was premiering, and at the time Suzanne Collins was to me what Jane Austen is to the rest of the world. I had read all three books in record time, and the thought of waiting until we returned home to see the film was just too much to bear. My dad, feeling particularly generous during our trip, bought five tickets to the eight o'clock show and made a reservation at a nearby restaurant beforehand.

"Lydia, what are you getting?" She wasn't sure. "Do you want to split the beef lava nachos and Awesome Appetizer Sampler?" I asked. Just then a lion roared and a gorilla pounded his fists against his chest. We had been seated in the very back, by a waterfall, in a cozy corner of the Rainforest Cafe.

"Oh, my God," I said shortly after, with a mouth full of food. "How good are these?"

"The steak on the nachos is unreal," Lydia agreed.

My mom looked over in total disgust. "You're eating like pigs."

Later, when we sat down in the movie theater, Lydia let out a long and monstrous belch. This was not unusual, but when she said her stomach felt funny, I had only just been thinking the same about my own.

"Do you want to go to the bathroom?" I asked.

She looked down the aisle. The row was packed, not an empty seat to be found. "That's okay," she decided. "I'll be fine."

The lights were turned down, and everyone in the cinema did a light cheer. Lydia was between my parents, with Jenna then me at the end. Katniss had not even volunteered as tribute when it happened.

"Hey," my dad whispered, "stop that."

"Phhoooooooo." Lydia let out another long and heavy sigh.

There was a pause of maybe two or three minutes, followed by another sigh. And then another.

"What is your..." Stew couldn't even finish his sentence before she blew.

Blat, blat, blat. Vomit seemed to cover every inch within eyesight. Anyone within three rows of us heard it, and, if they didn't hear it, they were about thirty seconds away from smelling it. Both my parents jumped up. My dad just picked up Lydia and began to carry her out. He turned back only when he realized Jenna and I were not following.

"Steph," he hissed, "come on."

I shook my head. "I'm not missing the movie."

He looked genuinely horrified. "Are you fucking kidding me? You're going to sit next to a seat of vomit for two hours?"

I shrugged because, yes, I was going to do that. I had waited a long time to see this movie and the tickets hadn't been cheap. "We'll meet you at the hotel later," I whispered, before covering my nose with a hoodie and settling back in.

Lydia and my parents were fast asleep by the time Jenna and I arrived back later that evening. By this point my stomach felt like it had been doing loops on a Hot Wheels track around my midsection. I tiptoed into the bathroom and made friends with the toilet. Sitting in the corner, I noticed a towel drenched in more puke.

I didn't get much sleep that night. Lydia and I were doing relay races to the bathroom and back. We were sick the remainder of the vacation.

"What a fucking way to end a trip. All done in true Kiser fashion," Stew joked at the airport. We were waiting at the Southwest counter for our section to be called.

Lydia and I, while nearly recovered, were still weak from our time with what we reckoned to be food poisoning. Still, we laugh,

already aware that this vacation is a memory our family will reference for years to come.

"I actually had a lot of fun," Jenna said.

I was surprised, but we were all pleased to see Jenna enjoying
herself for once.

That trip, disastrous as it was, was my first real taste of travel and
one of the few times our family wasn't angry, stressed, or both. My
sisters and I got henna tattoos on a boardwalk, my dad ate turkey
legs on Main Street. Stew never stopped talking about how one
morning at Denny's I ordered two breakfasts, which was not true
then and remains untrue now but became a running joke.

"You know what?" I said to Jenna. "Same. This was the best time
I've ever had." The vacation was the happiest my family had ever
been together. It felt good.

We arrived home late that evening. For the next month my parents fought nearly every day. We'd gone over budget on the trip,
and my dad had maxed out every single credit card. We didn't have
a cent for groceries, but I didn't mind. They were some of the best
memories of our family that I'd ever have.

•••••

The first time the baby cries out for a pacifier, it's 9:56 p.m. I do the
math. Tate went down at 7:15 and has already woken before the
three-hour mark. I know this night will be anything but restful.

At four months old, Tate regularly sleeps eight hours straight,
but a new crib and new environment in the Disney hotel wreaks
havoc on his circadian rhythm. I'm in the bed closest to the rollaway

crib and hear him toss and turn all night. He scratches at his sheets and, when he does sleep, snores louder than an English Mastiff. He wakes for the day at five thirty a.m. after being up four times during the night, once so distressed I had to calm him with a warm bottle. I rub my eyes and estimate I slept maybe a total of four hours.

For the next sixty minutes, the baby and I roam the halls of the Four Seasons aimlessly. It's too early for most vacationers to be up, and we encounter only hotel staff and others with early-rising toddlers and nothing to do. Each time I pass a mom, we exchange sympathetic smiles. These moms think we're one and the same but we're not, and so far this experience has made me want to be a mother less than ever. Vacationing with small children isn't a vacation at all. It's just a bunch of mundane tasks and tantrums with a bad sunburn. The moms I see are rarely without a child in tow. While I often observe fathers drinking beers by the pool and chatting with friends on the phone, the moms never seem to stop being mothers.

When the rest of the family arrives downstairs for breakfast, everyone is in better spirits than the day before. They are confident their day at Magic Kingdom will be far more pleasant with the VIP tour guide they've hired for seven hundred dollars an hour on top of ticket prices.

"But we won't have to wait in any lines for rides, and honestly that's way better. It was too hard yesterday for the kids having to stand in line for thirty minutes every time they wanted to get on something," Theo says.

I glance at Theo's mom, who raises an inquisitive eyebrow toward me. Having grown up an only child in the Bronx in the 1940s,

Nana is the only fully down-to-earth person on this trip. The thing is that nobody wants to wait in line for rides at Disney World. The lines and the crowds are the unappealing parts, but they come with the privilege of being there. I worry about the sense of superiority being modeled for Rei and Russ when they can walk past the crowds onto any ride they choose. I imagine the way Rei's little brain thinks, scanning children the same age as her, an hour away from a ride they so desperately want to go on. It is one of the rare instances in which I disagree with Devon on something, and I'm relieved when we all decide it's best that the baby and I skip the park.

"It was too hot for him yesterday, and it's going to be ten degrees worse today," Devon says.

"I think so too. I'll take him to the pool this morning, and then we'll grab lunch before nap."

"That's great. Obviously get whatever food and drinks you want today. Just give them our room number, and they'll put it on our tab."

"Great," I say, and on our way down to the cabanas, I purchase four Coke Zeros and a Donald Duck cupcake.

Tate requires a great deal of attention at this age. I settle us into a cabana, but before we can even think of moving out of the shade, the baby needs organic sunscreen, a rash guard, a swimming diaper, and the waterproof hat that makes him look like a safari ranger.

"Oh, my God, how cute is that baby," I hear a woman say.

I have Tate propped up on my knees by the shallow end of the pool, and every few minutes I dip his toes in the water. Each dip is unexpected, and he looks startled, then unsure, but eventually pleased.

"In his little hat," I hear another woman respond, and I stop, certain I'm familiar with the second voice.

I turn and watch Tina Fey walk by. Tina is wearing exactly what I would have pictured. A one-piece and a baseball cap, the most mom poolside getup there is. I smile, for once thrilled to be misidentified as Tate's mother. *Oh, yes!* I want to tell them. *MY baby IS adorable! Would you like to hold, hug, or raise him!?* Of course, I'm far too starstruck to even say hello, and the moment passes, but I do immediately text everyone I have ever known about my terrific encounter.

By the time Tate's family returns, we've had a long but happy day at the resort. Time can drag when your only company is a few dozen days old. Their attention spans are short or nonexistent, and the majority of the day is spent just keeping them awake until their next nap. It's tedious and boring but, without the big kids, *quiet.* Peace is a luxury I no longer take for granted.

"How was it?" I ask the big kids.

They hardly respond, already racing toward the water slides, Uncle Arlo following closely behind them.

"It was amazing," Theo says. "The guide planned everything. We did the entire park in five hours. Worth the money."

I'm nodding my head in unsure agreement when Devon calls over from the poolside bar, "Steph, you want a glass of wine?"

"Yeah, I'll take a white, please."

"It sounds like today went much better," I say to Theo. "I'm surprised you guys are already back." When my family went to the parks, my sisters and I never wanted to leave.

"Oh, well the kids got bored. It's really hot for them there. They can only do so much park time before they're over it, you know?" Theo says. "Disney World's not an easy place for kids this young. Next year, we'll take them somewhere better for little kids."

27

MINDY THE MOUSE

I NEED TO PEE, BUT I am wearing the baby. As always, not *my* baby, just *a* baby.

It is nearly ninety degrees, and the four-block walk to 96th Street has left Tate and me soaked in one another's sweat, drool, and anger. He screamed the entire walk to pick up Russ. I doubt I'll get Tate back into his Baby Björn peacefully if I take him out, so I enter a tiny bathroom stall, keep him in the carrier, and pee as he awkwardly bops around my chest. It is uncomfortable, both mentally and physically.

We maneuver into the camp pickup area and are immediately met with a gust of air-conditioning. It feels good after a sweltering walk through the humid New York City streets, but I am wearing a tank top that's both tight and white. I'd come to work in a far more appropriate gray-and-black T-shirt, but the baby had regurgitated approximately two liters of formula onto it. So now here I am:

wearing my boss's tank, peeing with her child attached to me, and trying unsuccessfully to keep my headlights from flashing on.

Russ is a camper at the Art Farm, held at a state-of-the-art private high school. They do no farming and very little art but have a brief visit from one small barnyard animal each morning. He goes three and a half hours a day, five days a week, and the cost for these seventeen hours is eight hundred dollars.

On the walk home, Russ is very vocal about Mindy the Mouse. "Was she a small mouse or big mouse?" I ask.

"She was so, so, so teeny-tiny. And she got on her wheel and run, run, run like super jet speed!"

"Did you get to hold her?"

"No, they wouldn't even let us! I ask the teacher and she just not heard me and then and then she did heard me! But then she said no."

"Oh, no, but did you want to hold Mindy?"

"No," he says flatly.

"But I thought you just said you liked her?"

"No, I didn't!" he yells. It is both a quick change of heart and the average cycle of love for a three-year-old.

We are nearly up the hill and approaching their building when I feel a warm dribble snaking down my neck. I think it is bird poop and let out a sigh of relief when I see it is instead baby vomit. I wipe it away with my hand before flicking it to the ground, and that's when the screaming starts up again. I pop a pacifier in Tate's mouth and he spits it back at me, then yells a little louder, just in case I haven't heard him well enough the first time.

"Ughhhh, make it stop," Russ whines.

I search in my purse for something, anything, that will keep this seven-month-old bag of jib jab quiet for eighty-five more seconds. *Bingo.* I find a quarter of a Mum-Mum, the baby version of a grown-up granola bar and my current lifeline.

As the baby settles, I explain the schedule for the next fifteen minutes to Russ as we enter his building's elevator. "I'm going to put on a show for you, get Tate ready for his nap, then put him down. When I come back out, we're going to go right to your room for pjs and books so you can rest too. Got it?"

"Got it!" he says, though when the time for his rest arrives, I know he will certainly not *got it.*

We are in the hall and nearly to the front door when Russ asks for his water. "Can you wait just one minute until we get inside the apartment?"

"No! I can't! I'm too thirsty."

"Russ, just wait one…" Now Tate was crying again.

"I CAN'T DO IT!! I need water NOW!"

"Okay, okay."

I push the last bite of Mum-Mum into Tate's mouth before shoving a cup of water toward his brother. We are one step inside their apartment when the baby begins making gagging noises.

In a different life, I would have used this moment to melt into the ground and become one with cement. The hair on my arms would have stood up, my face would have grown hot, and my limbs would have frozen, but today I just do what I have to do. I pry open Tate's mouth with one hand and scrape the tiny bite of cracker out of his throat with the other. I wonder, *Is there a way to list finger CPR as a skill on LinkedIn?* Within ten seconds, the entire scene is over. The baby does not seem particularly bothered, and neither do I.

It's been two and a half years since Sasha brought home a newborn for me to care for, and perhaps, like with all new things, the fear disappeared with time. I imagine this feeling isn't so different from that of a new mother. The first child seems so dependent and fragile that it's hard to believe they will ever be anything other than terrifying. Then comes the second child, and maybe a third, and suddenly you have this acute understanding that it is unlikely you will kill the children. In fact, it's far more likely that the children are going to kill you.

Though I am managing with reasonable success, balancing three children under the age of five is as delicate as baby nurse Esther had warned.

I am outnumbered and often outwitted, but I do have the power of youth on my side. At twenty-seven, I can chase around two kids while holding a baby for twelve hours straight. Of course, by the time the day ends, I am exhausted. Just like a real mom, I find myself too tired to meet friends downtown for dinner and rarely go out for drinks on a weekday. I am beginning to feel prematurely aged, every ounce of energy I have dedicated to freeze tag, playgrounds, and pushing a triple stroller up and down Fifth Avenue. I miss stopping into a trendy East Village restaurant on a Tuesday without the fear of suffering through a hangover with a baby looming over me.

There is an intimacy with Rei, Russ, and Tate that I never had with Sasha's children. Unlike Ruby, when Rei needs a snuggle, it is me that curls up on the couch with her. And when the baby is ill and his pediatrician needs someone to hold him down for a flu swab, I'm the one pinning down his tiny arms and listening as he screams. My attachment to these children is greater and more intense, but I'm beginning to feel like I am living a life I'm not yet destined for. I am wasting the last of my free years with anything but freedom.

"Stephanie!" I hear only moments after I tuck Russ in for his afternoon nap. I throw my head back and sigh. Ever since he reached three and a half, getting Russ to nap has become a battle. If he refuses, I lose any semblance of a break in my shift.

"Stephanie! Come now!"

I push open his door quietly. "Russ, it's nap time, buddy. What do you need?"

Russ looks so small in his new twin-sized bed. His lip quivers as he holds his stuffed owl, Who-Who-Ay, tight against his chest. I ask again what he needs.

"Will you lay with me?" he asks.

Most days I refuse the request, afraid this will only prolong the process. But today he is sweet and tiny, the stereotypical adorable little boy protesting sleep.

"All right, but just for a minute," I say.

As I lie down against the cool comforter, Russ grabs on to my hand. In a few months, he'll find this sort of thing childish, but for now he slips his fingers between mine before he drifts off to sleep. It's a moment I should cherish, and I do, but I am also missing my only opportunity to scroll Instagram by lying here.

"Steph?" Russ whispers.

"Yes?"

"I love you."

There are rare instances of nannying that feel more like a privilege than anything else. The sort of unconditional love children offer is different from the affection we share as adults. It's given without judgment or boundaries. Their love is pure and simple. There's a generosity to it that they quickly outgrow. It is the one thing I get from this job that I could not possibly find anywhere else. And it is no small thing.

"I love you, too," I say, and as I occasionally do, I think of how lucky I am to be here and wonder how I'll ever leave.

But this feeling is fleeting.

Because for every blissful moment with a child comes ten more of hell.

●●●●●

I am boiling water on the stove when Russ's friend Pearl pops out of his room.

"Stephanie," she screams, though we are only twelve feet apart, "can I play with this?"

Pearl is a real piece of work at only three and a half. She has boundless energy and a sharp tongue. Pearl also has a personal chauffeur, a nanny, three babysitters, and a close family friend named Chelsea Handler. Pearl holds a paper doll kit out for me to see, and I think, *Kid, play with whatever you want. Just please don't bother me.*

"Sure, be careful with it though, okay?"

"Okay!" she shrieks before sliding back into the bedroom.

It is the first day of my period, and my entire body throbs from PMS and a long workday. My midsection feels as if it is filled with three hundred papercuts and one very full S'well water bottle. Everything hurts. But Pearl is here now, entertaining my dear Russ, and it is the first moment of the day when a child is not touching, climbing on, or wiping something on my body. I glance at the clock as I stir some pasta. There are three and a half hours of the eleven-hour shift left. I nearly throw up.

Pearl and Russ continue popping in and out as I work around the kitchen. I hear their muffled chatter; nonsense I assume, and then one of them has another question.

"Can we use these markers?"

"Yes."

"Can we use these magna tiles?"

"Yes."

"Can we cut the cat open and check out his insides?"

"No."

In the first ten or so minutes they are playing in Russ's bedroom there is nothing suspicious. Nothing out of the ordinary. I could do this day a million times over and I still wouldn't suspect a thing. It seems like a peaceful Wednesday afternoon. I am surprised and appreciative of my good fortune. And then the doorbell rings.

I crack open the door. "Yes?" I ask impatiently. The baby has only been sleeping half an hour, and I'm worried he'll wake from the bell.

"Is everything all right in here?" Jimmy asks.

Jimmy is the doorman. He is a husky guy, not dissimilar to a brown bear, and I watch as a bead of sweat slides down his forehead.

"Yeah, everything's fine." I laugh. *What is he so worked up for?*

His coworker slides forward. "Are you sure?"

"Yes, I'm sure we're all..."

"Okay, listen, is anyone throwing things out the window?" Jimmy interrupts. I laugh again.

"No, no one is..." but then I stop. Suddenly, I just know.

When the three of us enter Russ's room, Pearl is giddy with excitement. I turn from Pearl to Russ, and I ask the question, but he is sitting by a slightly open window, so I don't need an answer.

"Russ," I say slowly, "did you throw something out the window?" We are on the twenty-fifth floor.

Russ looks me in the eye but does not respond, so I ask again. "Did you...Russ...throw something out the window?"

"Actually," Jimmy interjects, "it wasn't something. It was a lot of things."

"What do you mean? Like how many?" I ask. He says he isn't sure, and I feel my skin turning hot. "An approximate number?"

"Maybe twenty toys," he admits, "plus an alarm clock. An art set. And two packages of printing paper."

Pearl shrieks with excitement, but I hardly hear a thing. I'm busy thinking about how fucked I am.

My greatest blessing this day will be that none of the toys fell twenty-five stories down to hit pedestrians. Most of the evidence could be found on the ninth floor, where it had been caught on a terrace that connected to the building's playroom. When Jimmy explains this, I wake the baby, grab Russ, and set out to collect as many undamaged items as possible.

As we enter the playroom, my heart is beating hard enough that I can feel it thumping, and I'm fighting back tears. *I can't believe I missed this,* I think to myself. *How could I let this happen?* But also, *How the fuck would I have thought this might ever happen?*

"Can you believe all these toys?" I hear Marilyn, a nanny and grandmother of two, exclaim. She's talking to another nanny, Veronica. Veronica often texts me long prayer chain messages, and I respond as if I am thrilled to be included in the list of strange phone numbers. I am not sure what most of the prayers are about, but Veronica is an adorably ancient Asian woman, and it seems wrong to opt out of her faith. While other phone numbers text back long paragraphs describing what this prayer means to them, I write things like Wow, great read! And Thanks for the share :). It occurs to me now, in this moment, that when Devon hears about this, I'll wish more than anything that I did in fact believe in a god.

"So he just threw all these toys out the window?" Marilyn asks.

"Yes," I mumble, mortified.

There are four nannies total in the playroom, and they all laugh before composing themselves. Then, without a word, each of these women begins to do what they always do: clean up someone else's mess. They collect broken toy cars and dispose of shattered action figures. They pile together whatever items have somehow survived the ordeal unharmed. No one questions me further about what transpired.

"I think that's the last of it," Marilyn says.

Sheepishly, I thank the women for the help, while anxiously anticipating the consequences I will face with Devon when she finds out.

"But thank you guys, seriously. I know you didn't have to do this."

"Don't worry, Steph. We've been doing this a long time. Kids are crazy. We've all been there," Marilyn smiles gently. "You're a good nanny, and we have your back."

By the time we get back upstairs, Devon has arrived home, and the doormen have so kindly reported the entire story before I've had the opportunity to explain. Although, I am unsure what sort of explanation I could provide. My work today, though not purposely so, was negligent. I stumble through a brief exchange with Devon before she decides it's best I just leave for the day.

I call my roommate Sara, a preschool teacher, the moment I step outside their building, and to my surprise, I immediately burst into tears.

"Steph, I can't—" Sara says, but I cut her off with another dramatic sob. "I can't understand you. Take a breath."

Once I manage to compose myself, I explain what happened. "How long was he alone?" she asks.

"A few minutes! That's all. And I didn't check on them because they were popping in and out to ask me questions! Why would I have ever assumed they were throwing all Russ's belongings out the window?" I say this and dissolve into tears once more.

"But, Steph, everyone makes mistakes at work. Literally everyone. Why are you this upset?"

"Because this was dangerous," I say. And it was. But also, I've let work down and, much more than that, I've let Devon down.

The boundaries between us have become blurred, and our friendship intensifies the stakes of my overall work performance. I am not upset because I might get fired. In fact, I'm tired of playing house. I was so obsessed with making money, and now even that isn't enough to keep me happy. I'm trying to write on weekends, but my free time is so limited and the work never goes anywhere. Sometimes it feels like my entire identity has become being a nanny. I am still lost.

I might even find it a relief to be free of children and playdates and diaper changes. *But my friend is upset with me*, I think. I have let Devon down by having a bad day at work, and these things that should be unrelated are completely intertwined. Every aspect of this situation is really *very* inappropriate. I go to sleep that night with my eyes stinging from nonstop tears. It's the most I've cried in ages. I pull down the shades and click off the TV, then I lie down and wonder, *Will I still have a job tomorrow?*

I can't decide what I hope the answer will be.

28

BURNOUT

I AM ON MY THIRD fourteen-hour shift of the week when it happens. I'm balancing Tate on one hip while pinching Rei's bloody nose closed. Tate is fifteen months old now, a carnivore, and thicker than a healthy baby needs to be. Russ is screaming beside me. It played out the way it always does toward the end of the day. Rei and Russ, exhausted and weary from their long day, were happily engaged in some roughhousing until suddenly it stopped being fun. They bashed heads right as Rei jumped from one couch cushion to the other, and now the laugh fest has turned into shrieks. I turn off the stove, where I am boiling water for pasta, and try to hand the baby off to the housekeeper, Anna, in an attempt to buy myself a moment with Russ. But the baby refuses. Now all the children are in ruins, and I have no choice but to ride this out. My voice is soothing when I tell them, "Shh, don't worry; it's okay." Anna passes with a Swiffer in hand and looks at me apologetically, but I know she's happy to be nothing more than a witness to this train wreck.

"*Mucho complain, los chicos,*" she says.

I nod, because despite our language barrier, I agree. I am tired. Mainly, I am tired of children.

Later that night, I give Devon a recap of the day on my way out. She's an hour later than usual, drinks with the junior associates having gone longer than she anticipated. I used to linger after I finished my shifts. Devon and I would swap stories from our day, discuss things we had texted about earlier, make fun of neurotic moms and their misbehaved children. But for weeks our conversations have been strictly information exchanges. They are boring and stiff and uncomfortable to execute. I miss my friend, but I've started to dislike my boss, and the two feelings have become inseparable. By the time I get home from work that evening it's nine fifteen p.m. I have to be back out the door and en route to their house again in nine hours.

●●●●●

I tell Devon that I need help, a break, some room to breathe apart from these three tiny humans who require so much of me. They hire a sitter, a college kid, who studies down by Union Square. I wait with great anticipation on her first afternoon. It will be an extra pair of hands, and the sitter will stay until seven, giving me the green light to leave at six. It's a rare treat to get out early, and I make a long and thrilling list of things I will do with my extra hour. I spent the prior evening texting everyone I know, Who wants to get dinner tomorrow? No one is interested, but I remain excited about the free time, nonetheless.

The doorbell rings, and I answer enthusiastically, "Hi, Maggie! I'm Stephanie."

As Maggie takes off her shoes and the children gather around her cautiously, like dogs sniffing out a new smell, I breathe a sigh of relief. If this sitter can cover just a handful of my hours, it will be exactly the break I need. It feels like the answer I've been looking for.

"What should we play today, guys?"

The big kids shout things like *cars* and *Mario Kart.* But as Russ grows excited, I feel the baby's hand tighten around the collar of my sweatshirt. I look down to find him eyeing Maggie carefully. She notices this and steps forward with a smile.

"Hi, baby Ta—" she says, but she's stopped by bloodcurdling screams.

I shush Tate, rubbing his back calmly, and explain that he just needs a moment to get acquainted.

But three weeks later Tate still clings to me each time Maggie enters the house. I want nothing more than for him to grow attached to someone else so that I can get more time to myself, and so I encourage Maggie to keep trying.

"We'll get there," I say. But I'm wrong. The baby never grows fond of her.

I've noticed you've been down lately and wanted to ask you about it. Devon texts one day. What's going on?

It's a Thursday afternoon, and I am lying on her and Theo's bed with their son in my arms. Russ is watching TV—the *PAW Patrol* pups are on the case. Ryder calls for Rubble to get his digger moving, and Russ snuggles a little closer to me. I love him so much, but I hate being his nanny.

I struggle to respond to Devon's text. For weeks we've been dancing around this subject. I type a few words, then erase them, and then type more out again.

After minutes of this, I consider not responding at all, but this issue is not going away. I've known that for some time, and it does no one any good to keep silent.

> Obviously I really love you guys, but I'm feeling burned out.
> I think realistically, I'm probably ready to do something
> different, something a little more normal. It might be time
> for me to move on soon.

I wait in anxious anticipation for a response. I find myself inching closer to Russ now, aware that just as he has grown to find comfort in me, the same is true on my end. I'm not just a big part of Russ's life. He's a huge part of mine. I wonder which of us will take my departure harder.

> Look, we obviously don't want you to leave but we want
> you to be happy. All I ask is that you give me a lot of notice
> to find a replacement for you. And you know I'll help you
> move forward in anything you want to do next. We will do
> whatever we can for you.

It's then that I imagine someone else taking my spot, filling my shoes, and replacing who I am to these three children. I don't want them to have a new nanny. I don't want a stranger taking care of them. But I also don't want to do it anymore. I have had this conversation with myself so many times. It's the problem with this job. You treat them like they're yours, but they never were. It was always meant to be temporary. It's like falling in love with a person you know you're incompatible with. You keep seeing them because in the moment it feels good, but the longer you do that, the worse the inevitable fallout.

I force myself to continue the conversation, working up the courage to send my response.

> Of course I would never leave you guys high and dry, which you know. I think in the next few weeks we should start discussing an end date. I know it'll be hard but there's no better time to start figuring things out.

I breathe a sigh of relief, happy to have gotten the conversation off my chest. This had been building up for weeks, months, or if I am being completely honest, the entirety of the last five years. Nannying was something I planned to dabble in to supplement my income. I'd wanted to be independent and have the ability to buy things that were out of reach in my childhood. In my mind, success equated to things. *Earning things, buying things, owning things.* I wanted more, and I got it, but now I wondered at what price?

On one hand, I lived in a luxury building and had a savings

account with thousands of dollars in it. I never missed a student loan payment. I could treat my sisters to vacations and concert tickets and did so regularly. The last time Gram visited the city, I took her uptown to see the kids, and she smiled more than I had seen in years. After we left, I surprised her with dinner at the top of Rockefeller Center. She was in awe of the view but couldn't help herself from asking, "Stephy, can we afford these prices?" I looked at the numbers on the menu. They no longer even seemed that high to me.

Here I was, with all the things I had wanted, and it felt anti-climactic. I thought I would feel a rush when I could buy a sweater without looking at the price tag, but the cashmere didn't feel all that different from cotton.

It also felt, in many ways, that no matter how well I did, most of my friends would never see me as their equal. My New York friends, some of whom lived off of their parents' millions, would meet my family and say things like, "You're a modern miracle." When I tried mussels for the first time, they'd joked, "White trash folk don't eat seafood." In many ways, this was on me, for using self-deprecating humor when discussing my upbringing. But I did that to feel better about not fitting in.

The thing was, I had never felt like I deserved to be here, and I was beginning to realize I probably never would.

I thought I'd proved myself by finding some sort of success in the big city, but now I was beginning to question what success was. The people I worked for had all the markers of success: savings, assets, a beautiful home, children they could easily provide for. I had a few thousand in the bank and a 24/7 work mentality. My life looked so much better than it had growing up, but I wondered now if I had lost more than I had gained. Was I *actually* doing well, or had people who had far more than I did just tricked me into *believing* I was?

Either way, it didn't matter. I just wanted my life back. I built my entire twenties around raising someone else's children, and if I ever wanted kids of my own, I needed a break from raising someone else's. I put my phone down and glance over at Russ. In reality, telling Devon how I felt was easy. Leaving her children would be the hard part. Still, the weight of anxiety has lifted, and beneath the sadness, I feel optimistic.

It is time for me to move forward. I come to this realization in the last week of February 2020.

29

COVID-19

I AM STANDING BEHIND LARGE glass doors overlooking a stunning pool. I sip a hot coffee out of an old mug and feel rustling as my dog lies down by my feet. It's early April, the weather has turned, and today the air will be warm. I watch a squirrel race up an oak tree, still bare of its leaves. The property that I look out onto—the miles of green grass, the pumpkins that grow in the fall—is so beautiful that I can't believe I'm here.

Truly, I cannot stress enough how much I do not believe that I am here.

Two weeks after Devon and I agree I should soon move on, the world is hit with a pandemic, and no place was hit harder in those early days than New York City.

Like most wealthy New Yorkers, Devon and her family do not need to stay in the virus-infested city, opting instead to flee to their Hamptons estate. Their law firms issue work-from-home orders that Devon and Theo cannot possibly comply with while also caring for their three children under five. The nannies who work in my building flood my phone with texts of where their employers will be taking them. I keep a running list: *Florida, Sag Harbor, Wyoming.* Russ's preschool teacher holds the class's Zoom calls from her parents' ten-bedroom estate on a beach in Mexico. Anyone who can afford to get out does, and most take their staff with them.

Now here I am, one day demanding distance from my job and the next finding myself and my canine moved into the office.

"Rei, you have gym class on Zoom in five minutes," I call.

Rei screams, then falls to the ground. She says something about how she absolutely will not be doing that and that she hates virtual school. I can't say that I blame her. The best part of school is your friends, and if you can't really see them, what's the point?

"Steph! I'm done."

I rush over to Russ to look over the letter tracing worksheets he's just completed. He's drawn all the letters correctly except for one.

"Uppies! Uppies!!!"

I feel a tug on my leg as the baby insists I pick him up. Only he's not really a baby anymore. Tate is eighteen months old and wants to be held constantly, growing hostile when his needs are not met. "One second, buddy," I say, while I show Russ an easier way to do an uppercase F. Tate erupts in anger before throwing his body to the ground theatrically.

"Steph, a timer on Alexa is going off."

"Thanks, Russ," I say, then quiet the Amazon robot. I walk over to the stove and dump pasta into the boiling water. "Rei, Zoom, right now."

Rei hollers about how I'm the worst and continues to berate me until her teacher finally makes her virtual appearance. The baby continues screeching "uppies" but quiets as soon as I comply.

"Steph? Steph!" Russ calls. I lower the burner to six then go to see what he needs.

"Is there something in my teeth?"

He opens wide and I look. "Just a little piece of food between two of them. It'll go away when you drink water or something."

"No! I need it out. I need it out now!"

"Russ, it's fine. We don't have any floss right now."

"Ahh... AHHHHHH... I need it out! Please, out!"

I think about all the ways in which I hate myself as I use my pinky nail to scrape the leftover whatever from his teeth.

Just then the front door swings open and I hear Devon shuffling in. She has a brief due in a few hours, but the line for the one and only grocery store in town is long by afternoon. She goes early to avoid the rush, but now she will be forced to work late into the night. Theo does not go to the grocery store, but he does work his normal hours.

"Well, that's it," she says firmly, "life is officially over. Starbucks has closed. I guess I'll just go fuck myself now." It feels like we're both starting to hit rock bottom. "How's everything going?" she asks while scrubbing her hands at the sink.

"Not bad. Rei's mad about PE, but other than that fine."

"She hates PE," Devon sighs then adds, "and frankly, she's not very good at it."

I nod. Rei is tragically unathletic.

"How was the grocery store? Better than last week?" For weeks Devon has come back with horror stories that reach far beyond the headlines of people hoarding cleaning supplies. In the world of the 1 percent, something far more alarming is unfolding: the virus is exposing a larger inequality issue among the wealthy and their help than even I had thought possible.

"Not really. Today I saw this little old Hispanic woman loading, I'm not kidding, like, fifteen cases of sparkling water into a black SUV. She was probably, I don't know, sixty-five? Seventy? You know some millionaire just has her doing their grocery shopping so they don't have to risk exposure."

The last time I had stopped at Citarella, a grocery store that sells watermelons for as much thirty dollars apiece, domestic workers filed out with carts packed full of meats and fish, fresh fruits, and paper towels. I glanced around the parking lot. Porches, Audis, and Range Rovers. I myself sat in a Mercedes Benz SUV. Just two hours west, people in Far Rockaway were dying of the coronavirus by the hundreds daily. Yet here I was wearing a mask in a parking lot that could have passed for a luxury car show. No one here feared they would be denied a bed if they entered Southampton Hospital. Everyone could afford the best care, and more importantly, they could afford to leave the pandemic hotspot in which they lived and have their staff risk exposure in order to keep themselves safe. And the staff couldn't afford to refuse.

"It's awful," I sigh. The thought of someone sacrificing their elderly help makes me sick, but it's nothing unusual.

Each day my phone explodes with texts from other nannies. Unlike me—young and responsibility-free—these nannies have children and grandchildren of their own. It wasn't possible for them to pack up and move in with their bosses during the pandemic because then who would take care of *their* family? Many were given a choice: join us in quarantine or don't get paid. Some didn't have the ability to say yes, while others couldn't afford to say no.

I know of employers who do pay their nannies, housekeepers, and drivers for months, even while it is not possible for their staff to work. They show compassion and humanity in a time when hopelessness feels unavoidable.

But more of the texts I receive are from nannies who also work in Devon and Theo's building and are simply being left to fend for themselves—not given the opportunity to come to the Hamptons and not getting paid their salaries when left behind.

My boss pay me two weeks then after that say they don't know how long this will last so they just let me go. Said they will hire someone again when it is over, a hard-working nanny of two years writes to me. Her schedule prior to the virus had been eight to six, but Rosa always worked until seven, doing an extra hour for free to ensure the house was left spotless. Now she's sixty-two years old and searching for a job when there aren't any. Another tells me, I still coming to work, Stephanie. But my boss is very kind; she get me in an Uber from Queens to the Upper East Side every day. The mother she refers to has one child and no job. The nanny is just shy of seventy and immunocompromised, but she lives paycheck to paycheck. *Kind* is not exactly the word that comes to mind.

"What do you want for dinner tonight, Steph?" Devon asks. "Theo could make steaks. Or we could order out."

"Anything's fine," I say, then Rei screams for me.

"Steph," she cries, "when will this class be over?"

"And what is your favorite snack, Cordelia?" I hear the teacher on the Zoom call ask. A six-year-old responds that she loves avocado toast and crispy rice. Then they all return to doing jumping jacks.

"Soon," I mouth to Rei, and she explodes in tears. "Rei, please," I say because I'm too tired of arguing.

It's been four weeks of living at work, and I am exhausted, scared, and—despite being surrounded by the people I work for—incredibly lonely. But my boss has just asked me what I prefer for dinner at a time when many nannies are being fired out of convenience. I'm tired of being here, but I have it better than any other nanny, so how can I possibly complain?

I miss the city, my friends, the comfort of my own bed. *What does it matter if you live at work now?* I ask myself. *Your life has stopped anyway.*

●●●●●

"Hey, are you going to make the clams soon?"

Theo has just popped his head out of his room. Devon, straight off her third all-nighter, looks tired enough to fall asleep on a pile of steak knives.

"Should we just do takeout tonight? I still haven't finished this brief, and I have to file by midnight. I really can't deal with dishes and all the rest tonight."

Theo, clearly disappointed, mutters, "Whatever you want."

I find it altogether ridiculous that he even considered asking this of Devon, but the more shocking aspect isn't the ask itself. It's that it never crossed Theo's mind as inappropriate. He has no idea how much less he does around the house or with the children, but apparently neither do most men in America. I read that only 3 percent of women during COVID find their husbands to be doing as much homeschooling as they are. That number seems high to me.

I wonder what would have happened to my mother had we been children during this time. When I was ten, I was diagnosed with recurrent strep throat and was out sick nine times that school year. They had just recommended having my tonsils removed when the condition suddenly vanished. Every single day I was home sick, my mother was home with me. I can't recall a single time my father took me to the doctor, gave me antibiotics, or drove me to McDonald's for a cold milkshake. I never even considered that he might.

What Devon was experiencing was the same as what my mother experienced throughout my childhood: pressure, demands, and, above all, unequal parenting responsibilities. Women of all shapes, sizes, and colors had it harder when it came to domestic life than men. COVID-19 did not start this. It brought it to light.

"Steph, can we come to your pool house to watch a movie tomorrow?" Rei asks.

Tomorrow is Saturday. My day off. Normally, our weekends take place on opposite ends of Manhattan. While Rei remains in the child-friendly hub of the Upper East Side, I barhop around the West Village and eat dinner at bistros in SoHo.

I never wanted to be a live-in nanny, and this is precisely why. The children do not understand the concept of days off, especially when their nanny is across the lawn. During COVID-19, these kids and this family are more than workplace responsibilities. They are now my entire life.

"Sure," I say, because what else can I say, and Rei cheers in delight.

A moment later Theo is back, and Devon asks if he can watch the baby while she runs to the bathroom. He says yes, but then immediately plops down on the couch and begins browsing Twitter on his phone. Within ninety seconds the baby has dumped someone's glass of wine on the floor. I am brushing Rei's hair when I notice this and, although I alert Theo, it is Devon who returns to clean the mess up.

Being a nanny has always struck me as an invasive profession. I know too much, specifically in this house, where my boss is now a personal friend. And as a live-in nanny, in a time when people are discouraged from leaving their homes, I'm exposed to every part of the family's day. I witness, and often participate in, moments that I shouldn't. While I do not know what particular pair of underwear Devon is wearing today, I do know all the options. When Theo and Devon have an argument over dinner about something ridiculous, I quietly excuse myself, then scurry to the pool house while my cheeks burn with embarrassment. *I don't need to know what goes on in their personal life,* I think. But, here, nothing is personal anymore. Not really. We're all just one big, fucked-up, happy family.

"Okay, Steph, you can go," Devon says after the wine is cleaned up. "Sorry it was another long one."

I look at the clock. The shift was twelve straight hours.

"I'm going to put the kids down, then we'll start cooking. Do you want to come back over to eat in an hour?"

You sure know I don't have any other plans, I think, but instead I say, "Okay."

I call my dog to follow me and head out, glad to be done with work for the day. On my walk across the yard, I look up at the cold April sky and wonder when it happened: when did so much of my life become no longer mine?

●●●●●

"Rei, come on! Follow me!"

I hear the commotion outside my pool house window. It's Saturday morning. Eight a.m. Burger hears the kids and runs to the door.

"Go back to sleep." I shush him.

Rei yells for Russ to hop on his ATV, and I hear them both speed off. So does the dog, who is now begging to be let free.

"Burger! Lie down!" I scream, but he does not.

The kids keep playing, and the dog keeps barking. A minute later I hear the screen door slide open and little giggles shushing one another. Both kids scream, "BOO" and explode with laughter, and already my weekend feels over.

Russ and Rei are watching *Scooby Doo* on my bed when my phone rings. I'm surprised but thrilled to see Elissa's name. It's been ages since we've been in touch, and I've been meaning to reach out.

"Hello?"

"Stephanie?" she says, and her voice sounds weak. I know right away it won't be the joyful reunion I had imagined.

"How are you?" I ask.

She tells me the whole story in just a few minutes. It's not all that different from the others that I've been hearing. A nanny works for a family for years, decades even. They are expected to keep their boss's children fed and clean *and safe*. But when COVID-19 hits and nannies ask for the same loyalty they've given families for years, most are met with disappointment. It wasn't that these families of significant wealth could no longer afford to pay their help; it was that they didn't want to.

"They just tell me if you can't commute to work, we can't keep you. Stephanie, I have diabetes. I can't be on the subway or the buses. I said to them, please. After so many years, please just pay me until it's safe to commute. But they just said, 'Elissa, we're sorry. We just can't.'"

"Can you go on unemployment?"

"I cannot," she cries, "because I was not on the books. I am not legal here."

The cracks in her voice are painful. I think of how deeply Elissa loved the children she took care of. I think of her braiding Katherine's hair and peeling her fruits. Then I think of their family's three-floor Upper East Side brownstone. The vacation home they own in Aspen. Elissa changed Katherine's diapers, bandaged her scraped knees, and told her fairy tales until she drifted off to sleep. She missed precious moments with her own family in order to take care of someone else's.

While my predicament of living with my employers was

unfortunate, I did not lose my job. I didn't make more money during this time. I didn't make less. Everything for me sort of stayed still, whereas most workers' lives were turned upside down. There would be more horror stories like Elissa's. Bosses who fired their nannies and gave them not even a week's severance. Housekeepers and baby nurses who came in one day to find the homes where they worked empty and their employers gone. Household staff who were paid off the books and could not file for the loss of a job it appeared they never had.

While their bosses hid in their country estates, these women went back to their apartments in Harlem and Flushing and wondered how they'd survive. Some employers, like Sasha, chose to leave their help behind to stay with their own families when they fled. They paid them every cent of their salary anyway. But there weren't enough Sashas. There never are.

30

THE RETURN

I'M SITTING IN THE PASSENGER seat of Lydia's Ford Focus. Burger is on my lap, and my sister's driving is so bad that it may be a greater threat than COVID itself.

"What's on your hand?" Lydia asks.

I look down at the red mark that is barely hanging on.

"It was a heart," I say of the temporary tattoo. "Rei gave me it. She has one too. She wrote GNE under it."

"GNE?"

"Goodest Nanny Ever."

We pull up to my family's ranch-style house to find that it is now painted two colors. I'm sure my father, always eager to start a home improvement project, at some point grew bored. So what I see today is a bicolored house with a mailbox that's been painted to look like a basketball and an American flag waving from the roof.

Hope's three dogs attack the living room window as we lug my

J.Crew duffel bags in. I'm concerned they'll get dirty on my parents' dusty floors and tell Lyd: "Just put them down on a carpeted area." As we enter the house, Stew is just leaving.

"Hey, dumbass. Welcome home," he says and then he's off to who knows where, but I'm pretty sure it's Dunkin' Donuts.

"How was the drive?" Hope asks Lydia.

"You only called her five times during it," I say, and Hope flashes me a scowl.

Sometimes my mother and I go months without any contact at all. Neither of us has ever been bothered by this arrangement, but Hope grows anxious if she doesn't hear from Lydia within a four-hour time span.

"Stephanie. Nice of you to leave the Hamptons to come visit us peasants."

"Yes, sorry I couldn't come sooner; some of us still have to work," I say.

"Oh, yes. You and your rich family getting fancy takeout every night," she taunts. I roll my eyes but don't bite, so she continues. "We don't serve eighty-dollar steaks here. I'm sure you remember what a Domino's looks like?"

I still order cheesy bread on my own in Manhattan, frequently, in fact. I nearly tell her this but instead let her keep her assumptions.

"From the looks of you, it appears you hardly eat at all," I say. "Not sure what you could possibly get at Domino's."

"Don't you worry, Stephanie," Hope says, proudly. "I never eat more than a slice."

By the time I came home from my three-months-in-the-

Hamptons lockdown, I realized there was more happening out there in the world than I thought. Not a whole lot more, but more than I saw while living in my nanny children's backyard. I'd become obsessed with getting a vehicle so I might commute back to the city on weekends, or at least drive myself to the beaches and coffee shops.

I really wasn't sure what I would do with a car once the pandemic ended but decided to buy one anyhow. I didn't feel safe using public transportation, so initially I considered it to be a purchase made out of necessity.

"Did you see the listing I sent you, though? Just look at the one I sent. It's a really great price for a Mini," I hounded Stew when he returned home later that morning.

Stew, who had grown up working with cars, knew good vehicle value when he saw it. I had never made a really big purchase on my own, and I was stressed about overspending and obsessed with staying within the arbitrary budget I'd decided on.

"Oh, this idiot," he sighed. "Hope, look what this kid sent me. She doesn't know her ass from her elbow."

I was about to defend the listing when he pointed to the words: stick shift.

Hmm.

"I can learn to drive a stick." I shrugged. He said I couldn't.

After a minute, I agreed.

At the dealer, my father tried to negotiate the price of an automatic Mini Cooper, but the sales agent wouldn't budge. In the end, I bought the car anyway. It was more than I had set out to pay, but Stew, never one to budget, convinced me.

"Steph, the car is basically new. For five thousand more than you wanted to pay, you can get this."

"Dad," I sighed, "the payment is going to be three fifty a month."

"But you can afford it!" he complained. "What's the point of making money if you won't spend it?"

It was that way of thinking that had gotten him into so many financial messes, I thought. But I didn't often splurge, and I knew this car would make me happy. I signed the paperwork an hour later and waited with anticipation. But when the sales agent returned he had some bad news.

"We just can't qualify you for that size loan," he said. "You have so much student debt, the bank just can't swing it."

"I can make a bigger down payment," I insisted. "Instead of five thousand down, I could do seven? Eight?"

The man smiled apologetically. "I'm sorry, Ms. Kiser. I just don't think we'll be able to make it work."

"I wish I could cosign it, Steph," Stew said. "I have too much credit out already. It wouldn't go through even if I tried."

I told him it was okay, not to worry, and it wasn't his fault. "Can you show me what you have around max ten thousand?" I asked.

The sales agent typed quickly into his computer then turned the screen. On it was a used 2009 Nissan Rogue, fully loaded, with 95,000 miles on it. It would only cost me seven thousand, and I had a feeling it would only last me about two years. I was just about to ask for what I imagined would be a very sad test ride when Hope interjected.

"I'll cosign it," she said.

Hope had been in the corner of the room, hood up, silent like always. If I was being honest, I had forgotten she was even there.

"Really?" both my father and I asked.

She nodded then held out her hand. "Give me the paperwork."

She read through the paperwork the sales agent handed us on our way out and perked up. "BMW is the maker of Mini?" she asked. "You know what this means? I own a BMW!"

We both laughed. I hadn't even made my first payment. Neither of us owned a damn thing.

"In all seriousness, I really appreciate you helping me," I told her when we pulled onto the highway. "It really means a lot."

"Well, I know you're good for the money," she said. "Besides, you shouldn't be punished for going to college. You pay your student loan every month; what more do they want?"

It was strange hearing her say these words to me. Hope and I would never have the traditional mother-daughter relationship. But there had been times that she had pulled through when I hadn't even considered seeking out her help. This was one of them.

Maybe we would never have the bond I wished for, but her heart was there and her intentions were good. Her life hadn't always been easy, and for the first time, I thought maybe she'd been doing the best she could all along. I felt sorry and ashamed that it had taken me this long to see that, but growing up is hard, and accepting people for who they are is even harder.

31

SMALL STEAKS ONLY

TATE IS RUNNING ACROSS THE patio when he trips and crashes down onto both knees. I hold my breath, aware that this can go one of two ways and praying for the more pleasant outcome.

"You okay, T?" I ask.

Tate hoists himself up and dusts his hands off as if nothing happened. "I fine, Ste," he announces. "I fine."

I walk over and pick him up just to be sure he didn't suffer any scrapes. As I look over his chubby arms and knees, he watches me intently. When I'm done, I meet his gaze.

"What?" I ask.

Tate points across the yard to the pool house. He has now begun to associate me and my pool house with the junk food I keep there. No matter what the sugary snack, Tate uses one universal word.

"Cookie?"

"You want a piece of candy?"

"YEAH!"

"Okay, fine," I tell him, as we stroll across the grass. "But only one."

The thought of candy is bliss to the baby, and he grins widely. As I slide open the front door, he claps his hands and waves toward the candy cupboard.

"One, Ste. Yeah. One," he says, then holds up three fingers.

I watch Rei and Russ run through their massive Bridgehampton lawn as I hand the baby his snack. There's a kiddie pool, a full-size pool, ATVs, a swing set. They have a bounce house, bikes, scooters, a zip line. They are the luckiest kids in the world, and I wonder if they'll ever know it.

"Come on, guys," I call. "It's time to go to Axel's house."

By now New York has begun to reopen enough that an outdoor playdate is acceptable. I'm grateful for the two hours the children spend with their friends but even more so to see an adult my own age during the workday. In the city, Mina and I would get our nanny children together nearly every day. But now, there are no random playdates and there is no adult interaction. We don't go to museums, and there is no stopping at Shake Shack for lunch. Even Central Park has become a distant memory. I spend all day between the same four walls entertaining the same three children with the same toys and games. Spontaneity had once been the best part of this job, but here and now every day is Groundhog Day.

"Axi, come," Mina calls when we pull up, "our friends are here!"

Rei and Russ rush out of the car and onto another massive property. While the older children play, Mina attempts to speak to Tate, who promptly buries his face in my shirt and screams.

"Oh, he is still very bad, this one, huh?" Mina asks.

I quickly say that he is not bad, though of course he is. I would just never admit it.

She shakes her head, "This one is your favorite. So so favorite."

"I love them all equally," I say, but this is a *big* lie.

Tate is the first child I've had this long from birth. I spend the same number of hours per day with the baby and his personality is no better than his siblings. In fact, it's worse. He yells constantly, never stops eating, and hasn't stopped saying no since the day he learned the word. But my love for him is absolute in a way it's never been for any of the other children. It's not that I don't love Rei and Russ; it's just that I love Tate more. It makes me think that Hope's favoritism toward Lydia wasn't so calculated after all.

Russ and Axel run through the yard toward the putting green on the other side. This rental home, which they only have for the month of June, has eight bedrooms, seven bathrooms, a pool, a firepit, and a basketball court. Rei finds Summer, Axel's cousin, who is also staying at the house. The extended family pooled together to afford this home that costs thirty thousand dollars for a thirty-day stay.

Summer's nanny, Magui, is an immigrant like Mina. Magui lives in Queens but hopes to retire back to Nepal, her home country, soon. Summer adores her, and Magui seems to reciprocate the adoration.

"Summer, do you and Rei want to swim?" she asks.

Rei swims like a fish and jumps at the opportunity, encouraging Summer to do the same. Tate and I settle into a spot by the side of the pool, where he eats pretzel sticks on my lap. We watch as the two girls test out who can hold their breath the longest underwater.

After three short competitions, all of which Rei wins immodestly, Summer's dad comes out to cheer his daughter on. She loses once again but smiles when her dad applauds the effort.

"How's it going, Stephanie?" he asks.

I have only met Summer's dad twice, both times in recent weeks at this house. Bruce is a stereotypical Upper East Side dad. Well dressed and charismatic—a frat boy with a five hundred *K* salary.

"The kids been good lately?" he asks.

We briefly discuss how much harder three are than two.

"Where'd you go to college, by the way?"

"I went to Emerson."

"Oh, I was a Boston guy too. A Harvard man," he says.

Aren't they all.

By the time we finish chatting, ten minutes have passed. When I finally return to the same side of the yard as my nanny friends, I mention how nice the conversation was.

"Mr. Bruce?"

I say, "Yes, Mr. Bruce," and Magui scoffs at my apparent misjudgment. "Mr. Bruce is not nice," she says. "Every day, Mr. Bruce expect me to treat his children like my family, but for me he never do the same."

When I ask her what she means, Magui grows upset, and it is Mina who explains.

"Last night, Mr. Bruce barbecue. When me and Magui come down to join, we reach for the steaks. But Mr. Bruce yelled for us to stop. He said he had different ones for us. He brought out two tiny pieces of meat. He told us, the big steaks are for everyone else."

It takes me a moment to comprehend this story. How could the same person who just chatted with me have such blatant disregard for the woman raising his own blood? I recall with clarity Theo making my favorite dishes when my friends visit and Devon being sure to keep my favorite drinks stocked in the fridge.

"But Axel's dad apologized to me after. He said he was so sorry Mr. Bruce did that to us. You know Axel's parents aren't like that," Mina continues.

I realize how little that matters. Shame on Axel's dad for apologizing later, rather than sticking up for his son's nanny in the moment. Shame on him for allowing his peer to be unkind to someone he refers to as *like family*. I wonder how many times this has happened to Mina or Magui. How often have they been made to feel out of place and less than, more like help and less like people? At this very moment, all around the country, people are taking to the streets, protesting, voicing support for people of color. So then why is the storyline here just more of the same?

"I'm so sorry," I finally say.

I have spent many years pretending and wanting to fit in with the 1 percent. But looks are deceiving. I can never be one of them. And I'm no longer sure I want to be.

●●●●●

We sit along an all-glass buffet table while savory smells waft from the kitchen throughout the ground floor of this four-thousand-square-foot townhouse. Two maids begin shuffling in with porcelain bowls of sauteed shrimps, chorizo, mango salsa, and what I suspect is cheese. I place my dinner napkin on my lap and glance around the table: four babies. Two elderly nannies. Two stay-at-home moms. And me.

"Happy Birthday, Reagan!" someone shouts, and one of the maids places a number two crown amid her blond curls.

"Please, everyone, eat. Carne asada tacos are Reagan's absolute favorite. She's delighted to share them with all her dearest friends."

I watch as Reagan pushes a taco off of her plate.

"Here, Tate," I say, offering him a shrimp. He swings a fist toward the fork.

"No, Ste! No. Chick nuggets, pease."

I explain that there are no chicken nuggets, to which he all but punches me in the mouth, and I pray that I can avert a tantrum. It's 12:25, and we're flirting with nap time.

"This food is delicious, Jodi," one of the moms says. "Did you make all of this?"

Jodi is Reagan's mother, and Reagan is the younger sibling of a boy Russ is friendly with. None of these babies actually know one another, but during COVID in the Hamptons, the elite learn to make do with whoever is available.

"Oh, God, no," Jodi laughs, although nothing is funny. "You know, all summer long, we were hosting, hosting, hosting. Friends here, friends there. Every week I was spending all day in the kitchen. Finally, my husband said, That's it. Enough's enough. You want to host, fine, but we're hiring a chef. So you know what? I did, because you know how it is. I can't do it all."

How had Jodi managed to cook for her closest friends last summer with only six staff members in her home and unlimited income? The thought is so burdensome, I send thoughts and prayers.

"Well, whoever you hired is excellent. The food is delicious."

"I can give you her info. Honestly, she's so reasonable you couldn't regret hiring her if you tried."

Tate begins to grow antsy, but luckily Jodi brings out a chocolate ganache cake topped with the letter R. The promise of dessert settles him. They place the beautiful cake in front of Reagan and snap hundreds of photos while she smashes it. When she's done, a maid deposits the culinary masterpiece in the trash.

"Our chef made the cake for photographic purposes. We have cupcakes to eat. I hate to waste, but you know what they say: a picture is worth a thousand words."

I laugh along. I think, *she means dollars.*

•••••

A white camera follows the car as it passes through the gates down a long and winding driveway. I pass a meadow of tall grass, then a freshly landscaped lawn, and finally arrive at a house so magnificent it's graced the pages of *Architectural Digest*. The mansion is similar to all the others I've come to know, except for the quiver tree, typically found only in the dry climate of Namibia, poking out from the middle. A twenty-five-million-dollar mansion built around an exotic tree. My only wish is that it shocked me.

"Don't forget your backpacks," I tell the big kids when we pull up behind the row of parked cars. Two Audis, a Range Rover, our Mercedes.

"Will there be an ice cream truck today?" Rei asks.

"No, because he came on Friday," I say.

While most of America's parents face a harsh reality—send your kids to camp and risk COVID or quit your job—the parents here wrestle with a different problem.

"What should we do?" they ask one another. "I don't want the children to miss out on social interaction, but I'm afraid of all that exposure."

These parents, whose wealth runs New York City, pooled their resources, and I now find myself dropping off Rei and Russ at Mansion Camp, a place where six children's families take turns offering up their Hamptons estate to provide their children with a normal version of summer. They have counselors, specialty coaches, pools, hot tubs, private beaches, and bounce houses. The counselors plan themes, take them on safaris, and give them daily prizes. The camp is so over the top, it's absurd.

"Can I have a playdate with Ava this week?" Rei asks as we make our way to the backyard.

Ava, whose grandfather founded TGI Fridays, is wild and a little unhinged, the sort of friend I dislike Rei mingling with.

"Sure, I'll talk to her nanny," I assure her, and then she and Russ bolt.

I wonder what these children will be like fifteen years from now. At a time when most children cannot leave their homes, these kids carry on as if the world is not standing still. They're so privileged and lucky, I can't imagine they will grow to be resilient or grounded. But maybe I'm wrong.

Perhaps the means to shield them from the pandemic or any of the harsher things in the world is what will keep them young. Allow them a childhood. Give them time to grow up.

Tate shields the sun from his eyes then buries his face in my shoulder. "Ste, go? Back car?" he asks.

"Yeah, buddy. Let's go back to the car."

I shout out to Rei and Russ that I'll see them this afternoon, and Rei gives a halfhearted wave. But Russ bolts over, arms outstretched, flying into a hug.

"I'll see you at pickup," I tell him.

"Okay," Russ says, unsure, but eventually shuffling back toward his now-vacant swing.

I start to go when he calls my name once more. "Yeah?" I turn around.

"I love you."

I love him too, but it doesn't feel like enough.

32

JUST LIKE GAYLE AND OPRAH
(WELL, ALMOST)

I HAD REACHED OUT TO Lila just a few weeks before COVID began. I had begun writing again, for the first time in ages, after joining a women's writers group. At first, it was a way to make new friends and challenge my brain (something my nannying job failed to do). But I began writing the bones of this book, and I could feel it slowly morphing into something real. I knew I'd need Lila's permission because, regardless of where we were at now, Lila was part of who I was, a now-missing piece in the jigsaw puzzle of my life. I could not tell my story without hers. I felt awkward popping in out of nowhere but knew that giving her a heads-up was the right thing to do. I wrote and rewrote a text message a dozen times before finally, nearly two years since we'd last spoken, finding the courage to press Send.

Now, we're together in Rhode Island, strolling the same narrow streets we had grown up on. No one could understand it, least of all us, but the moment we reconnected, it was as if we'd never spent a second apart.

But because walking is generally very boring, we've decided to get margaritas.

I'd heard from friends over the years that Lila's life was better than ever. They showed me pictures of her on vacation in Ecuador or driving a boat in the Caribbean. In all of them she looked carefree and beautiful, and I struggled with the idea that my life still wouldn't compare. Lila would have incredible stories of her travels and her experiences at an innovative tech firm. *What could I catch her up on?* All I had done since we'd fallen out of touch was consort with toddlers and try my hand at an assortment of casual and failed relationships. Was I *afraid* to reconnect with Lila or *embarrassed*?

Maybe we can at least be friendly, I told myself, *no bad blood.*

"Please," I said after she mentioned that the last few years had been tough, "I've seen your social media pages. Every week before COVID you had some kind of fun night out."

I was admittedly jealous. These past years, I'd worked and saved but had hardly done anything that I looked back on and thought, *Thank God I did that.* Lila's life had always been more magical than mine. She was young when we met and had already seen so much of the world. Now we were older, and she was still seeing more.

"Things aren't always that simple," Lila said after a moment.

"I don't know," I disagreed. "Bermuda seems like an undeniably good time, if you ask me."

She nodded. "I really have had a lot of fun the last few years, and I do have a lot of good memories, but Instagram isn't always what it seems. Like the pictures from Ecuador. It was an amazing trip, but the first two days my friend had a million errands to do. She was from Quito, so we went to the dentist and the tailor and to visit her cousins. I didn't see a single thing those days," Lila continued. "And the picture from the Catskills? I fought with my boyfriend that entire trip."

It took me a moment to register that I was seeing a different side of Lila: vulnerability. Lila had always seemed perfect. Her personality was captivating; she was brilliant and fun. She had the rare ability to come off as shy yet still command a room. But the last two years had been hard for Lila, I learned that night. She'd lost touch with her mother completely, Joie having fallen back into bad habits and moved away to Florida, and her family had struggled to move past her absence. She'd landed a new job as an executive assistant, but after two years of hard work had failed to be promoted. I had been so busy worrying that I needed to appear better off that I had overlooked how she really was.

We spent the next hours filling each other in. Lila told me she'd felt confused—so weighed down with life's hardships that she'd lost sight of who she was, what she stood for, and the things she wanted. I couldn't imagine Lila, the most self-assured person I'd ever known, somehow not confident.

"But in all the years I was always soul-searching, feeling torn between where I came from and where I was now; it was you who always knew yourself," I said.

How foolish I had been, worried about what Lila would think of my life now, when she'd been the one person who had never judged me. Lila and I understood one another. We were adults who thrived in chaos, having come from homes laced with dysfunction.

Growing up, I'd watched Lila entangle herself with friend groups and relationships that didn't know the real her. She would dilute herself when they were around but could never hide from herself for long. I sometimes thought Lila sought out bad fits for the roller coaster highs and lows. A distraction from the bigger issues in her life, the ones she couldn't control.

Coming to terms with yourself is hard for everyone, no matter who you are or where you come from. I didn't need to prove to Lila that my life was better than hers, but I knew mine was better with her in it.

"I hit twenty-seven, and suddenly things got hard. I had a lot of stuff happening with my family, I broke up with my boyfriend, and I lost so many friends. I just felt like fuck, you know, what do I do now? Maybe I am doing things all wrong, I don't know!"

I realized that's how I'd felt throughout my entire twenties. Like I was doing things wrong. Maybe that's how everyone feels. Maybe my father had thought that, at the age I was now, with four children to support. Or my mother, who found herself single with three children at twenty-eight. Even Devon, who'd married young in a time when that was no longer the norm—did she ever doubt her choices?

Perhaps there was no "right way" to do things. Maybe I was doing okay after all.

33

TOOTHLESS

WE RETURNED TO THE CITY at the end of the summer, and New York existed for the next few months as a shell of its former self. The lights of Times Square shined for tourists who did not show. Lines at local food pantries wrapped around avenues, leaving people waiting in the cold for hours. Businesses by Madison Square Garden shuttered their windows. Even the block of 7th Avenue where my apartment sat, once reliably lively, was now desolate. Only in one neighborhood of Manhattan did things almost carry on as usual: the Upper East Side.

"Is there any chance we're moving back to the Hamptons, though?" I asked Devon one morning.

The lease on my Chelsea apartment was up at the end of the month, and I wasn't sure what to do. I had just spent half a year shelling out two thousand dollars a month for a place I hadn't stepped foot in.

"Look, if the schools stay open, for sure we're staying here," Devon said, "but if they don't have school we'll go back."

I needed to find a place but even in COVID times, I could not afford the sort of one-bedrooms my old Chelsea building offered, which were close to four thousand a month. But I also did not want roommates during a global pandemic.

"Come look in Astoria," Lila insisted. "You can live in the same kind of luxury building for half the price. At least check it out."

I wasn't interested in Queens. Besides Elliot Stabler (who must be a wizard, as he only becomes more attractive with age!), I had no idea what kind of people lived there, and I wasn't keen to find out. I gave Lila an endless list of reasons it would be nearly impossible for me to move outside of Manhattan but began to worry that, really, I was just a snob. Lila had grown up wealthy and loved living in Queens. In the end, I agreed to look in Astoria to prove to myself that I was still the low-maintenance kid I had been in North Providence.

Some of the reasons I loved where I lived were trivial: I liked telling my family or friends who'd never left my hometown that my apartment was blocks from the trains of Penn Station. Even my parents, disenchanted with New York, would brag about this. Lydia, now a student at Bard College, loved bringing her friends to visit me there. It was the first time I lived somewhere that we could be proud of. *But did that apartment actually feel like home, or did I just like what the address represented?*

Finally, during a thunderstorm on a Sunday evening in late October, I found somewhere with potential in Astoria. I filled it with sleek new furniture from Pottery Barn and a pink couch I found online. The living room was lined with framed pictures: Aunt Patty and my grandma drinking wine on a porch in New Hampshire, my dog on his birthday, Lydia and me in London, where I'd taken her for her nineteenth birthday, the first time she'd ever left the country. Piece by piece, the apartment started to look like more than just a testament to what I could afford; it started to feel like mine. I hung an Andy Warhol photo above my bed and, for Christmas, Lila bought me a desk from West Elm that I could sit at to write. Looking around I thought, *Maybe I could learn to like this place after all.*

●●●●●

"Oh, my God, Stephanie!" Rei gasped, "look at that! The train is above ground!"

She had her head sticking fully out the window of my Mini Cooper. Cold winter air smacked her in the face, but Rei seemed unbothered. Besides attending a Mets game, Rei had never been to Queens, but it had been a tough year, and Devon wanted to do something special for Russ's birthday.

"He's going to have his first sleepover with William," Devon said, "but William will have to sleep in Rei's bed. I don't know where she'll sleep. I guess with me and Theo?"

I told her four children, two adults, and a couple of cats would be a tight squeeze in a three-bedroom apartment. "Rei can stay at my house if she wants," I said. That night we were set to leave for my place when I finished work at six. Rei started packing her bag at noon.

"Let's get a treat before we go home to watch our movie," I said. "Should we do cupcakes? Munchkins?"

"How about ice cream?" Rei asked. "Because, Steph, don't forget. I can't bite into stuff. My tooth is too wiggly!"

Like me, Rei was on the late bloomers train of losing teeth. All of her friends had two or three visits from the tooth fairy, and Rei spent a portion of each day examining her mouth. You'd catch her in a mirror trying to knock one loose or pull a very firm molar sideways. Nothing. But finally, just before her seventh birthday, a wobbly incisor.

Rei's eyes were wide as we crossed the street to the Ample Hills on 30th Avenue. She surveyed the crowds and the places, commenting on the cookie place on the corner and asking why she hadn't seen any taxis.

"Guess people like Ubers in Astoria, huh, Steph?"

"Guess so, kid."

By the time we got home at eight, I had worked all day and wanted nothing more than to lie down, but Rei couldn't sit still. She ran from room to room shrieking in delight. She'd toss my dog a tennis ball, then investigate what was in the fridge. "Stephanie," she'd sigh, "why is there so much soda in here?" Rei was convinced my memory was poor on account of how much Coke Zero I drank, when, in fact, I believed my constant brain fog was caused by so much time with her and her brothers.

Rei stepped out onto the balcony. She had asked me to open the door so that she could look down and watch the cars on 21st Street zoom by. When she came back in, Rei searched every cupboard and closet until she finally reached my room. Then she stopped, paused, and looked at me.

"Wow," she said as she ran her hand along the side of my desk, "you really are a real writer. Hey! Let's write together."

I glanced at the clock. 8:43. *Oh, let's please not,* I thought. But how could I say no? Rei and I each had twenty minutes to write a story then share it with each other. When we finally finished, we went to the bathroom and brushed our teeth, I washed my face, and she gave my dog a kiss goodnight. When I got into bed, Rei, not one for affection, cuddled close. She was quiet and, after a few minutes, I thought she'd fallen asleep.

"Hey, Steph…"

"Yes?"

"This is the best apartment ever."

I laughed. "Do you love the apartment or the stuff in it?"

"Both," she said, thoughtfully. "I'm going to live here too one day."

She wouldn't, of course, but at the moment that hardly mattered. At six, Rei was wiser about what made a home special than I was. Rei loved my apartment simply because it was mine and she felt special being there. I realized it *was* mine and *I* should have felt it was special, because, regardless of the neighborhood, I wasn't splitting rent between three people. I wasn't lounging on furniture inherited from a roommate's dad's cousin. Everything in this place I had paid for, chosen, and, most importantly, earned.

So, why had I seen this place as a failure? Because I had never been looking for an apartment that impressed me. I'd been looking for one that would impress everyone else.

"Hey, Steph…" Rei whispered once more.

"Yeah?"

"When do you think my tooth is going to fall out?"

"Soon," I said, "sooner than you think."

●●●●●

On my very last day as Rei, Russ, and Tate's nanny, Devon and I are sitting outside sharing a bottle of wine after my shift has ended.

"I know you don't want to hear this," Devon says, "but I don't think Tate will be the one to miss you most."

I scoff. Tate is an angel, and, as he often proclaims, I am his "best girl." I cannot imagine a world where it is not he who suffers most from the separation.

"I'm telling you it's going to be Rei."

"Rei?" I say with surprise. Rei is many things, but sensitive does not rank high among her list of traits. "Why Rei?"

"Rei doesn't care what many people think, but she does care what you and I think." Devon stops to sip her wine. "Remember when you got a tie-dye sweat set? Then she had to have one. And when her teacher asked her what she wanted to be when she grew up, what did she say? A writer."

She also offered me several pointers on how to improve my writing skills, I think to myself, but I don't say anything. I'm too busy reflecting on the last few years with these kids. These hyper, sassy, complicated, absolutely wonderfully beautiful kids.

A few months from now, Devon will make partner at her firm, her years of hard work finally paying off. She'll have all the things a successful lawyer strives for: status, influence, and an equity partnership. Her all-nighters and long work days will no longer seem pointless because the achievement will be so great, and the honor will be what she's dreamed of.

Over the last six years, I too have worked hard. Like Devon, I have never shied away from overtime or extra responsibilities. When the job has asked more of me, I've risen to the occasion and given it my all, but in the end, Devon's hard work will mean something. She will advance and move forward, her career just beginning. When my time as a nanny concludes, there won't be a big payoff. No higher salaries. No congratulatory celebrations. It'll mean nothing. It will just be over.

34

NANNY NO MORE

I HEARD ABOUT A JOB through a friend who swore I'd be perfect for it. The position was a personal assistant to a tech genius whose net worth topped two billion. I wasn't sure what made me a good candidate since my only assistant experience was to a small army of toddlers and involved spreading rash cream on their behinds.

Much to my surprise, they call a few days later for me to come in to meet with the CEO, offering an evening time so it won't conflict with my current work schedule.

My whole body feels sick with nerves on my cab ride down Fifth that Tuesday.

The CEO walks in and, as I imagine he had most of his life, got right down to business. He fires questions off so quickly I'm hardly through an answer before he asks the next. I can't imagine he's even listening to the answers and feel myself grow flustered.

"So you've never been an assistant?" he scans my resume.

"Well no…but…"

"But what do you do for these people you work for now?" I haven't even opened my mouth when he thinks of something else to ask. "Walk me through an average day in the life."

I describe half my duties when he interrupts, asking, Where am I from? Where do I live now? Do I like it?

"I've got a few properties over there," he says. "I like that street. Good food. Anyway, can you use QuickBooks?"

"I actually haven't before," I say, and by the time we reach his next question, I know things are not going well. I knew I wasn't truly qualified for this position. It's too big a leap from the nannying world to an office job. If I want to make the money I did now, maybe I'm stuck as household staff forever.

"We're like a team here," he says. "You know anything about basketball? It's like that. We need every player and all the coaches to make it work. No one player can carry the team."

I can't believe it, but I've found a window of opportunity in the most unlikely place. It's a topic I rarely think of these days but one I built my entire young life around. In a spectacular turn of events, I reach deep into my past and reference the sport that perhaps brought me to this very moment.

"Except for LeBron James."

The CEO glances over at me suddenly. "What was that?"

"LeBron. LeBron can carry a team on his own," I begin. "I mean he's not loyal to a team, which is why he's always changing jerseys. But four championships and ten NBA finals. There's a reason he's a four-time finals MVP."

For a moment, I'm not sure if he's confused or offended (after all, LeBron can be controversial), but then he begins to laugh.

I nail the rest of the brief interview using an important lesson I learned at Lincoln School for Girls: how to convince a rich person I belong in the same room as them.

I receive a ninety-thousand-dollar starting offer with full health benefits, which made me think maybe I *was* good enough to be there.

Epilogue

MY PHONE HAD GONE OFF so many times that morning that it died by noon. If I wasn't being Slacked or called, then someone was messaging me on WhatsApp. To try reaching me by email would have been useless, but anyone who really needed to get in touch would know that. I'd been so desperate for a place in the corporate world, and now here I *finally* was: facing a barrage of notifications from every communication platform on the World Wide Web.

The conference was three days long if you didn't count the eight hours I'd spent on my boss' private plane getting to it. We'd just come from a quick trip to Europe and were scheduled to go from here straight to LAX. I now spent the majority of my time rescheduling already rescheduled meetings and sprinkling carbon emissions between destinations. When we arrived at the hotel, my boss directed me to fetch him "something keto."

"How else am I going to live forever?" he laughed.

Immortality for this man was the last thing the world needed.

While I was out ordering a salad, a younger assistant unpacked his suitcase. Another made reservations at every Michelin star restaurant in town. The fourth assistant was busy setting up his computer station, which we took turns dragging around the globe. Three monitors, two laptops, a webcam, a mouse, and a special chair for his bad back. But there was nothing unique about us. Every assistant here in the hotel was working this way today. That's how things were at a conference for billionaires. Suddenly, all of Rei's meltdowns that I had endured over the years weren't seeming so bad after all. In fact, I *nearly* missed them.

It turned out that being an executive assistant was a lot like being a nanny. It required incredible amounts of patience, vigilance, and an abandonment of any sort of ego. Instead of scheduling playdates, I scheduled luncheons. Here, I didn't cut the crust off anyone's sandwich, but I did know exactly how many sugars should go in an Earl Grey tea.

I knew I was one of the lucky ones. My boss wasn't so bad. He did berate his staff and his requests were outlandish, degrading even, but he paid us well, and the job had perks. I saw and heard stories from others who had it far worse and was disgusted by how inhumanely they were treated.

I was still thinking this when later that night I began chatting with a guy who worked as a junior assistant to a hedge fund manager.

"What's the worst thing he's ever asked you to do?" I asked over a third glass of prosecco.

"Okay, well, you know how I said he has his assistants lay out his outfits for him before dinner?"

I nodded.

"Well, one day they need to buy him some new clothes, so they lay out a few options of new outfits, but he loses his mind when sees them."

"Why?"

"Because he couldn't believe we'd thought he'd have time in his day to try on new clothes. So the next day, he sent us to the place that makes stunt bodies for Hollywood to get a custom mannequin of him so we could always try his clothes on the mannequin beforehand. One assistant used to Uber with it to his stylist at Bloomingdale's and dress it in the fitting rooms."

I burst out laughing, but I wasn't sure if it was because the story left me entertained or uncomfortable.

"Oh, but he's actually really generous. I mean he's demanding, but he gives me a bonus of five grand every year," the assistant continued on. But while he gushed, I wondered something that I often did. *Why do people with so much often choose to treat those who work for them as so little?*

I finished the glass of wine before returning to my room. Tailored suits and flashy white smiles. Rolex watches and sparkling champagne. The only women I passed seemed to be working for the men. *How rich* it all still was.

"Hey, Steph," my boss called just before I reached the lobby elevator.

He walked over with the two suits he'd been schmoozing with for the last hour. "Do me a favor. Run to the nearest liquor store and get us some alcohol for my hotel suite. We'll be up in ten."

"Sure," I sighed, exhausted from the long day and disappointed to be headed in the opposite direction of my bed.

"Oh, and can you buy duct tape? We're going to play Edward Fortyhands. You'll just need to duct tape the beers to my buddies' hands while we play." He paused. "Get some latex gloves too, so that you don't rip out our arm hair with the duct tape."

One of the men with him nodded to me. The other winked. All three walked back toward the bar for another round.

And that's when it finally hit me. I had been lying to myself. This man wasn't a decent boss. I didn't like this job. I thought, *Fuck this.*

I was making the same mistake I'd made in the past, only now I didn't have to make it; I was choosing to. I wasn't trapped. I was not boxed in. I had spent my twenties doing jobs I never intended to do, for people I loved but in a career I did not want, that had met a financial need but not a mental one. I didn't have to do that anymore. I could make slightly less and be comfortable now, having created a sturdy foundation for myself. It was possible for me to do a less demanding job, one that allowed me more time to write, that I felt respected doing. *Respect.* I had been so desperate for people to give me that, but how could I seek it from others when I refused to give it to myself?

For years, I had been so obsessed with what I wanted that I had forgotten to notice what I had gained. I wasn't born into wealth, that was true, and I didn't have as easy a start as most of my friends. So what? Whether or not my parents had stumbled through raising me, they'd helped me obtain a better education and future than they had. Nannying had allowed me to begin building a life I never imagined possible. I was now a thirty-year-old single woman with unlimited freedom and countless resources. I had the best friend one could have, a person so fiercely loyal, so devoted, I never faced any difficulty in my life alone. I had the most adorable dog, my beloved Gram, and a place I called home in what was in my opinion the best city in the world. My life was beautiful.

But did I ever get my dream of writing for television? No, I'm afraid I didn't, but if you're reading this, you must know I'm no longer all that far off. I decided to email my building to say I wouldn't be renewing my lease. It hadn't been that long ago when even this apartment seemed below what I wanted, but I realized there was more I was willing to do without if it meant I would no longer have to dedicate every minute of my life to someone else's.

I decided to find a cheaper place because, in order to be happy, I'd need a new job. I would have to make a little less to feel like more.

I applied for an executive assistant position at a small tech company. The salary was less than I made now, so I'd have to give up some things, but that was okay.

I called my parents on the way out of the apartment viewing to tell them the news.

A few days later, HR onboarded me and said the company kept to a strict nine-to-six schedule. On that first weekend, I kept my phone close, waiting for a call or a text, a reservation that needed to be adjusted, a contract that had slipped through the cracks and needed to be faxed. But it never came.

"Your life's going to be real different, you know," my father had said at the end of our call.

He was right.

People say that I am living proof you can climb the class ladder, do anything, become anyone. My social circle is evidence of my success. If I need a distinguished doctor, I know just who to call, and if I need a good lawyer, I'm familiar with a couple of those too. My network is filled with CEOs and founders, geniuses whose work centers around saving a heating planet, men who swipe badges each morning at Google, and women who code the World Wide Web. In many ways, I have made it, but I'm still paying a thousand dollars a month on a student loan that never seems to get smaller. I'll be questioning if I can afford children because I'd opted to have a good education. I have a lingering bill from a hospital emergency visit from a period when I couldn't access healthcare, despite how much and how hard I worked.

Life for me had been like starting a game of Monopoly with half a dice and five one-dollar bills. My opponents, like the ones whose homes I had worked in, had begun the game with six properties and a hundred thousand dollars. The only miracle for them would be if they *didn't* end up successful. Life in America was rigged, but I had done well enough in the game to find a happy medium. My feet were firmly planted on the bridge between less and more. It was *everything* I could have hoped for.

If wealth has taught me anything, it is that friendship holds more value than money ever will and that dignity has no price tag. The only thing truly precious in this world is having people who love you, and success and happiness often have no correlation whatsoever. If I know one thing, it is that the old saying rings true: Money can't buy happiness. Though I can absolutely see why you'd be tempted to believe that it can get you pretty darned close.

Acknowledgments

Thank you to my agent, Jen. I found Jen at a time when publication seemed hopeless, after I had received more rejection letters than I care to remember, and when I had all but given up on this story. Publishing is a long and lonely road, but once I found Jen, I never once felt like I was on the journey alone. Her feedback, gentle and encouraging, constructive yet kind, has undoubtedly made me a better writer, storyteller, and, most importantly, collaborator. It had been on my bucket list to be published by thirty. I signed with Jen two days after I exited my twenties. She got me close enough.

Thank you to my editors, Anna and Diane—Anna for legitimizing my absolute dread of having to play another round of Peppa Pig and Diane for writing such wonderful tidbits in the comments section of our edits. (It's because of you that revisions never grew dull!) Of all the books in the world, you two chose this one. It still doesn't feel real even as I write this.

Many thanks to my small but mighty marketing and publicity team: Liz and Kayleigh. Kayleigh for seeing something special in this story and Liz for her help starting from the very beginning of my time with Sourcebooks.

And to all the rest of the folks at Sourcebooks who played a role in making this happen, thank you. My dream has come true because of you.

Thank you to all of my children: Ruby and Hunter, for showing me how to care about something other than myself at an age when people often exist in a state of selfishness. Rei, whose boldness never ceased to surprise me and whose vivaciousness kept me on my toes; Russ, who made me patient and gentle. And Tate, who I loved most dearly—watching you grow was something I'll treasure forever. And to all the other kiddos I had the privilege of loving throughout the years: Charlotte, Elizabeth, Miles, and Will—every minute I spent with each of you made me a better person.

To all the moms I've worked alongside: I hope to take the best lessons from each of you if and when I become a mom myself. Sasha, who showed me how to mother selflessly; Devon, who embraced motherhood realistically; and to the rest of you: you're doing the hardest job in the world. You should be so proud of yourselves.

To my writing group, who read the most raw version of these chapters: Anastasia, Norma, and Louise, thank you for seeing potential. Thank you for steering me in the right direction.

To Cynthia, who I sent this manuscript to when I was flat on ideas, thank you for your feedback. I hope one day to be a matriarch just half as strong as you.

To AD, who opened the door that gave me the chance, thank you. I wish every kid received the same chance as me. My wish is that one day we'll live in a world where they do.

To ODW, whose hand helped guide me through the darkest period of my life. Who reminds me that most—if not all—families are complicated. And who is always just a phone call away no matter how much time has passed.

Cat, for sending me the most delicious cake when I signed my first publishing contract. (Might be good manners to send the same one on the release date too, no??)

To Sara Rosie, it's been the greatest gift to grow into ourselves together and to see so much of the world with you. Our friendship and our travels have made me more accepting and more compassionate; they remind me that we know both everything and nothing at all. Our adventures have given me something I didn't know existed, and because of them, I am reminded how good I have it.

To Lana, who's always there for me with a glass of wine on both the good days and bad.

AP and Gram, thank you two, who have always been my biggest fans, who saw *humor* where others saw *sass*, who called me *different* when others said *difficult*. You've seen the best in me from the very beginning. You're two hands of a compass that never let me stray. I hope I've made you proud.

To the Kisers: it's been a roller coaster. Give me the whole theme park, and I'd choose this ride every time. Well…probably. But it would definitely be in my top three choices! I know allowing me to write this wasn't easy, but many things in your life haven't been, and my greatest wish is that your story will comfort those facing difficult times of their own. And whatever anyone ever says, Dad, you made it. I'm proud to be your daughter.

Al and Lid, the very first children I ever helped raise! I have no idea why we look nothing alike, and we really should get to the bottom of it. But even if we weren't related, I'd love you both anyway.

And finally, to Lila, who read this manuscript nearly as many times as I did and (hardly) ever complained. Thank you for letting me write freely and openly, for always accepting both the best and worst parts of me, and for telling me I could do this long before I ever believed I could.

Knowing you has made me smarter, kinder, and stronger, and because of you, I even know how to put concealer on correctly. For more reasons than one, this book is not possible without you. I could search this whole world twice over and never find a friend quite as good as you.

Reading Group Guide

1. In the first chapter Stephanie recounts conversations she over-
    hears while waiting to pick up Ruby at her exclusive Upper East
    Side school. As the wealthy mothers lament the traffic and other
    minor inconveniences they "suffered" during their summer in the
    Hamptons, Stephanie imagines what her life would be like if these
    were her concerns. Have you ever found yourself wishing you were
    in someone else's Jimmy Choos? Do you believe that extreme
    wealth would leave you with nothing but trivial complaints?

2. Stephanie's childhood in working class Rhode Island was the
    opposite of the lives of the various children she nannies. While
    she states that her experiences gave her grit, she also wonders
    what she might have accomplished if she'd had the advantages of
    her young charges. Do you think her achievements are because
    of or in spite of her often-harsh upbringing?

3. Stephanie laments early on in her nannying gig that she finds her situation humiliating: "I want so desperately to have a respected job…something that excites people, that they respond to with admiration…but now I'm someone's domestic staff. No matter how I try and spin it, I am simply the help. And no one respects that." Do you agree with this assessment? Why or why not?

4. Stephanie's friendship with Lila is the relationship she counts on most throughout high school and into adulthood. Why do you think it fractures after Stephanie's abortion? Have you ever been through a similar "breakup?" If so, were you able to resolve it? Was your relationship weaker or stronger afterwards? Why?

5. After her abortion, Stephanie begins a downward spiral of depression that ultimately results in her decision to leave her profession to pursue a career more aligned with her original goals—and some work-life balance. Can you think of a time when a negative experience was a catalyst for your personal or professional change and growth?

6. As an adult, Stephanie espouses her parents' worldview and politics—until she travels abroad and her experiences make her question everything she's accepted as true to that point. Do you think travel and exposure to other cultures are integral to an effective education?

7. Several people in Stephanie's circle suffer from mental health issues. Stephanie observes that among the rich, it's almost a point of pride to be in therapy. Do you think there's a social stigma attached to mental health counseling? Would you encourage a loved one to seek therapy if they were having issues? Why or why not?

8. The biggest emotional hurdle Stephanie faces when she decides to quit nannying is saying goodbye to the children she has grown to love. Have you ever been paralyzed with ambivalence when facing a major decision? What helped you resolve the situation?

A Conversation with the Author

At what age did you decide you wanted to be a writer? Did doubts along the way hinder your progress or inspire you to prove them wrong?

I think I knew when I was a senior in high school, but it was just an idea then. I wasn't confident I had any writing talent until I was in my midtwenties, and even today I still sometimes feel like I'm not sure! Most of my friends grew up believing they could be anyone or do anything, but my family didn't have the luxury of instilling that in us, so I think I had to adopt a sort of underdog mentality. But I've learned over the years not to try and accomplish things because you think it'll impress people or make them respect you more—because that can lead to disappointments. You have to do it because it'll make *you* proud.

Do you think your college degree, with its massive debt load, helped or hurt your progress as a writer? Why?

People ask me this question a lot, and the answer is complicated. I took out a massive amount of debt, and while it is a burden, it worked out for me. If given the chance to go back in time, I would do it all over again because college exposed me to so many things that ultimately molded me into who I am now.

Today I have a great job, brilliant and incredible friends, and I'm a published author. I don't know that college benefited me specifically as a writer, but it allowed me to build a life I couldn't have otherwise dreamed of. But I think it's important to be mindful that it doesn't work out this way for a lot of people.

You lay bare a great many intimate details about your family and upbringing in this book. Was it your intention to do so when you began writing, or did your tell-all honesty occur organically as the story took shape? Has your family been supportive of this project?

No, it wasn't my plan, but the more time I spent nannying, the more I began to see a misunderstanding between classes, and I wanted to write something that didn't villainize either side. However, inequality is alive and well, and I think it's important we recognize that. It's been really challenging for my family. It's one thing for me to choose to lay out the most personal and difficult moments of my life. It's another to allow someone else to do that for me. So in a lot of ways I think my family has been a lot braver than me. I also think that your early twenties are filled with so many growing pains, and it's helpful for people that age to be able to read something as honest as this so that they don't feel so alone.

Which writers have influenced you the most? Why?

Almost all of my favorite writers are women whose writing so realistically captures the triumphs and tragedies of the female experience. When I first started at Emerson, Lena Dunham and Greta Gerwig were just emerging, and both were writing these really raw, realistic scripts of life as a twentysomething. Taylor Swift, Stephanie Land, and Roxanne Gay all also do this particularly well. I love how comforting their work feels to me, and I wanted to write something that felt similarly authentic.

What are you reading now?

The Once and Future Witches.

About the Author

AVANI/SHOOTT PHOTOGRAPHY

Stephanie Kiser is a former nanny living in New York City. She grew up in North Providence, Rhode Island, before moving to Boston to attend Emerson College, where she studied Writing for Film and Television. For seven years, Stephanie worked as a nanny to some of Manhattan's wealthiest families before pivoting careers. Currently, Stephanie is the senior executive assistant to the engineering team at an NYC ad-tech company. She is in no way an engineer and has little clue as to how coding works (though luckily this does not affect her ability to be successful in her role).

She lives in Astoria with her Cavalier King Charles spaniel, Burger Clinton.